The Official Rails-to-Trails
Conservancy Guidebook

Rail-Trails
Michigan &
Wisconsin

The definitive guide to the region's top multiuse trails

🦬 **WILDERNESS PRESS** . . . *on the trail since 1967*

Rail-Trails: Michigan & Wisconsin

Copyright © 2017 by Rails-to-Trails Conservancy
1st edition, 3rd printing 2018

Maps: Lohnes+Wright; map data courtesy of Environmental Systems Research Institute
Cover design: Scott McGrew
Book design: Annie Long; book layout: Leslie Shaw

Cataloging-in-Publication Data is available from the Library of Congress.

ISBN: 978-0-89997-873-4; eISBN: 978-0-89997-874-1

Manufactured in China

Published by: 🐾 **WILDERNESS PRESS**
              An imprint of AdventureKEEN
              2204 First Ave. S., Suite 102
              Birmingham, AL 35233
              800-443-7227; fax 205-326-1012

Visit **wildernesspress.com** for a complete listing of our books and for ordering information. Contact us at our website, at **facebook.com/wildernesspress1967,** or at **twitter
.com/wilderness1967** with questions or comments. To find out more about who we are
and what we're doing, visit our blog, **blog.wildernesspress.com.**

Distributed by Publishers Group West

Front cover photo: Biking the Chippewa State Trail in Wisconsin (Trail 35, page 133),
photo by Ken Bryan; *back cover photo*: Bridge over the Bad River on the Saginaw Valley
Rail Trail in Michigan (Trail 23, page 89), photo by Ed Beaumont

SAFETY NOTICE: Although Wilderness Press and Rails-to-Trails Conservancy have
made every attempt to ensure that the information in this book is accurate at press time,
they are not responsible for any loss, damage, injury, or inconvenience that may occur to
anyone while using this book. You are responsible for your own safety and health while in
the wilderness. The fact that a trail is described in this book does not mean that it will be
safe for you. Be aware that trail conditions can change from day to day. Always check local
conditions, know your own limitations, and consult a map.

About Rails-to-Trails Conservancy

Headquartered in Washington, DC, Rails-to-Trails Conservancy (RTC) is a nonprofit organization dedicated to creating a nationwide network of trails from former rail lines and connecting corridors to build healthier places for healthier people.

Railways helped build America. Spanning from coast to coast, these ribbons of steel linked people, communities, and enterprises, spurring commerce and forging a single nation that bridges a continent. But in recent decades, many of these routes have fallen into disuse, severing communal ties that helped bind Americans together.

When RTC opened its doors in 1986, the rail-trail movement was in its infancy. Most projects focused on single, linear routes in rural areas, created for recreation and conservation. RTC sought broader protection for the unused corridors, incorporating rural, suburban, and urban routes.

Year after year, RTC's efforts to protect and align public funding with trail building created an environment that allowed trail advocates in communities across the country to initiate trail projects. These ever-growing ranks of trail professionals, volunteers, and RTC supporters have built momentum for the national rail-trail movement. As the number of supporters multiplied, so too did the number of rail-trails.

Americans now enjoy more than 22,000 miles of open rail-trails, and as they flock to the trails to connect with family members and friends, enjoy nature, and get to places in their local neighborhoods and beyond, their economic prosperity, health, and overall well-being continue to flourish.

A signature endeavor of RTC is **TrailLink.com,** America's portal to these rail-trails as well as other multiuse trails. When RTC launched TrailLink.com in 2000, our organization was one of the first to compile such detailed trail information on a national scale. Today, the website continues to play a critical role in both encouraging and satisfying the country's growing need for opportunities to ride, walk, skate, or run for recreation or transportation. This free trail-finder database—which includes detailed descriptions, interactive maps, photo galleries, and firsthand ratings and reviews—can be used as a companion resource to the trails in this guidebook.

The national voice for more than 160,000 members and supporters, RTC is committed to ensuring a better future for America made possible by trails and the connections they inspire. Learn more at **railstotrails.org.**

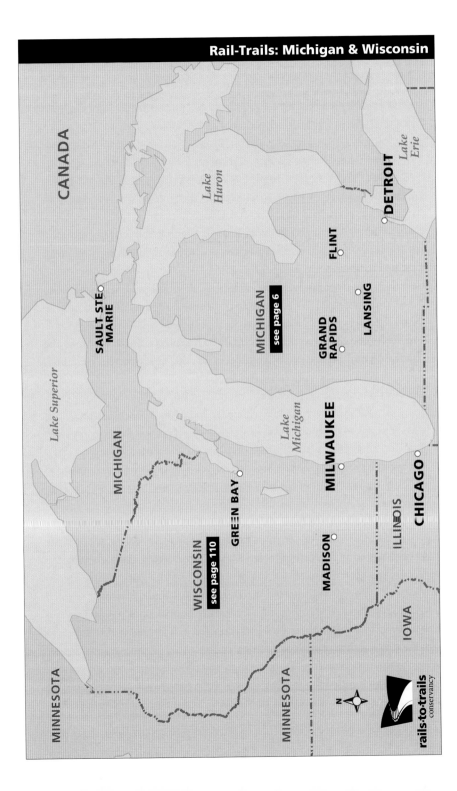

Rail-Trails: Michigan & Wisconsin

Table of Contents

MICHIGAN 6

Foreword

For those of you who have already experienced the sheer enjoyment and freedom of riding on a rail-trail, welcome back! You'll find this *Rail-Trails: Michigan and Wisconsin* guidebook to be a useful and fun guide to your favorite trails, as well as an introduction to pathways you have yet to travel.

For readers who are discovering for the first time the adventures possible on a rail-trail, thank you for joining the rail-trail movement. Since 1986, Rails-to-Trails Conservancy has been the leading supporter and defender of these priceless public corridors. We are excited to bring you *Rail-Trails: Michigan and Wisconsin* so you, too, can enjoy some of the region's premier rail-trails and multiuse trails. These hiking and biking trails are ideal ways to connect with your community, with nature, and with your friends and family.

I've found that trails have a way of bringing people together, and as you'll see from this book, you have opportunities in every state you visit to get on a great trail. Whether you're looking for a place to exercise, explore, commute, or play, there is a trail in this book for you.

So I invite you to sit back, relax, pick a trail that piques your interest—and then get out, get active, and have some fun. I'll be out on the trails, too, so be sure to wave as you go by.

Happy trails,

Keith Laughlin

Keith Laughlin, President
Rails-to-Trails Conservancy

Acknowledgments

S pecial thanks to writer Gene Bisbee, who contributed a substantial number of trail descriptions for this book.

We are also appreciative of the following contributors and to all the trail managers we called on for assistance to ensure that the maps, photographs, and trail descriptions are as accurate as possible.

Kevin Belanger

Tracy Conoboy

Brian Housh

Jake Laughlin

Kevin Mills

Patrick Wojahn

Derek Strout

Ken Bryan

Andrew Dupuy

Amy Kapp

Keith Laughlin

Mary O'Connor

John Siegert

A hidden bridge along the Omaha Trail (Trail 53, page 201)

Introduction

*R*ail-Trails: Michigan & Wisconsin highlights 63 of the region's top rail-trails and other multiuse pathways; they offer a broad range of experiences from bucolic Midwestern farmland to woodsy parks and river valleys to vibrant urban centers and friendly small towns.

It was here in the Midwest that the origins of the rail-trail movement began as an intriguing idea that quietly took hold in the 1960s and eventually spread across the country.

The 33.8-mile Elroy-Sparta State Trail, which claims its origins from Wisconsin's 1965 purchase of a disused piece of right-of-way of the Chicago and North Western Railway, is widely considered to be the oldest multiuse rail-trail in America. Rail-trail aficionados around the country flock to the trail to view the historic 20-foot-tall wooden double doors that still hang from its three famous tunnels.

For a more urban experience, Milwaukee's Oak Leaf Trail provides 120 miles of access to the city's most popular attractions, including museums, sports complexes, parks, and neighborhoods, as well as numerous access points to Lake Michigan.

Though many of the trails in this book span well over 20 or 30 miles and beyond, there are also smaller gems like the 8.9-mile Paint Creek Trail—Michigan's oldest nonmotorized rail-trail—which offers a short, scenic experience with a variety of charms, including wildlife, historical sites, a pleasant creek, and a few places to relax and refuel. As Michigan seeks to make biking and walking connections across the state, it has welcomed the 8.9-mile pathway into its larger 2,000-mile-plus Iron Belle Trail network, one of the most ambitious trail-network projects in America to date, spanning from Detroit to Ironwood in the Upper Peninsula.

For a wider variety of trail amenities and experiences, the Fred Meijer Heartland Trail rolls for 42 miles through farmland and woods in central Michigan as it links a half dozen towns with parks and historical sites; it is also one component of the 125-mile Fred Meijer Mid-West Michigan Trail Network.

And car-history buffs might appreciate the 19.5-mile Hines Park Trail/Rouge River Gateway Greenway, which, on its path from Dearborn to Northville, passes the Henry Ford Estate and his iconic Greenfield Village, an 80-acre open-air museum featuring 300 years of American life.

No matter which routes in *Rail-Trails: Michigan & Wisconsin* you choose, you'll experience the unique history, culture, and geography of each as well as the communities that have built and embraced them.

What Is a Rail-Trail?

Rail-trails are multiuse public paths built along former railroad corridors. Most often flat or following a gentle grade, they are suited to walking, running, cycling, mountain biking, in-line skating, cross-country skiing, horseback riding, and wheelchair use. Since the 1960s, Americans have created more than 22,000 miles of rail-trails throughout the country.

These extremely popular recreation and transportation corridors traverse urban, suburban, and rural landscapes. Many preserve historical landmarks, while others serve as wildlife conservation corridors, linking isolated parks and establishing greenways in developed areas. Rail-trails also stimulate local economies by boosting tourism and promoting trailside businesses.

What Is a Rail-with-Trail?

A rail-with-trail is a public path that parallels a still-active rail line. Some run adjacent to high-speed scheduled trains, often linking public transportation stations, while others follow tourist routes and slow-moving excursion trains. Many share an easement, separated from the rails by extensive fencing. More than 275 rails-with-trails exist in the United States.

How to Use This Book

Rail-Trails: Michigan & Wisconsin provides the information you'll need to plan a rewarding trek on a rail-trail or other multiuse trail in the region. With words to inspire you and maps to chart your path, it makes choosing the best route a breeze. Following are some of the highlights.

Maps

You'll find three levels of maps in this book: an **overall regional map, state locator maps,** and **detailed trail maps.**

The trails in this book are located in Michigan and Wisconsin. Each chapter details a particular state's network of trails, marked on locator maps in the chapter introduction. Use these maps to find the trails nearest you, or select several neighboring trails and plan a weekend hiking or biking excursion. Once you find a trail on a state locator map, simply flip to the corresponding page number for a full description. Accompanying trail maps mark each route's access roads, trailheads, parking areas, restrooms, and other defining features.

Key to Map Icons

P	🚶	🚻	- - - -	- - -	┼┼┼┼┼
parking	drinking water	restrooms	featured trail	connecting trail	active railroad

Trail Descriptions

Trails are listed in alphabetical order within each chapter. Each description leads off with a set of summary information, including trail endpoints and mileage, a roughness index, the trail surface, and possible uses.

The map and summary information list the trail endpoints (either a city, street, or more specific location), with suggested points from which to start and finish. Additional access points are marked on the maps and mentioned in the trail descriptions. The maps and descriptions also highlight available amenities, including parking and restrooms, as well as such area attractions as shops, services, museums, parks, and stadiums. Trail length is listed in miles.

Each trail bears a **roughness index** rating from 1 to 3. A rating of 1 indicates a smooth, level surface that is accessible to users of all ages and abilities. A 2 rating means the surface may be loose and/or uneven and could pose a

problem for road bikes and wheelchairs. A 3 rating suggests a rough surface that is only recommended for mountain bikers and hikers. Surfaces can range from asphalt or concrete to ballast, boardwalk, cinder, crushed stone, gravel, grass, dirt, sand, and/or woodchips. Where relevant, trail descriptions address alternating surface conditions.

All trails are open to pedestrians, and most allow bicycles, except where noted in the trail summary or description. The summary also indicates wheelchair access. Other possible uses include in-line skating, mountain biking, hiking, horseback riding, fishing, and cross-country skiing. While most trails are off-limits to motor vehicles, some local trail organizations do allow ATVs and snowmobiles.

The trail descriptions themselves suggest an ideal itinerary for each route, including the best parking areas and access points, where to begin, your direction of travel, and any highlights along the way. Following each description are directions to the recommended trailheads.

Each trail description also lists a local website for further information. Be sure to visit these websites in advance for updates and current conditions. **TrailLink .com** is another great resource for updated content on the trails in this guidebook.

Trail Use

Rail-trails are popular destinations for a range of users, often making them busy places to enjoy the outdoors. Following basic trail etiquette and safety guidelines will make your experience more pleasant.

➤ **Keep to the right,** except when passing.

➤ **Pass on the left,** and give a clear audible warning: "Passing on your left."

➤ **Be aware of other trail users,** particularly around corners and blind spots, and be especially careful when entering a trail, changing direction, or passing so that you don't collide with traffic.

➤ **Respect wildlife** and public and private property; leave no trace and take out litter.

➤ **Control your speed,** especially near pedestrians, playgrounds, and heavily congested areas.

➤ **Travel single file.** Cyclists and pedestrians should ride or walk single file in congested areas or areas with reduced visibility.

➤ **Cross carefully** at intersections; always look both ways and yield to through traffic. Pedestrians have the right-of-way.

➤ **Keep one ear open and volume low** on portable listening devices to increase your awareness of your surroundings.

➤ **Wear a helmet** and other safety gear if you're cycling or in-line skating.

➤ **Consider visibility.** Wear reflective clothing, use bicycle lights, or bring flashlights or helmet-mounted lights for tunnel passages or twilight excursions.

➤ **Keep moving,** and don't block the trail. When taking a rest, turn off the trail to the right. Groups should avoid congregating on or blocking the trails. If you have an accident on the trail, move to the right as soon as possible.

➤ **Bicyclists yield** to all other trail users. Pedestrians yield to horses. If in doubt, yield to all other trail users.

➤ **Check whether dogs are permitted on the trail.** Pets are allowed on most trails, but some trails through parks, wildlife refuges, or other sensitive areas may prohibit them; it's best to check the trail website before your visit. If pets are permitted, keep your dog on a short leash and under your control at all times. Remove dog waste in a designated trash receptacle.

➤ **Teach your children** these trail essentials, and be especially diligent to keep them out of faster-moving trail traffic.

➤ **Be prepared,** especially on long-distance rural trails. Bring water, snacks, maps, a light source, matches, and other equipment you may need. Because some areas may not have good reception for mobile phones, know where you're going, and tell someone else your plan.

Key to Trail Use

ATV	UTV	cycling	in-line skating	fishing	wheelchair access
horseback riding	mountain biking	snowmobiling	walking	cross-country skiing	snowshoeing

Learn More

To learn about additional multiuse trails in your area or to plan a trip to an area beyond the scope of this book, visit Rails-to-Trails Conservancy's trail-finder website, **TrailLink.com,** a free resource with information on more than 30,000 miles of trails nationwide.

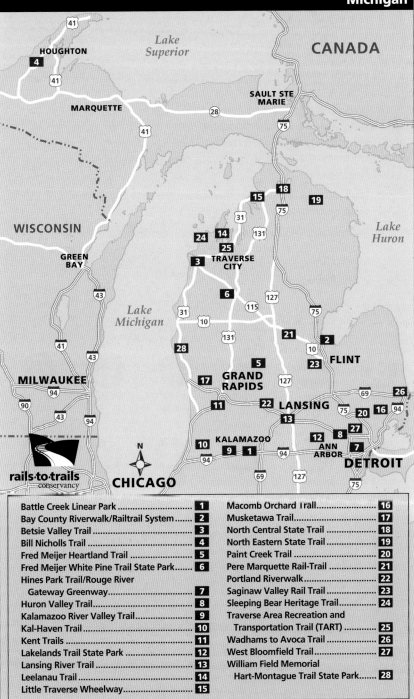

HOUGHTON

4

Lake
Superior

CANADA

MARQUETTE

SAULT STE
MARIE

28

75

41

WISCONSIN

18

15

19

75

31

24 **14**

131

25

3 TRAVERSE
CITY

GREEN
BAY

43

Lake
Michigan

31

6

127

115

10

75

41

131

21

2

43

28

10

FLINT

5

23

MILWAUKEE

94

17

GRAND
RAPIDS

127

90

43

94

11

22 LANSING

75 **20** **16**

69

26

94

13

27

8

10

KALAMAZOO

12

ANN
ARBOR

7

rails·to·trails
conservancy

N

CHICAGO

9 **1**

94

DETROIT

69

127

75

Lake
Huron

Michigan

North Eastern State Trail (Trail 19, page 75)

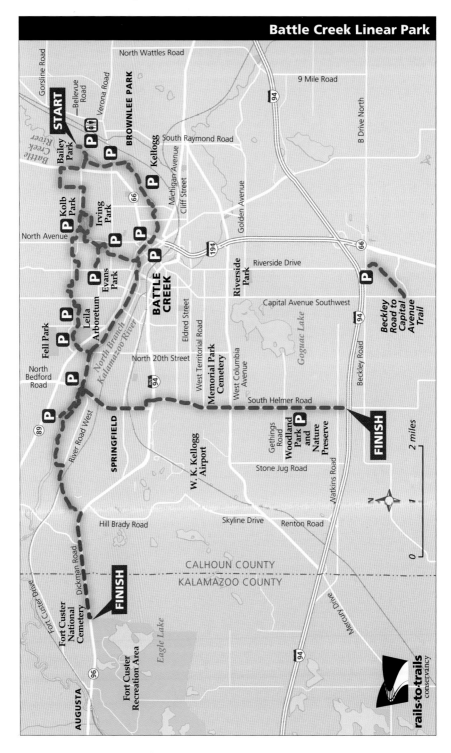

Battle Creek Linear Park

North Wattles Road

Gorsline Road

Bellevue Road

Verona Road

BROWNLEE PARK

START

Bailey Park

Kellogg

South Raymond Road

Battle Creek River

Kolb Park

66

Irving Park

North Avenue

Michigan Avenue

Cliff Street

9 Mile Road

94

B Drive North

Golden Avenue

194

66

Evans Park

BATTLE CREEK

Leila Arboretum

Eldred Street

North Branch Kalamazoo River

Riverside Park

Riverside Drive

Capital Avenue Southwest

94

Beckley Road to Capital Avenue Trail

Fell Park

94

North Bedford Road

North 20th Street

West Territorial Road

Memorial Park Cemetery

West Columbia Avenue

Goguac Lake

Beckley Road

89

River Road West

SPRINGFIELD

South Helmer Road

FINISH

W. K. Kellogg Airport

Gethings Road

Woodland Park and Nature Preserve

Stone Jug Road

Watkins Road

2 miles

Hill Brady Road

Skyline Drive

Renton Road

N

1

0

Dickman Road

FINISH

Fort Custer National Cemetery

Eagle Lake

CALHOUN COUNTY

KALAMAZOO COUNTY

Mercury Drive

94

Fort Custer Drive

96

AUGUSTA

Fort Custer Recreation Area

rails-to-trails conservancy

1 Battle Creek Linear Park

The Battle Creek Linear Park trail encompasses nearly 26 miles of connected trails in Battle Creek. Residents use the loop trails to put some snap, crackle, and pop in their exercise routines, while visitors to "America's Cereal City" can trek to parks, monuments, and museums located near the paths.

The city sits at the confluence of the North Branch Kalamazoo and Battle Creek Rivers, where the first settlers arrived in the 1830s and which remains a scenic part of the trail. The city later became home to the Kellogg brothers, who developed a way to make flaked breakfast cereals, launching an empire. The Kelloggs' interests embraced general health and wellness, a theme that inspired city leaders in the 1990s to create a linear park system of trails to encourage exercise.

View of the Battle Creek River

Counties
Calhoun, Kalamazoo

Endpoints
Bailey Park at Wagner Dr. and Eaton St. (Battle Creek) to Fort Custer National Cemetery at Battle Creek Blvd. and W. Dickman Road (Augusta) or Helmer Road S. and I-94 (Battle Creek)

Mileage
25.9

Type
Rail-Trail/Greenway

Roughness Index
1

Surface
Asphalt

The route offers a quaint journey through America's Cereal City.

Self-propelled visitors can take a 10.5-mile loop that encircles the city, or shorter loops of 6.6 or 6.9 miles by splitting the long loop. Other trails head south toward Woodland Park or west toward Fort Custer State Recreation Area. Along the way, look for gardens, gazebos, benches, fountains, and historical markers. Maps are available in boxes along the trail or online at the Battle Creek Parks and Recreation website.

Beginning at the Bailey Park trailhead in the eastern end, head south (left) when you arrive at the main loop to take a clockwise tour. You'll pass through the woods along the Battle Creek River, just across from the sprawling Kellogg Co. facility.

About 3 miles from your trailhead, you arrive at Division Street. Just off the trail, two blocks south, is Monument Park's Sojourner Truth statue, which commemorates the ex-slave who moved to the city in 1858 and tirelessly crusaded for the abolition of slavery. Returning to the trail, you'll see more evidence of Battle Creek's efforts to end slavery at the Underground Railroad Sculpture. Across the park is the historic Kellogg House.

You'll pass the 1888 Michigan Central Railroad Depot in the next block. It was later used by the New York Central and Penn Central Railroads, and lastly by Amtrak until 1982, when track owner Conrail stopped using this part of the

line. In 0.5 mile, just before the Battle Creek Area Math and Science Center, a side trail heads across town to the north side of the loop at Kolb Park.

Traveling along the Kalamazoo River now, you'll reach a junction where a branch of the Linear Park Trail heads west for just under 6 miles to the Fort Custer National Cemetery, where the trail ends. Here, you can access the northeast section of the Fort Custer State Recreation Area, a 3,000-acre park with three lakes, 200 campsites, and miles of mountain biking and hiking trails through woodland and restored prairies.

Another branch off this trail heads south for 5 miles along Helmer Road past Woodland Park and Nature Preserve.

Turning north on the loop trail, you'll enter the 85-acre Leila Arboretum, home to ornamental trees and shrubs, numerous perennial gardens, and the Kingman Museum. Continuing on the loop trail, you'll take a serpentine route eastward for 4.1 miles back to Bailey Park. About halfway through this segment, you'll pass Kolb Park, which has its own 1-mile loop around two lakes.

CONTACT: bcparks.org/134/linear-park

DIRECTIONS

To reach the eastern trailhead parking lot at Bailey Park from I-94, take Exit 98B from the west, or Exit 98A from the east, onto northbound I-194. Go 3.8 miles—I-194 becomes Division St.—and turn right onto MI 66 E./Capital Ave. NE. Follow Capital for 2.1 miles, and turn right on E. Roosevelt Ave.; the entrance and parking area for Bailey Park will be just ahead on your left.

The best official parking for the western end of the trail is on Jackson St. W./Stringham Road, south of Babcock St. and just north of the North Branch Kalamazoo River. To reach the parking lot from MI 89 in Battle Creek, head south 0.2 mile, and look for a small parking lot on your right, just past Stringham Road. The trail begins on the north side of the river and heads southeast.

To reach the westernmost endpoint for the trail, located north of the state recreation area, take the trail southeast along the river for 0.6 mile, turn right on the trail at S. Bedford Road, and turn right onto the trail, heading west for 5 miles.

To reach parking for the southern endpoint on Helmer Road from I-94, take Exit 95, head north on Helmer Road S. for 1 mile, and turn left into the parking lot at Woodland Park and Nature Preserve. The trail endpoint is located 1 mile south along the trail, just north of I-94.

Bay County Riverwalk/Railtrail System

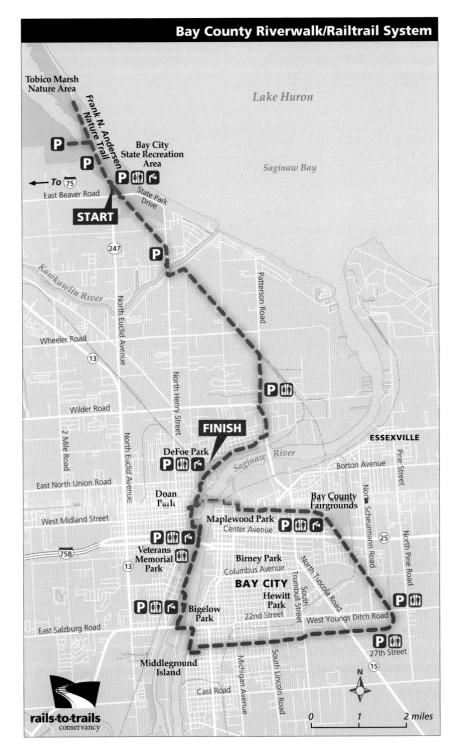

The Bay County Riverwalk/Railtrail System connects a nature trail in a wildlife refuge on the shores of Lake Huron to a loop trail around the bustling port of Bay City. From the same 17-mile paved trail, visitors can see thousands of migratory waterfowl on Saginaw Bay, cargo and naval vessels in the Saginaw River, and lumber barons' homes in the city's historic district.

A 7.7-mile-long rail corridor links the Tobico Marsh Nature Area in the north with the 9.8-mile Bay City loop in the south. Originally created in the 1880s as the Detroit, Bay City & Alpena Railroad, the rail line hauled pine from northern forests to the growing port of Bay City. Renamed

County
Bay

Endpoints
Killarney Beach Road near Athlone Beach Road at Bay City State Recreation Area to N. Tuscola Road between 27th St. and 22nd St. (Bay City)

Mileage
17.8

Type
Rail-Trail

Roughness Index
1

Surface
Asphalt, Boardwalk, Concrete

Experience the serenity of the Bay County Riverwalk/Railtrail System.

Great for bikers, the Bay County Riverwalk has diverse landscapes including serene waterfront views.

the Detroit and Mackinac Railroad in 1894, the railway was acquired in 1992 by Lake State Railway, which stopped using some sections.

Shaped overall like a lasso, the trail has many access points. It is mostly paved with asphalt as a separate path, although there are sidewalk sections alongside roads and boardwalks on the waterfront. Follow the directional arrows to stay on the path through Bay City.

Beginning at the Bay City State Recreation Area trailhead just off East Beaver Road/State Park Drive, you can visit the Tobico Marsh Nature Area by heading north for 1 mile on the Frank N. Andersen Nature Trail (part of the Bay County trail system). Bird-watchers use the two observation towers and 2.7-mile nature trail loop to view migratory birds.

Heading south from the Bay City State Recreation Area, you'll cross the Kawkawlin River and leave the rail corridor in 3.2 miles. From here, travel begins on paved paths separated from city streets or sidewalks. Just past the riverfront DeFoe Park, you'll arrive at the start of the Bay City loop. Going south to make a counterclockwise loop, you'll find many tempting eateries specializing in ethnic cuisine.

The trail continues past a bustling marina to the popular waterfront Veterans Memorial Park, featuring gardens in the Kantzler Memorial Arboretum, riverside benches, and memorials of bygone shipbuilding days. Bird-watchers will enjoy the riverfront boardwalk and pedestrian bridge over to Middleground Island and Bigelow Park. (Another pedestrian bridge at Hotchkiss Road is planned to link with the Saginaw County to Bay County Connector trail, which begins at the easternmost end of East Hotchkiss Road.) Taking the Lafayette Street Bridge, the route continues south past waterfront businesses before heading into the residential district.

After Trumbull Street, the corridor opens up for a smooth pass through farmland and woodlots for a couple of miles on a former Penn Central Railroad corridor. Heading north, you'll brush the eastern edge of Bay City's Center Avenue Historic District, where the local 19th-century elite built homes that still survive. In 2.4 miles, you'll close the loop after crossing the Saginaw River on the Liberty Bridge's sidewalk. DeFoe Park is 0.6 mile north.

CONTACT: bayfoundation.org/about-us/riverwalkrailtrail

DIRECTIONS

To reach the Bay City State Recreation Area trailhead from I-75, take Exit 168 (about 7.4 miles northwest of Bay City) onto Beaver Road/State Park Dr., heading east. Follow for 5.1 miles, and turn left to find parking in the recreation area.

To reach the DeFoe Park trailhead from I-75, take Exit 164 (about 2.7 miles northwest of Bay City) onto Wilder Road, heading east. Go 2.1 miles, and turn right onto N. Henry St. Follow Henry for 0.8 mile, and turn left onto W. Hart St. Go 0.6 mile, and turn right onto Marquette Ave.; then go 0.2 mile, and turn right into DeFoe Park.

To reach the southern trailhead at N. Tuscola Road from I-75, take Exit 160 for MI 84/ Saginaw Road, just southwest of Bay City. Continue onto MI 84 N. for 2 miles, and bear right to continue east for 1.1 miles on MI 84/Salzburg Ave., crossing the Saginaw River. Continue straight on Lafayette Ave. for 0.6 mile, and then continue onto 22nd St./Kosciuszko Ave. for 1.5 miles. Turn right onto MI 15 S./Tuscola Road, and follow for 0.3 mile. Make a U-turn at 27th St., and look for parking immediately to your right, just past the RAILTRAIL sign.

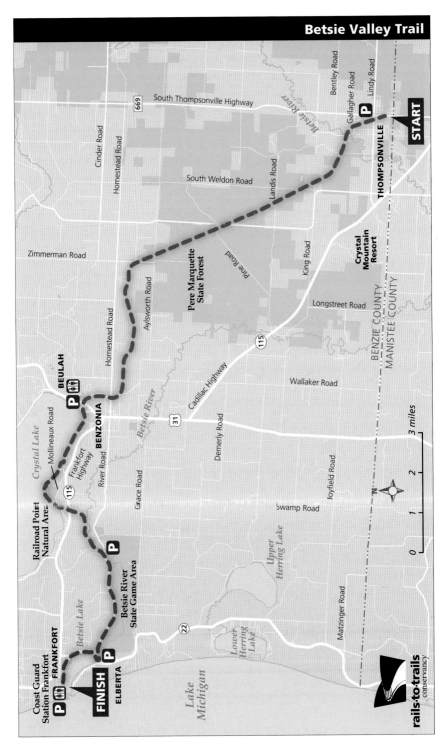

Betsie Valley Trail

Remoteness and solitude describe a trip along the 22-mile Betsie Valley Trail in Michigan's northern Lower Peninsula. Starting at the old logging town of Thompsonville, the trail slopes gently downhill in the Betsie River Valley through a state forest, a natural area, and a game refuge on its way to the port of Frankfort on Lake Michigan. The western 6 miles are paved, while the rest of the trail is covered in crushed limestone (which may be soft in some spots). Snowmobiles are allowed in season between Thompsonville and Beulah.

The trail follows the corridor of a railroad line that opened operations between Cadillac and Frankfort in 1888 and became part of the Ann Arbor Railroad in 1895. The railroad struggled; a railroad car ferry across Lake Michigan from 1892 to 1982 was its most profitable business. The railroad went through a series of owners after World War II. The section that is now the Betsie Valley Trail became disused in the early 1990s and began its transformation into a trail in 1992.

Wetland views at the mouth of the Betsie River

County
Benzie

Endpoints
County Road 669/ Michigan Ave. north of E. Easy St. (Thompsonville) to Waterfront Dr. east of Frankfurter St. (Frankfort)

Mileage
22.1

Type
Rail-Trail

Roughness Index
2

Surface
Asphalt, Crushed Stone

Beginning in Thompsonville, you'll head north through farmland for about a mile until you cross a renovated railroad bridge and enter a 7-mile stretch of pine and hardwood in the Pere Marquette State Forest. Along the way, you'll see the old turbine that supplied the sole source of electricity in this area. Near Aylsworth and Zimmerman Roads, you'll pass the ghost town of Homestead, where railroad maintenance workers lived at the turn of the 19th century.

The trail offers a gradual descent along the 5.3-mile stretch between Aylsworth Road and Beulah, where you can stop by the replica railroad depot for visitor information, restrooms, and memorabilia. Just west of Beulah, the trail meets the south shore of Crystal Lake and winds through a row of beachside cottages. Dogs are not allowed on the trail between Beulah and Mollineaux Road (about 3 miles). Trail users must stay within the 10-foot trail easement for a 2-mile stretch west of Beulah to Railroad Point Natural Area, a 200-acre refuge that offers a 1-mile stretch of preserved beach along Crystal Lake.

At Mollineaux Road, near mile 15, the trail surface becomes asphalt, and the route veers into the woods and follows the Betsie River and adjacent marshland past the Betsie River State Game Area. About 7 miles past Beulah, you cross the Betsie River into Elberta, which has cafés and visitors' services. You can take Frankfort Avenue north for a mile to see ruins at the old railyard at the mouth of Betsie Lake. Crossing the river again on MI 22, the trail takes a 2-mile run into Frankfort along the lake and past marinas to the Lake Michigan shoreline.

Several towns, including Beulah, Elberta, and Frankfort, as well as the Crystal Mountain resort near Thompsonville, have bike rentals, and you can shuttle between towns on the Benzie Bus.

CONTACT: betsievalleytrail.org

DIRECTIONS

To reach the Thompsonville trailhead from US 131, take Exit 176 toward Frankfort onto MI 115/55 in Cadillac, heading northwest. After 34.4 miles, turn right onto Thompsonville Road. Go 2 miles, and turn left onto County Road 602/Lincoln St. In 0.1 mile, turn right into the park (entrance will be before the Betsie Valley Trail and Front St.); look for parking straight ahead in about 0.1 mile. The trail's endpoint is located 0.4 miles south along the trail.

To reach the Frankfort trailhead from US 131, take Exit 176 toward Frankfort onto MI 115/55 in Cadillac, heading northwest. Go 44.8 miles and bear right as US 31 joins MI 115. Go 2.3 miles and turn left onto MI 115/Frankfort Hwy. Go 7.3 miles, continuing onto Forest Ave., and turn left onto Fifth St. Go 0.1 mile (you'll cross Main St. and head into the marina), and look for parking to the left or right off Waterfront Dr.

The Bill Nicholls Trail wanders for 41 miles through the Upper Peninsula's scenic Copper Country, where visitors can spot wildlife and see remnants of the copper mining that flourished for more than 100 years. The soft-surface trail is a popular destination for motorized off-road vehicles such as all-terrain vehicles and snowmobiles, so mountain bikers and hikers should be prepared to deal with wear and tear on the trail.

Most of the trail follows the route of the Copper Range Railroad, built between 1899 and 1901 to haul copper ore from the mines that proliferated on the peninsula from the mid-19th century until the 1960s. When the state acquired the line in 1974, it was among the first disused railroad corridors in Michigan converted to a public trail.

Beginning at the Ontonagon County Fairgrounds outside of Greenland, the first couple of miles can be challenging for trail users. A rock escarpment, steep grades, and mine tailings placed on the trail to prevent erosion will force you to watch your progress. You'll soon pass the Adventure Mine, a copper mine (1850–1920) that's now open for tours as part of the Keweenaw National Historical Park, a collection of heritage sites celebrating the region's copper-mining history.

Counties
Houghton, Ontonagon

Endpoints
Depot St. (Greenland) between Ridge Road and Adventure Ave. to Raymond C. Kestner Waterfront Park at Houghton Canal Road west of W. Lakeshore Dr. (Houghton)

Mileage
41.5

Type
Rail-Trail

Roughness Index
3

Surface
Ballast, Dirt, Gravel, Sand

The Bill Nicholls Trail takes you near Twin Lakes.

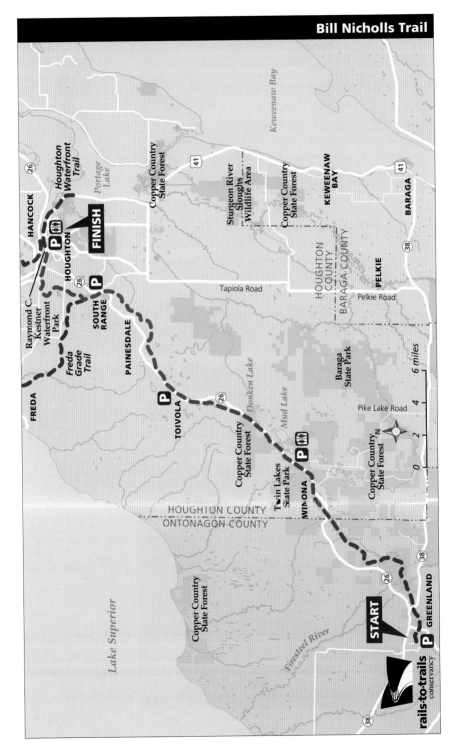

Bill Nicholls Trail

At 2 miles, the trail heads northeast and merges with the former railroad line and its level surface. Not long after crossing MI 38, you'll cross the first of three steel bridges over the Firesteel River, which total 1,300 feet in length and clear the rivers by 85 feet, creating one of the trail's scenic highlights.

The trail passes through a remote stretch of pine and hardwood forests as you reach Twin Lakes State Park near mile 16.4, where the trail parallels MI 26 and allows access to the park and nearby businesses. After the state park, the trail passes several small lakes, traverses scenic woodlands, and is periodically lined with wild blackberry and thimbleberry bushes.

With a tower as your beacon, you arrive at the crossroads community of Toivola, which offers a restaurant and grocery store near mile 25.2. You'll pass old ruins of the mining era and piles of mine tailings. After crossing MI 26 into South Range at mile 34.4, you can visit the Copper Range Historical Museum and check out local offerings.

The last 4 miles into Houghton are all downhill. About 1.5 miles from the trail's end is a scenic overlook at the Portage Lake Ship Canal, which played a big role in the copper industry by removing an obstacle for shipping. The final leg of the trail parallels the canal. About 1 mile from the end, you'll encounter a steep slope with loose stone. The trail ends at the city's RV park in Houghton, near the Raymond C. Kestner Waterfront Park, which provides picnic facilities, restrooms, a beach, and a playground. Here, you can also connect with the 4.5-mile Houghton Waterfront Trail, a paved pathway that links a series of small waterfront parks along an inlet of Portage Lake.

CONTACT: exploringthenorth.com/keweenaw/billnichols.html

DIRECTIONS

To reach the southern trailhead in Greenland from the intersection of US 45 and MI 26 near Rockland, head right (northeast) on MI 26. Go 5.5 miles, and turn left on MI 38 W. Go 0.5 mile, and turn left onto Plank Road. Follow Plank for 0.7 mile, and turn left onto Depot St. in Greenland. Parking at the fairgrounds is in 0.3 mile on the right; the trail is another 0.3 mile on the left.

To reach the northern trailhead in Houghton from the intersection of US 45 and MI 26, head right (northeast) on MI 26. Go 43.1 miles to Houghton—MI 26 joins W. Memorial Dr.—and turn left at W. Lakeshore Dr. Parking is available in the park on your left. The trail starts about 0.3 mile west through the RV park.

The northern trailhead is also accessible via US 41, a trip of 28 miles north from the intersection with MI 38 in Baraga. Heading into Houghton, US 41 will eventually turn into Memorial Dr. After 0.3 mile, turn right onto W. Lakeshore Dr. Parking is available in the park on your left. The trail starts about 0.3 mile west through the RV park.

Fred Meijer Heartland Trail

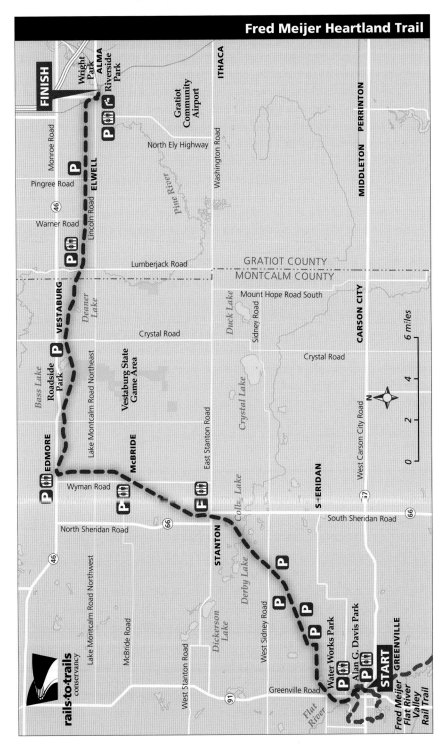

FINISH

Wright Park

ALMA

Riverside Park

ITHACA

Gratiot Community Airport

PERRINTON

North Ely Highway

Monroe Road

Pingree Road

ELWELL

Washington Road

Pine River

MIDDLETON

46

Warner Road

Lincoln Road

Lumberjack Road

GRATIOT COUNTY

MONTCALM COUNTY

VESTABURG

Deaner Lake

Crystal Road

Duck Lake

Mount Hope Road South

Sidney Road

CARSON CITY

Crystal Road

6 miles

Bass Lake

Roadside Park

Lake Montcalm Road Northeast

Vestaburg State Game Area

Crystal Lake

West Carson City Road

N

4

EDMORE

McBRIDE

East Stanton Road

2

Wyman Road

Colby Lake

0

North Sheridan Road

66

S ERIDAN

South Sheridan Road

66

46

STANTON

Derby Lake

37

Lake Montcalm Road Northwest

McBride Road

West Stanton Road

Dickerson Lake

West Sidney Road

Water Works Park

Alan G. Davis Park

GREENVILLE

START

Greenville Road

91

Flat River

Fred Meijer Flat River Valley Rail Trail

rails-to-trails
conservancy

The paved Fred Meijer Heartland Trail rolls for 42 miles through farmland and forests in central Michigan as it links a half-dozen rural towns with recreational opportunities. Its route follows the corridors of two Pere Marquette Railroad branches that crossed in Edmore with connections to Grand Rapids in the south and Saginaw in the east. In 1947, the railroad merged into the Chesapeake and Ohio Railway, later to become the Chessie System. CSX Transportation ended up with the rail lines in 1986, and they fell into disuse by 1994.

Midwest grocery-store magnate Fred Meijer, who got his start working in the family store in Greenville, and his wife, Lena, helped buy the former rail bed, which Rails-to-Trails Conservancy held until a citizens group could take over the trail's development and operation in 2000. Another purchase in 2005 completed the trail from Greenville to Edmore to Alma.

Bridges make for a nice escape into gorgeous foliage.

Counties
Gratiot, Montcalm

Endpoints
E. Washington St. between Flat River and S. Cedar St./Fred Meijer Flat River Valley Rail Trail (Greenville) to Prospect Ave. between W. Center St. and Mechanic St. (Alma)

Mileage
41.8

Type
Rail-Trail

Roughness Index
1

Surface
Asphalt

The Fred Meijer Heartland Trail runs through rural Michigan.

The trail meets both the Fred Meijer Flat River Trail and the Fred Meijer Flat River Valley Rail Trail in Greenville. The three trails, along with the Fred Meijer Grand River Valley Rail Trail and the Fred Meijer Clinton-Ionia-Shiawassee Trail farther south, are components of the Fred Meijer Mid-West Michigan Trail Network, which will eventually stretch 125 miles from Owosso to Alma.

Technically, the trail begins on the north side of East Washington Street, just north of Jackson's Landing Park, but note that parking near the endpoint is

available only on the south side of East Washington Street. Here, the trail meets with the northern endpoint of the Fred Meijer Flat River Valley Rail Trail, which heads south to Lowell and crosses the Fred Meijer Flat River Trail, which circles Greenville. Heading north, you'll pass an old railroad depot at East Grove and North Court Streets and cross the Flat River on a restored trestle. Here, at Water Works Park, you'll find Little League fields and more public parking.

A trail interruption creates a 2.1-mile detour on bike lanes on Peck and South Lake Roads until you regain the trail for a peaceful stretch through prime farmland, woods, wildlife areas, wetlands, and small historic towns. A side trip on Sidney Road visits the Heritage Village at Montcalm Community College, where a cluster of 28 historical buildings depict life at the turn of the 20th century.

Before arriving in Stanton, you'll cross Fish Creek on an 1880 trestle that was relocated here from Greenville. You'll find a variety of eateries in Stanton and McBride, and in between you may be surprised by roaring dragsters at the Mid Michigan Motorplex.

The railroad crossroads town of Edmore is roughly halfway. You'll find more places to eat here, as well as eclectic memorabilia at the Old Fence Rider Historical Center on South Sheldon Street. In about 3 miles, you'll cross County Road 575 just 200 feet south of the trail's oddest landmark, a two-story outhouse. Legend has it that a local businessman built it next to his two-story office/home so his family could have a private upstairs entrance.

The trail passes through Vestaburg State Game Area for 2.5 miles. Many white-tailed deer, foxes, muskrats, and other animals can be seen here. Ten miles past Edmore, you'll pass a restored one-room schoolhouse in Riverdale. The town of Elwell, 2 miles farther, has limited services for trail users, but your journey ends 4 miles later in Alma, home of Alma College and the Highland Festival, as well as cafés, grocery stores, and a bike shop.

CONTACT: mitrails.org/Fred-Meijer-Heartland-Trail-62.php or facebook.com
/fred-meijer-heartland-trail-106243959468119

DIRECTIONS

To reach the southern trailhead at Jackson's Landing in Greenville from US 131 in Cedar Springs, take Exit 101 for MI 57 toward Kent B72/Greenville/Sparta, and head east on MI 57/14 Mile Road NE/E. Washington St. for 16.9 miles. Turn right into Jackson's Landing Park, which is just before the intersection with the Fred Meijer Heartland Trail.

To reach parking at the northern endpoint in Alma from US 127, take Exit 123 in Alma, and head west on Bus. US 27/E. Lincoln Road. Go 2.9 miles, and turn left onto N. State St. Go 2 blocks, turn right onto Mechanic St., and then go 2 more blocks and turn right onto Park Ave. Turn right into the parking area.

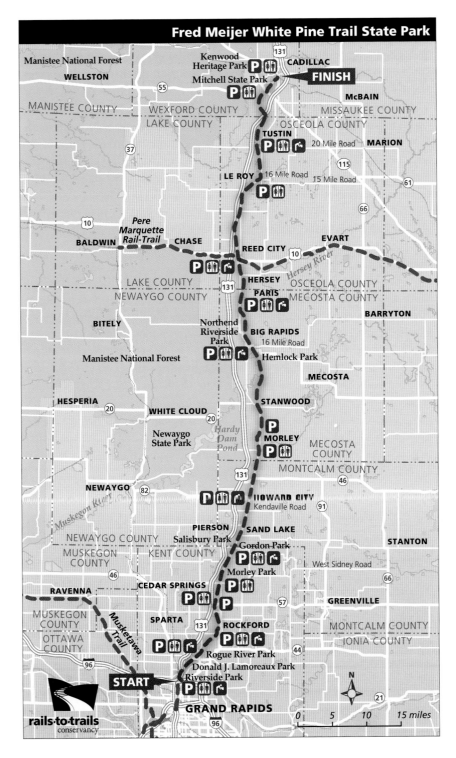

Fred Meijer White Pine Trail State Park

Fred Meijer White Pine Trail State Park makes tracks from a bustling Grand Rapids community to the forests, farmlands, and friendly towns of Northern Lower Michigan. At nearly 93 miles, it is the state's second longest rail-trail (the State Line Trail on the Upper Peninsula is longer, at 107 miles) and the state's longest linear park. More than a dozen towns that tended to trains running between Grand Rapids and Cadillac now cater to hikers and bikers by offering food, lodging, or camping.

Asphalt covers about 52 miles of the trail, while two sections of about 10 miles (Reed City to Le Roy) and about 30 miles (Sand Lake to Big Rapids, with the exception of blacktop in Howard City) are packed ballast or gravel. Long-range plans call for paving the entire trail with asphalt as funds become available.

Fred Meijer White Pine Trail State Park is one of the longest rail-trails in Michigan.

Counties
Kent, Mecosta, Montcalm, Osceola, Wexford

Endpoints
N, Park St. NE at Mill Creek Ave. NE (Walker) to S. Lake St. at W. Chapin St. (Cadillac)

Mileage
92.6

Type
Rail-Trail

Roughness Index
2

Surface
Asphalt, Ballast, Crushed Stone, Gravel

The route follows the former rail line of the Grand Rapids and Indiana Railroad.

Horses are prohibited from the trail, but snowmobiles are allowed from Russell Road (north of downtown Rockford) to the trail's north endpoint in Cadillac. The trail isn't groomed for cross-country skiing, although it is an approved use.

Officially opened in 1995, the trail follows the rail bed of the Grand Rapids and Indiana Railroad that laid the first tracks from Grand Rapids to Cedar Springs in 1867. By 1873, the railroad ran from Cincinnati to Little Traverse Bay. Its prime business of hauling lumber out of Michigan's old-growth forests dwindled at the end of the century, replaced by a brisk tourism trade to northern fishing camps and resorts. Subsequent owners include the Pennsylvania Railroad in 1918 and the state in 1975. Operations ceased between Grand Rapids and Cadillac in 1984.

Beginning near the stadium for the West Michigan Whitecaps Minor League Baseball team just north of Grand Rapids, you'll head north on 21 miles of paved trail through mostly rural terrain. The first of several historic railroad trestles crosses the Rogue River as you enter Rockford about 8.2 miles from the trail's start. Rockford has many opportunities for dining; you can also enjoy a picnic at the scenic overlook of the Rogue River Dam. After passing through Cedar Springs, the pavement ends as you approach Sand Lake, about 12 miles past Rockford.

It's another 7 miles to Howard City; a short stretch of asphalt heads through town, where you'll find groceries and cafés. Morley, in 7 miles, has an ice-cream shop, and Stanwood, in 6 miles, has a convenience store and café. You'll enter

the Muskegon River Valley and return to paved trail before you arrive in Big Rapids in 9 miles. You can connect to the Big Rapids Riverwalk to head into town to grab a bite or take a rest stop. Leaving town, a 319-foot bridge provides a scenic Muskegon River crossing.

Six miles north is Paris, where the trail runs through Paris Park, featuring camp-in cabins, a canoe launch, and a fishing concession along the banks of the Muskegon River. Continuing 6.4 miles to Reed City, trail users can catch a view of the Yoplait Yogurt factory and cross the junction with the Pere Marquette Rail-Trail (Trail 21, page 81) before taking a covered bridge over the Hersey River.

The trail is ballast and gravel for the next 12 miles to just south of Le Roy, and in another 5 miles you'll arrive in Tustin, which has railroad memorabilia at the Pine River Museum. Heading north another 11.2 miles takes you to the trail's end in Cadillac on Lake Cadillac, where you can enjoy swimming beaches and an outdoor amphitheater for concerts.

CONTACT: www.whitepinetrail.com

DIRECTIONS

Parking and access to the trail are provided at each community along the trail. Camping is available in Belmont, Cedar Springs, Sand Lake, Morley, Paris, Reed City, and Cadillac, and Hersey and Evart (both on the Pere Marquette State Trail).

To reach the trailhead in Comstock Park from I-96, take Exit 31B, and drive 1.5 miles north on US 131. Take Exit 91 to West River Dr., and turn right. Go 0.8 mile, turn left onto Lamoreaux Dr. NE, and look for the parking lot immediately on the right. The trail endpoint is just over a half mile south, in Walker, at N. Park St. NE.

To reach the trailhead in Cadillac from US 131, take Exit 177 onto northbound Bus. US 131/ S. 43 Mile Road toward Cadillac. Go 1.9 miles, turn left onto South St., and then turn right onto S. Lake St. Go 0.2 mile, and look for parking on the left, just across W. Chapin St. Take the pathway in the back of the parking lot 0.2 mile south to reach the trail endpoint at South St. and S. Lake St.

Hines Park Trail/Rouge River Gateway Greenway

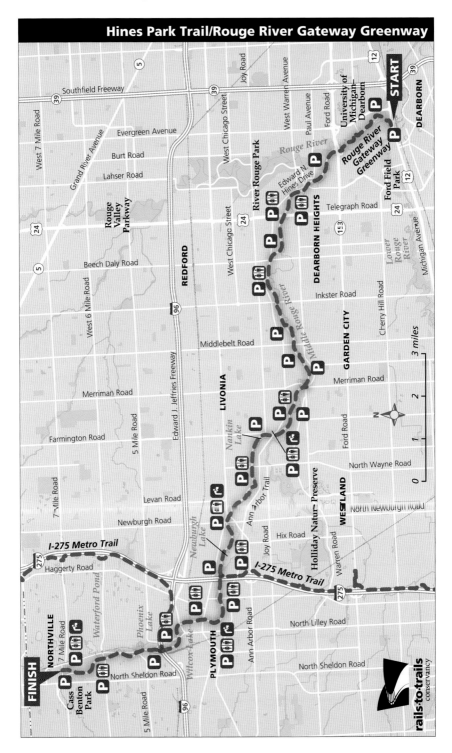

This trail is actually composed of two trails: the 2-mile Rouge River Gateway Greenway and the 17.5-mile Hines Park Trail, which create a seamless 19.5-mile connection between Dearborn and Northville.

Starting at the Michigan Avenue trailhead in Dearborn, the Rouge River Gateway Greenway winds north through the University of Michigan–Dearborn campus for 2 miles. Just south is Henry Ford's popular yesteryear tourist attraction, Greenfield Village, an 80-acre open-air museum featuring seven historic districts covering 300 years of American life.

Heading north toward the university, you'll cross the Lower Rouge River and Fair Lane Drive, where the historic Henry Ford Estate sits to your left. The trail then runs along Fair Lane Drive and past the university and its affiliated environmental interpretive center, and

You're likely to see vintage cars of all kinds along the Hines Park Trail.

County
Wayne

Endpoints
Michigan Ave. north of Elm St. and Dearborn Station (Dearborn) to W. Seven Mile Road and River St. (Northville)

Mileage
19.5

Type
Greenway

Roughness Index
1

Surface
Asphalt

then crosses the Rouge River again near Kingfisher Bluff—a bend in the river that is now a storm-water management project with an observation overlook and interpretive signage.

Crossing over Ford Road, the trail turns into the Hines Park Trail, which takes you 17.5 miles to Northville. Automotive history is not confined to Greenfield Village, as classic-car buffs tend to flock to Edward N. Hines Drive, which runs adjacent to the trail, for official and unofficial events; don't be surprised to see Model T Fords and flashy cars of all vintages along this historic stretch of trail.

The trail travels through Wayne County's linear Hines Park, which has a dog park and plentiful picnic facilities, gazebos, sports fields, exercise equipment, ponds, playgrounds, restrooms, and parking. Near the middle of the trail, just before reaching Ann Arbor Trail, is historic Nankin Mills, a gristmill turned natural and cultural interpretive center, which has indoor restrooms and tanks with local wildlife, such as turtles. You can rent bikes and Segways and purchase snacks at the private establishment next to the gristmill.

Before reaching mile 11, the trail intersects the 33.2-mile I-275 Metro Trail, which runs north to Novi and south to New Boston.

Restrooms and parking are accessible in very short intervals throughout the park, but water is less plentiful; those planning to travel the entire length of the park should bring a bottle and fill up when possible.

The trail repeatedly intersects the Rouge River—historically embattled by industrial waste but making a comeback (note that on portions of the trail near the river, flooding can be an issue). Although the river and woods create a nice backdrop, the trail runs next to the 40-mile-per-hour park road, Edward N. Hines Drive, for most of the way to Northville, creating not the away-from-it-all experience preferred by some trail users. However, its proximity to thousands of adjacent suburban homes makes it an ideal "close-to-home" gem for recreation, fitness, and travel.

CONTACT: mitrails.org/Hines-Park-Trail-81.php or mitrails.org/Rouge-River
-Gateway-Trail-82.php

DIRECTIONS

To reach the southern trailhead in Dearborn from I-94 in Taylor, take Exit 204 for MI 39 N./ Southfield Fwy. N. Merge onto Southfield Fwy. N. and go 2.5 miles. Take Exit 6 toward US 12/ Michigan Ave., and go 0.2 mile. Merge onto Southfield Road, and go 0.3 mile. Take the ramp onto US 12 W./Michigan Ave. heading west, and go 1.4 miles. Turn right into the trailhead parking lot, which is located north of Dearborn Station.

To reach the northern trailhead in Northville from MI 14 in Plymouth, take Exit 20 for Sheldon Road, head north on Sheldon Road, and go 2.7 miles. Turn right onto Edward N. Hines Dr., and go 0.4 mile (you'll pass W. Seven Mile Road on your left). Turn left into the parking lot. The northern endpoint is about 0.3 mile north on the Hines Park Trail.

The trail can also be accessed at many points along Edward N. Hines Dr. between Dearborn and Northville, with parking lots at frequent intervals.

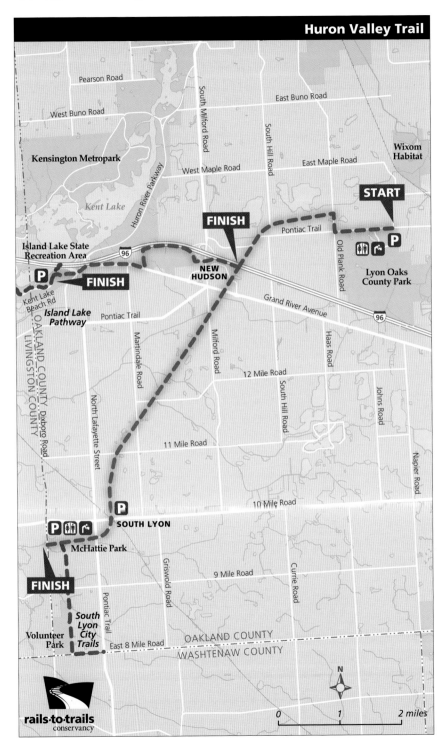

Huron Valley Trail

Pearson Road

West Buno Road

East Buno Road

South Milford Road

South Hill Road

East Maple Road

West Maple Road

Kensington Metropark

Kent Lake

Huron River Parkway

Wixom Habitat

START

Island Lake State Recreation Area

96

Pontiac Trail

Old Plank Road

FINISH

NEW HUDSON

Grand River Avenue

96

Lyon Oaks County Park

Kent Lake Beach Rd

FINISH

Island Lake Pathway

Pontiac Trail

Martindale Road

Milford Road

12 Mile Road

South Hill Road

Haas Road

Johns Road

OAKLAND COUNTY Dixboro Road

LIVINGSTON COUNTY

North Lafayette Street

11 Mile Road

Napier Road

SOUTH LYON

10 Mile Road

McHattie Park

Griswold Road

9 Mile Road

Currie Road

FINISH

Pontiac Trail

South Lyon City Trails

Volunteer Park

East 8 Mile Road

OAKLAND COUNTY

WASHTENAW COUNTY

N

rails-to-trails
conservancy

0   1   2 miles

Paved and mostly flat, the Huron Valley Trail links several suburban communities, parks, and a large recreation area while providing connections to a growing network of trails.

Forming a lowercase *y* shape, the trail can be divided into three sections—northeast, west, and south—of fairly equal lengths. From the northeast to the south, the trail is flat and passes through wooded areas bordering residential neighborhoods and travels across creeks, past ponds, and along a surface street. The western branch features

County
Oakland

Endpoints
Pontiac Trail and Product Dr. at Lyon Oaks County Park (Wixom) to Dixboro Road north of Londonderry Dr., west of McHattie Park; Island Lake Pathway at Kent Lake Beach Road in Island Lake State Recreation Area (South Lyon) to the Huron Valley Trail just south of I-96 and north of Lyon Center Dr. (South Lyon)

Mileage
12.2

Type
Rail-Trail, Greenway/Non-Rail-Trail

Roughness Index
1–2

Surface
Asphalt

Trekkers are treated to fields of flowers along the Huron Valley Trail.

The trail's natural setting and mostly flat surface make for a pleasant journey.

more hills and ends at the Island Lake State Recreation Area, where it meets the Island Lake Pathway at Kent Lake Beach Road. The trail contains bumpy and potholed pavement in some sections, and some road crossings are gravel.

The trail's northeastern endpoint begins in Wixom at the edge of Lyon Oaks County Park. Flat, it passes fields of flowers and stands of trees and other foliage and periodically crosses wooden footbridges. Note for all trail users: Among several road crossings in the northeast branch, one requires extra vigilance. After crossing South Hill Road, you'll head southwest and cross a curved section of Pontiac Trail—a high-speed road. There is a crosswalk but no traffic light. Traffic from the west (to your right) comes around a blind curve just before the crossing. Use extra caution here.

Near the midpoint of the trail in New Hudson, users can choose to continue south toward Dixboro Road or turn right onto a western segment of trail toward the 4,000-acre Island Lake State Recreation Area. Heading west, you'll pass strip malls and a former industrial park; here the trail surface is rocky and uneven and requires extra care to navigate. The western branch terminates inside the state recreation area at Kent Lake Beach Road, where you can pick up the 4-mile Island Lake Pathway. The popular park also offers canoeing, volleyball courts, picnic shelters, swimming, and cabin rentals.

The southern branch of the *y* is similar to the northeast branch, featuring wooded areas interspersed with suburban neighborhoods. Entering the city of South Lyon, the Huron Valley Trail overlaps a portion of the South Lyon city trail system. Signage—limited throughout—can be confusing in this area. At

10 Mile Road, the trail parallels Reynoldsweet Street a short distance toward McHattie Park, which has parking, restrooms, and a drinking fountain near the trail's terminus.

Just before the terminus at Dixboro Road north of Londonderry Drive, users can continue south along another city trail that passes over wetlands and along extended wooden footbridges, through suburban neighborhoods, and past a park containing athletic fields.

CONTACT: southlyonmi.org/residents/community/rail_trail.php

DIRECTIONS

To reach the northeast trailhead at Lyon Oaks County Park in Wixom from I-96, take Exit 155 from the west, or Exit 155B from the east, toward New Hudson/Milford, and head north on Milford Road for 0.3 mile. Turn right onto Pontiac Trail, and go 2.7 miles. Turn right at Holtz Drive, go 0.4 mile, and turn at the dead end into the trail parking area.

To reach the western trailhead at the Island Lake State Recreation Area from I-96 heading east, take Exit 151 for Kensington Road, and head south for 0.5 mile. Turn left onto State Pkwy. and go 0.2 mile. State Pkwy. turns slightly right and becomes State Park Road, then Kent Lake Beach Road. Continue onto Kent Lake Beach Road for 1.3 miles to its dead end and a parking lot. Just northwest of the parking lot, look for the short connection to the Island Lake Pathway heading west or the Huron Valley Trail heading east.

To reach McHattie Park in South Lyon from I-96, take Exit 153 toward South Lyon/Kent Lake Road, head south on Kent Lake Road, and go 0.9 mile. Turn right onto Silver Lake Road, go 0.5 mile, and turn left onto Dixboro Road. After 1.9 miles, swing left to continue onto 11 Mile Road for 0.8 mile, and turn right onto N. Lafayette St. Go 1.2 miles, turn right onto W. McHattie St. Go 2 blocks, turn left onto S. Warren St., and look for parking on your left where the street dead-ends. Look for trail access adjacent to the south side of the parking lot.

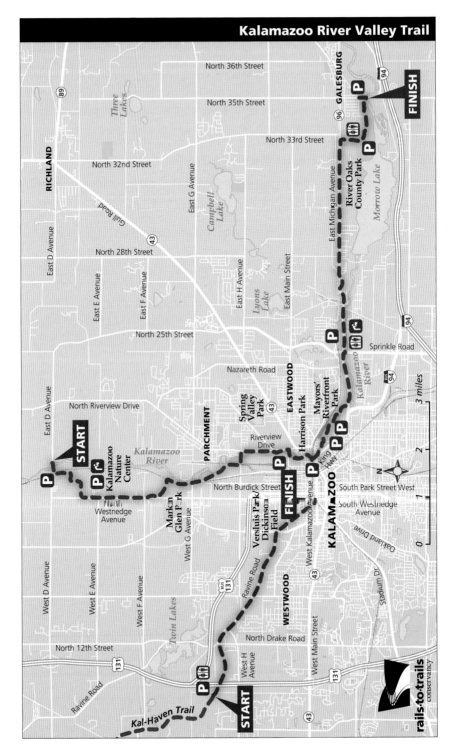

Kalamazoo River Valley Trail

When complete, the Kalamazoo River Valley Trail will run for 35 miles throughout Kalamazoo County. Currently, the trail consists of two continuous segments connected by bike lanes: one segment extends from 10th Street and the Kal-Haven Trail (see next profile) to North Westnedge Avenue in downtown Kalamazoo, and another extends from East D Avenue in Kalamazoo (near the Kalamazoo River) south through downtown and then east to the town of Galesburg.

The western trail segment passes through suburbs and farmland of Kalamazoo.

County
Kalamazoo

Endpoints
Kal-Haven Trail /10th St. N. between W. H Ave. and W. G Ave. to Bus. US 131/N. Westnedge Ave. and W. Kalamazoo Ave. (Kalamazoo); E. D Ave. just east of the Kalamazoo River and west of N. Riverview Drive (Kalamazoo) to Galesburg-Augusta Primary School at S. 35th St. and W. Battle Creek St. (Galesburg)

Mileage
20.9

Type
Greenway/Non-Rail-Trail

Roughness Index
1

Surface
Asphalt

10th Street to North Westnedge Avenue (Kalamazoo): 4.8 miles

The 4.8-mile western segment of the Kalamazoo River Valley Trail begins at the eastern terminus of the Kal-Haven Trail, which runs 34.5 miles west to South Haven near the shores of Lake Michigan. Heading east on the Kalamazoo River Valley Trail, you'll pass through scenic wooded areas and gently rolling hills, and then through a tunnel underneath US 131 and into the western suburbs of Kalamazoo. You'll find a lot of shade in this portion of the trail.

The route parallels but is separated from Ravine Road for 3 miles, after which it runs as a bike lane along the road for a half-mile stretch through a residential area. The trail then returns off road and heads into downtown Kalamazoo, where the buildings and the trail itself are a bit more rundown, and ends at Westnedge Avenue and Kalamazoo Road.

Here, you can continue along a designated bike lane route through downtown to the northeast segment of the trail, or you can stop in Kalamazoo and enjoy some of its many great eateries and microbreweries.

CONTACT: kalcounty.com/parks/krvt/index.html

DIRECTIONS

The western trailhead for the Kalamazoo River Valley Trail is shared by the eastern trailhead of the Kal-Haven Trail, which is profiled starting on page 43. To reach the western trailhead in Kalamazoo from I-94 in Portage, take Exit 74B for US 131 N./Bus. Loop I-94 toward Kalamazoo and Grand Rapids. Merge onto US 131 N./Bus. Loop I-94 E., and continue for 2 miles. Continue on US 131 N. for another 2.4 miles, and then take Exit 38B for MI 43 W. toward South Haven. Merge onto MI 43. Turn right onto 10th St. N., and then drive another 2.1 miles. Turn left into the trailhead and parking area.

East D Avenue (Kalamazoo) to West Battle Creek Street (Galesburg): 16 miles

The 16-mile northern segment of the Kalamazoo River Valley Trail follows the Kalamazoo River for a large portion of its length and provides many scenic views of the river itself. A good starting point is at the Cooper Township trailhead in northern Kalamazoo near the East D Avenue Bridge (which runs across the Kalamazoo River). The trail's endpoint is on the east side of the bridge, while the official trailhead and parking are just west of the bridge.

Heading south from East D Avenue, the first mile of the trail is hilly and winding as it leads toward Westnedge Avenue and then connects with the Kalamazoo Nature Center, which offers outdoor environmental education and exhibits for children and adults, as well as more than 14 miles of hiking trails.

The Kalamazoo River Valley Trail follows Westnedge Avenue for about 1.5 miles and then heads back toward the river and goes through Markin Glen County Park, a 160-acre space with campsites, fishing and swimming areas, trails, picnic shelters, and sports fields. You'll continue along the river for a scenic, 3-mile stretch before reaching downtown Kalamazoo; in the eastern downtown area, the trail passes by several points of historical interest, including a former railroad depot for the Grand Rapids and Indiana Railroad and the Haymarket Historic District. There are many places to stop for lunch or a snack along this segment, including picnic areas and downtown businesses, and several parks provide restroom and water facilities.

Once the trail leaves downtown Kalamazoo, it continues along King Highway to the east toward Comstock. In this area, the trail alternates between suburban neighborhoods and more industrial areas. The route here is nicely graded and enjoyably curvy, and it has several small boardwalk bridges from which trail users can enjoy scenic views of the river.

The trail leads into the suburbs, where you'll wind through a meadow and wooded park with a good view of the Kalamazoo River, before reaching the eastern terminus at Galesburg-Augusta Primary School.

CONTACT: kalcounty.com/parks/krvt/index.html

DIRECTIONS

To reach the northern trailhead in Kalamazoo from US 131, take Exit 44 for D Ave. and head east for 4 miles. Turn right into the small trailhead parking lot, just after the railroad tracks and before the bridge over the Kalamazoo River.

To reach parking near the eastern endpoint from the intersection of US 131/I-94BL and I-94, take Exit 34 for I-94 W. Keep left at the fork, follow signs for I-94 E./Detroit, and merge onto I-94 E. Go 11.6 miles, and take Exit 85 toward Galesburg/Augusta. Turn left onto S. 35th St., go 1.1 miles, and turn left onto E. Michigan Ave. After 0.8 mile, turn left into River Oaks County Park. Go 0.5 mile, and bear right at the V (you'll cross over the trail); look for parking spaces immediately to your right. Head back out a few hundred feet to where the trail crosses over the park access road. Head left on the trail to go toward Kalamazoo, or head right on the trail for approximately 1.25 miles to reach the southeastern endpoint, at the corner of S. 35th St. and W. Battle Creek St.

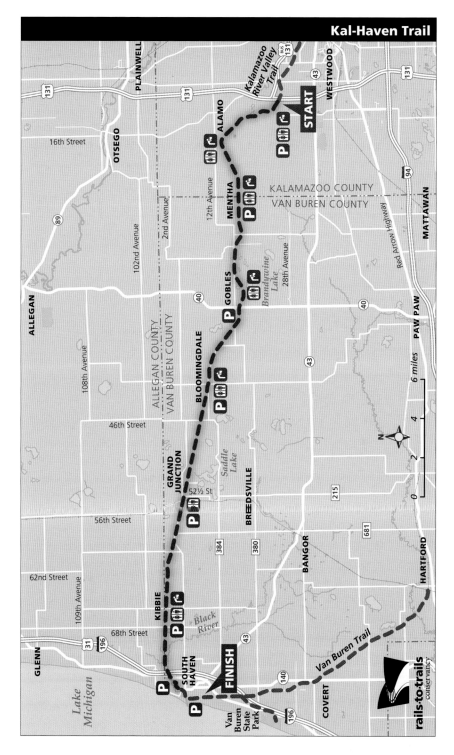

More than a half-dozen old railroad towns between Kalamazoo and South Haven offer rest and replenishment to travelers using the Kal-Haven Trail. The 34-mile crushed-limestone rail-trail links these towns as it rolls across the bucolic landscape of southwestern Michigan, from the outskirts of the bustling city to the resort town on Lake Michigan.

The trail follows the rail bed laid down in 1870 for the Kalamazoo & South Haven Railroad, which was almost immediately purchased by the Michigan Central Railroad. The New York Central Railroad took over the line in 1950 and ran trains on it until a 1968 merger to create the Penn Central led to the line becoming disused in 1970.

Opened in 1991, the trail is one of the oldest conversions in Michigan. Old depots serve as trailside visitor centers in Bloomingdale and South Haven, and an old red caboose offers trailhead services on the outskirts of Kalamazoo. The majority of the route is crushed slag and limestone and slopes gently down toward the lake; note that while the trail can accommodate road bikes, the crushed stone may prove challenging in a few sections.

Counties
Kalamazoo, Van Buren

Endpoints
10th St. N. between
W. G Ave. and W. H Ave.,
where it connects to
the Kalamazoo River
Valley Trail (Kalamazoo),
to to just north of N.
Bailey Ave. and E. Wells
St. (South Haven)

Mileage
34.0

Type
Rail-Trail

Roughness Index
1–2

Surface
Crushed Stone, Asphalt
(half mile at South
Haven)

The trail offers a spectacular outing for leaf peeping in the fall.

Beginning on the outskirts of Kalamazoo, where the trail meets the western endpoint for the Kalamazoo River Valley Trail (see previous profile), you'll pass through 7 miles of tree shade before entering the open fields of Mentha. Almost nothing remains of the old Mentha Plantation, which built this area's reputation for producing the world's finest peppermint oil in the early 20th century.

You'll pass the south edge of Gobles, which has services, before you arrive at the restored Bloomingdale Depot that houses a museum filled with railroad and local history at about mile 18. An adjacent bridle trail starts about 5 miles past Bloomingdale, at the trail intersection with 52½ Street, and runs for 7.5 miles to 68th Street, a mile beyond the town of Kibbie.

Here, the blueberry industry is going strong. Look for signs for "pick yourself" blueberry farms around Grand Junction and west to South Haven, which hosts the annual National Blueberry Festival in August. Just 2 miles past Grand Junction, you'll cross the Camelback Bridge, named for its unique midspan hump that was a structural support common in the 1920s.

Another bridge, this one covered, about 9 miles past Grand Junction signals that you are nearing the end of the trail. Head uphill to the South Haven staging area alongside the Black River. A bike route leads into town where you can see the South Pier Lighthouse, dating back to the early 1870s, standing over the mouth of the Black River. To either side of the river, North Beach and South Beach offer fun places to play and take a dip in Lake Michigan.

A trail connector/streetscaping route heads about 2 miles through downtown South Haven to the northern side of Aylworth Avenue and the northern endpoint of Van Buren Trail State Park. Here, you can head 14 miles south to Hartford or take a short spur southwest to Van Buren State Park, adjacent to Lake Michigan.

CONTACT: michigandnr.com/parksandtrails/#list (choose "Kal Haven Trail State Park") or **vbco.org/downloads/trail_map_1.pdf**

DIRECTIONS

To reach the Kalamazoo trailhead from I-94, take Exit 74B for US 131 N./Bus. Loop I-94 toward Kalamazoo/Grand Rapids. Merge onto US 131 N./Bus. Loop I-94 E., and continue for 2 miles. Continue on US 131 N. for another 2.4 miles, and then take Exit 38B for MI 43 W. toward South Haven. Merge onto MI 43. Turn right onto 10th St. N., and then go 2.1 miles. Turn left into the trailhead and parking area.

To reach the South Haven trailhead from I-196, take Exit 20 onto Phoenix St., heading west. Go 0.4 mile, and turn right onto Blue Star Hwy. Go 0.5 mile, and turn left onto E. Wells St./Second Ave. After 0.3 mile, turn right on N. Bailey Ave., the first street off the traffic circle. Go north about 300 feet and turn right into the trailhead parking lot.

An easy, flat, and well-maintained trail system, the Kent Trails provide transportation and access to nature in the bustling, second-largest metropolitan area in Michigan. The southern trail section passes through residential areas intermingled with woods, creeks, and fields, while the northern section runs along Grand Rapids' namesake river through a large urban park featuring wetlands, recreational areas, and a historic bridge. The trail system provides connectivity to numerous other trails.

Users can choose one of two trailheads in Byron Center at the southern end of the trail: one at 84th Street Southwest and another just farther east at Douglas Walker

A view of the Grand River from the northern branch of the Kent Trails

County
Kent

Endpoints
Douglas Walker Park SW at 84th St. SW (Byron Center) or 84th St. SW between Sunny Ln. SW and Merton Ave. SW (Byron Center) to Baldwin St. north of I-196 (Jenison) or Butterworth St. SW just east of I-196 near Millennium Park (Grand Rapids)

Mileage
22.2

Type
Rail-Trail, Greenway/Non-Rail-Trail

Roughness Index
1

Surface
Asphalt

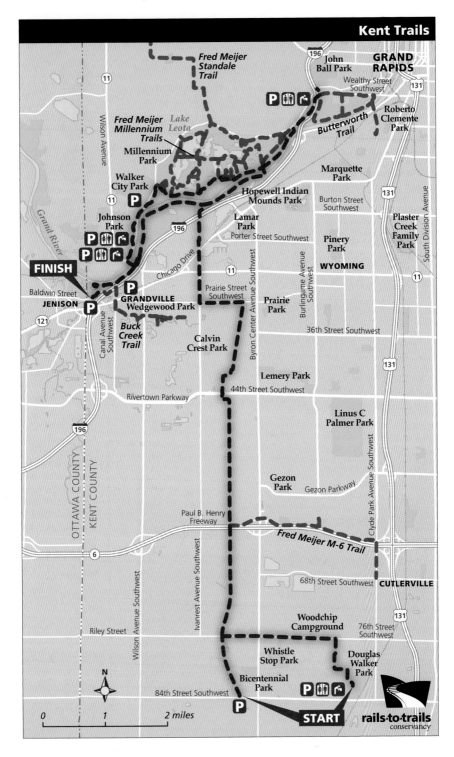

Park. Starting from the trailhead at 84th Street Southwest, the first few miles are heavily wooded, despite the suburban development that surrounds the trail. Charming footbridges cross the trail periodically. Heading north, the foliage eventually grows thinner and reveals a more suburban environment interspersed with cornfields. At MI 6/Paul B. Henry Freeway, the trail links to the Fred Meijer M-6 Trail, which is well marked.

At 44th Street Southwest, you'll proceed along Spartan Industrial Drive to Pine Creek Drive along sharrows; note that trail signage is limited. You'll then reach another heavily wooded section and cross over Buck Creek. The trail cuts left onto Prairie Street Southwest—a high-traffic area—before heading north on Ivanrest Avenue Southwest in East Grandville toward the Grand River. (This road segment has a 40-mile-per-hour speed limit and poorly signed sharrows, and in one short section at its northern end, there is no sidewalk.)

You can avoid Ivanrest Avenue via a longer but more scenic detour on the Buck Creek Trail and Grand River Pathway. To access the Buck Creek Trail, stay on Prairie Street Southwest for two blocks past Ivanrest Avenue, and turn left onto Wayburn Avenue Southwest. After one block, turn right onto the Buck Creek Trail. Head west on the trail and then north along Canal Avenue Southwest, cross Chicago Drive Southwest, and then turn right followed by an immediate left onto Broadway Avenue Southwest. You will need to either ride in traffic or use sidewalks along these short sections of Canal Avenue, Chicago Drive, and Broadway Avenue. Cross the railroad tracks and turn left onto the trail as Broadway approaches the Gerald R. Ford Freeway. The trail veers right underneath the freeway and then intersects again with the Grand River Pathway, which provides a scenic route along the river.

Returning to the Kent Trails, you'll enter Hopewell Indian Mounds Park. A heavily wooded section of the trail parallels I-196 and the Grand River and eventually crosses left over a scenic truss bridge—a high point of the route. Upon entering the 1,500-acre Millennium Park, you may continue along two forks of the Kent Trails or take one of multiple connections to the Fred Meijer Millennium Trails (pay close attention to signage).

The western fork wends along the northern bank of the Grand River and through wetlands until reaching its endpoint at Johnson Park, which offers picnic areas, parking, restrooms, and water. The eastern fork features a beautiful wooded area along the Grand River, which transitions to meadow and a connection to the Butterworth Trail, a reclaimed landfill site featuring pathways and wildflowers along the Grand River.

CONTACT: kentcountyparks.org/kenttrails.php or trailsmichigan.com /Kent-Trails-52.php

DIRECTIONS

To reach the southern trailhead at 84th St. from US 131, take Exit 74 for 84th St. toward Byron Center, heading west. After 3 miles, turn right into the trailhead parking lot (immediately beyond a small hotel and across the street from a fast-food restaurant).

To access the southeast trailhead at Douglas Walker Park, start by following the above directions to the 84th St. trailhead. After you exit onto 84th St., go west 1.2 miles. Turn right onto Douglas Walker Park SW and then right again into the parking lot.

To reach the Butterworth St. trailhead from US 131, take Exit 84A, and head west on Wealthy St. SW, crossing the Grand River. After 1.3 miles, bear right onto Garfield Ave. SW, then immediately left onto Butterworth St. SW, crossing under I-196. In 0.6 mile, turn left into the parking lot at the Kent County Parks Department. The trailhead is approximately 0.2 mile north along the trail at Butterworth St. SW.

Tradition says that Michigan has 11,000 lakes. The eastern section of the Lakelands Trail State Park passes through a chain of them as it rolls from the town of Hamburg and Lakeland to Munith some 26 miles away. In fact, Hamburg Township, where the trail starts, is 10% covered in water.

The trail, dating to the 1990s, is in various stages of improvement. Asphalt covers the eastern 7.5 miles from Hamburg to MI 36 west of Pinckney; the next 4 miles to the township line near Barton Road and MI 36 is hard

Counties
Ingham, Jackson, Livingston

Endpoints
Hall Road between Forest Creek Court and Howard St. (Hamburg) to Musbach Road between Fourth St. and Third St. (Munith)

Mileage
26.0

Type
Rail-Trail

Roughness Index
1–2

Surface
Asphalt, Ballast, Crushed Stone

A picturesque fog often shrouds the marshland along the path early in the morning.

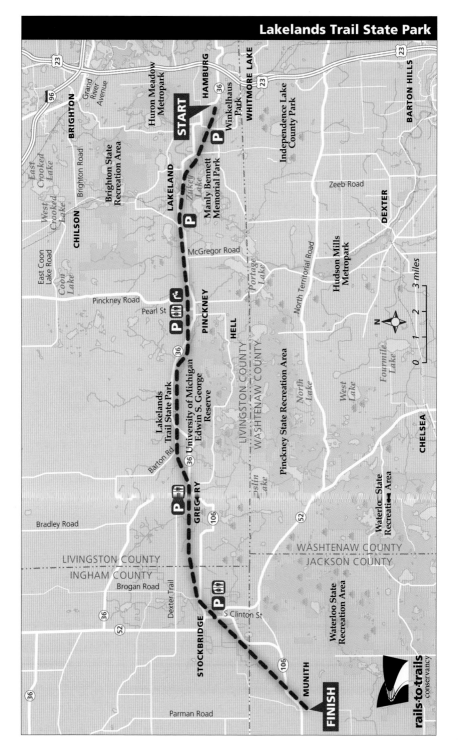

Horseback riding is permitted along the 26-mile rail-trail.

limestone; slag and sand comprise the surface for the next 9 miles into Stockbridge; and the final 5 miles southwest to Munith is open but mostly unimproved. Horseback riding is permitted in the trail corridor, but snowmobiles and off-road vehicles are prohibited.

Short-range plans call for extending the trail southwest to Parnall Road in Jackson and improving the soft surface to hard limestone. Also, connections to the cross-state Iron Belle Trail (north–south) and Great Lake-to-Lake Trail (east–west) are in the works.

The Lakelands Trail follows a section of the former Michigan Air Line Railroad opened in 1884 as part of a planned rail line across southern Michigan. It was absorbed by the Grand Trunk Western Railroad in 1928 and became disused in the 1970s.

Beginning at the trailhead on Hamburg Road, you'll leave from Winkelhaus Park, the site of the old Hamburg House Hotel from about 1835 to 1968. The trail heads east for 0.7 mile and ends in the woods. A future connection to South Lyon is planned.

Heading west, the trail is paved as it passes sports fields at Manly Bennett Park and Zukey Lake, one of a chain of eight lakes in the Huron River watershed, and home to a well-known lakeside tavern dating back to the 1930s. You'll continue through a growing residential area to a trailhead and old railroad depot at Pearl

Street in Pinckney, about 7.5 miles from the eastern trailhead. Four miles south is the 11,000-acre Pinckney Recreation Area, known for its mountain biking trails.

The Lakelands Trail changes to hard-packed limestone about a mile west of Pinckney as the countryside becomes mostly farmland and forest. The trail brushes the northern edge of the 535-acre University of Michigan Edwin S. George Reserve, a fenced research and educational preserve.

Crossing MI 36 again, the trail surface deteriorates and is more suitable for horseback riding, hiking, and mountain biking for the next 8 miles through the small burg of Gregory to Stockbridge, where the trail veers southwest. You'll find trail parking on South Clinton Street and places to eat a few blocks north.

Very few improvements have been made to the trail past Stockbridge, and it's impassable after Munith. Plans to replace bridges, improve the trail surface, and extend it to Jackson are proposed for 2018.

CONTACT: hamburg.mi.us/lakelands_trail_state_park

DIRECTIONS

To reach the eastern trailhead on Hamburg Road from US 23 heading north, take Exit 53 toward Hamburg/Whitmore Lake. Turn left onto Eight Mile Road, and go 1.3 miles. Bear right to continue onto Hall Road for 0.2 mile, and then bear left at the Y onto Sheldon Road for 0.4 mile. Keep right to continue onto Hamburg Road for 1.2 miles. Look for parking at Winkelhaus Park, on your right. The trail dead-ends 0.7 mile to the east.

The best access point for the western endpoint is the Stockbridge trailhead, as few improvements to the trail have been made between Stockbridge and Munith, and there is no dedicated parking lot for the trail in Munith. From I-94, take Exit 150 onto Mount Hope Road, heading north. Go 5.7 miles, and veer right at the intersection to stay on Mount Hope Road. Go 2.5 miles and turn right onto MI 106 N. Go 3.6 miles to Stockbridge, where MI 106 becomes S. Clinton St., and turn right onto S. Center St. Look for parking on the right. The trail's western endpoint is 5 miles farther west, at Musbach Road in Munith.

The Lansing River Trail traces the course of three water-ways for more than 25 miles across Michigan's capital city. Visiting all four main points of the compass in Lansing, the trail provides a route for self-propelled transportation to numerous parks, cultural and commercial attractions, workplaces, and a major university.

The trail rolls through waterfront parks on the Grand River from Moores Park in the west to Dietrich Park in the north. It follows the Red Cedar River from Elm Park to Michigan State University in the east. A branch along the woodsy Sycamore Creek tributary goes south to Maguire Park, where it joins the Sycamore Trail. Another trail branch from Maguire Park heads west on a utility

County
Ingham

Endpoints
Dietrich Park at
N. Grand River Ave. near
Willis Court (Lansing,
north) to Moores Park
at Moores River Dr.
(Lansing, west); *or*
S. Waverly Road south of
W. Jolly Road (Lansing,
west), *or* E. Cavanaugh
Road east of Chicory Ln.
(Lansing, south),
or Crego Park east of
N. Aurelius Road
(Lansing, east), *or*
Hagadorn Road between
E. Grand River Ave.
and E. Shaw Ln. (East
Lansing), *or* Frances Park
between Moores River
Dr. and N. Cambridge
Road/N. Nottingham
Road (Lansing,
west) to S. Waverly
Road and Maybel St.
(Lansing, west)

Mileage
25.3

Type
Rail-Trail

Roughness Index
1

Surface
Asphalt

True to its name, much of the trail lines Lansing's riverfront.

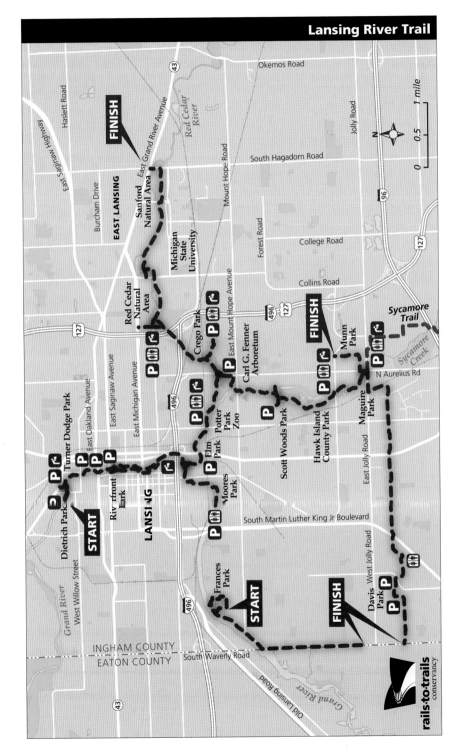

Lansing River Trail

The trail traces three waterways for 25 miles across Michigan's capital.

right-of-way to South Waverly Road. An orphaned trail section heads north along Waverly Road back to the Grand River and Frances Park.

The trail started as a paved path through the downtown Riverfront Park redevelopment project in 1975. In 1983, the city added a half-mile section of former railroad and later extended the trail to include passage to the zoo and university in the east and Maguire Park in the south. The park district completed the nearly 5-mile South Lansing Pathway south of Jolly Road in 2014 and rebranded it as part of the Lansing River Trail.

Despite the urban setting, you will experience wetlands and woodlands and probably catch sight of the trail's resident ducks, squirrels, and butterflies. The path has sections of wooden boardwalk passing under highways and skirting out over the water, avoiding almost all contact with motorized traffic.

Starting at Dietrich Park, head south along the Grand River to Turner Dodge Park, where you'll find the circa 1855 Turner-Dodge House, which offers tours. Past that, the eclectic Old Town area represents a revitalized arts and entertainment district. You'll pass the Brenke Fish Ladder, which gives migratory fish a route around the dam.

Still traveling along Grand River, you'll come to the Lansing City Market where residents have been buying locally sourced food for more than a century. In 0.3 mile, you come to the hands-on Impression 5 Science Center and the R. E. Olds Transportation Museum.

Just past the zoo you'll arrive at another junction; a left goes 4.8 miles through the Michigan State University campus, passing wooded Crego Park and the Red Cedar Natural Area along the way. A right turn at the junction heads south through forest and wetlands alongside Sycamore Creek, visiting Scott Woods Park and Hawk Island County Park.

After 3 miles, you'll arrive at another junction at Maguire Park near North Aurelius and East Jolly Roads. The left fork takes you to Munn Park, while the right fork crosses Jolly Road and heads west for 5 miles through a utility corridor. It's the only section of the Lansing River Trail that doesn't run next to water. At Jolly Road, you can also opt to head east on the 2.1-mile Sycamore Trail, which cuts south to East Willoughby Road and the 1.3-mile Valhalla Trail.

CONTACT: lansingmi.gov/1296/lansing-river-trail or **lansingtrails.org**

DIRECTIONS

To reach the northern trailhead at Dietrich Park from I-496, take Exit 6 to northbound S. Walnut St. Go 1.6 miles, and turn right onto W. Willow St.; then go 1 block, and turn left onto N. Grand River Ave. Go 0.1 mile, and look for parking on the left immediately after crossing the Grand River.

To reach the southern trailhead at Maguire Park from I-496, take Exit 11 and head west on Dunckel Road. Go 0.9 mile, and turn right onto E. Jolly Road. Go 0.5 mile and, after crossing Sycamore Creek, turn right onto N. Aurelius Road. After 390 feet, turn left into Maguire Park.

To reach the western trailhead at Moores Park from I-496, take Exit 3 toward MI 99/ Martin Luther King Jr. Blvd. for 0.3 mile. Merge onto W. St. Joseph St. and, at the first intersection, turn left (south) onto S. Martin Luther King Jr. Blvd. to cross the Grand River. After 0.6 mile, take a sharp left, and then make a U-turn north to stay on S. Martin Luther King. Jr. Blvd. Turn right at the first cross street onto Moores River Dr. After 0.3 mile, look for parking on your left at the park entrance.

To reach parking for the S. Waverly Road endpoint from I-496, take Exit 3 for Waverly Road. Head south on S. Waverly Road, crossing the Grand River along the way. After 2.8 miles, turn left onto W. Jolly Road. Go 1.1 miles, and turn right onto Pleasant Grove Road. In 0.4 mile, turn right into Benjamin F. Davis Park. The endpoint is located by heading west on the trail past Wise Road to S. Waverly Road.

You can also park at Lansing City Market, Crego Park, Hawk Island County Park, Lot 56/ Cesar Chavez Plaza, Municipal Park, the Oakland Ave. lot, Potter Park, and Turner Dodge Park.

The 17-mile Leelanau Trail runs up a Lake Michigan peninsula that is known for its abundance of cherry orchards and Riesling grape vineyards. Located in northern Michigan, the paved trail connects the popular tourist destinations of Suttons Bay and Traverse City.

The trail uses a former railroad corridor that got its start by hauling timber out of old-growth forests and ended its life as a scenic railroad. The Traverse City, Leelanau & Manistique Railway opened for business in 1903 by running up the peninsula from Traverse City and then crossing the lake by ferry to Manistique on the Upper Peninsula. The railroad went through some ownership changes and fell on hard times after a fire wiped out a large lumber mill. It limped along for decades and finally found use as an excursion train run by railroad enthusiasts from 1989 until 1995, when it was bought by a trail association.

About 2 miles northwest of Traverse City, at the Leelanau Conservancy's DeYoung Farm and at a location next

The Leelanau Trail offers year-round outdoor recreation.

County
Leelanau

Endpoints
N. Dumas Road west of N. West Bay Shore Dr. (Suttons Bay) to E. Carter Road between S. Thorn Creek Dr. and SW Bay Shore Dr./Traverse Area Recreation and Transportation Trail (Greilickville)

Mileage
16.6

Type
Rail-Trail

Roughness Index
1

Surface
Asphalt

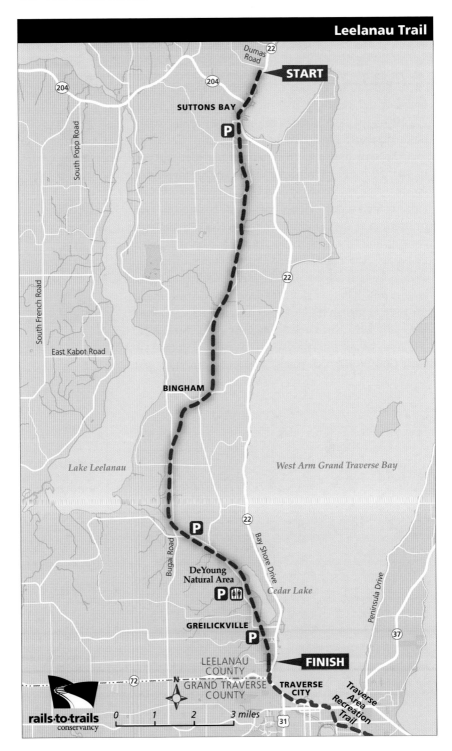

to Realeyes Homestead, visitors can enjoy edible forests offering free browsing for blueberries, plums, apples, and more.

Parking is available on Fourth Street in the village of Suttons Bay, about 1.8 miles from the northern endpoint. In addition to being a railroad stop, the town has served as a safe harbor for passing boats since the 1850s. Walking around the marina, you might see a tall ship schooner that serves as a hands-on vessel for the Inland Seas Education Association. Elsewhere in town, boutiques, galleries, bed-and-breakfast inns, and restaurants cater to visitors.

From the trailhead, you can head north along the bay (separated from the waterfront by Northwest Bay Shore Drive) to North Dumas Road or south through the middle of the peninsula toward Traverse City.

After heading south about 7 miles, you'll arrive in Bingham, which sits atop the spine of the peninsula and is roughly between Lake Leelanau in the west and the West Arm Grand Traverse Bay in the east. From here the route heads downhill toward Traverse City.

About 6 miles past Bingham, you'll arrive at the DeYoung Natural Area. This 145-acre preserve, one of 25 natural areas owned by the Leelanau Conservancy, provides hiking trails through a former farmstead and access to Cedar Lake. Drinking water and restrooms are available.

In 1.2 miles, you'll arrive at a trailhead on Cherry Bend Road that is marked by a historic caboose from the Leelanau Scenic Railroad. The trail officially ends 0.9 mile farther south on East Carter Road in Greilickville, but there is no parking here. South of Carter Road, the Leelanau Trail connects seamlessly to the Traverse Area Recreation and Transportation Trail (Trail 25, page 97).

CONTACT: traversetrails.org/trail/leelanau-trail

DIRECTIONS

To reach the northern trailhead and parking in Suttons Bay from US 31, take the highway north into Traverse City, where it becomes Division St. Where Division dead-ends at the intersection with W. Grandview Pkwy., near the waterfront, turn left onto Grandview, follow it north for 15.1 miles, and then turn left onto Fourth St. Go 0.1 mile, and turn left into the signed trailhead parking lot. The northern endpoint is 1.8 miles north; the southern endpoint, in Greilickville, is 14.9 miles south.

To reach the southern trailhead and parking in Greilickville, follow the directions above, but after turning left onto Grandview Pkwy., follow it just 1.9 miles, and then turn left onto E. Cherry Bend Road. After 0.4 mile, turn right into the trailhead parking lot after passing S. Cedar Ln. and where the trail intersects the road. The southern endpoint is 0.9 mile south.

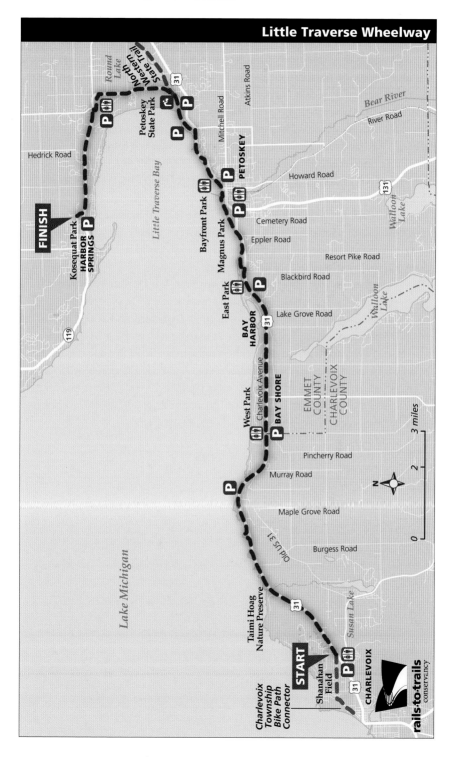

Picture-postcard-worthy views of Lake Michigan and its shoreline greet visitors to the Little Traverse Wheelway in Michigan's northern Lower Peninsula. The paved trail rolls for 24 miles from Charlevoix to Petoskey to Harbor Springs as it follows the curve of Little Traverse Bay.

"Trail-to-rail-to-trail" describes the background of the Little Traverse Wheelway in this historic resort getaway. A section of trail dates to the 1880s when high-wheeled penny farthings were a popular, though risky, form of recreation and transportation. The Chicago and West Michigan Railway and the Grand Rapids and Indiana Railroad adopted the corridor for rail traffic in the

Beautiful views of the water make a ride down the Little Traverse Wheelway one to remember.

Counties
Charlevoix, Emmet

Endpoints
Waller Road and
US 31 (Charlevoix) to
Kosequat Park at
Park Ln. and E. Lake
Road (Harbor Springs)

Mileage
23.7 miles

Type
Rail-Trail

Roughness Index
1

Surface
Asphalt

The Little Traverse Wheelway in Michigan

1890s, but by the 1970s the surviving railroads were no longer using segments of rail bed. By the 1990s, the first 2-mile section of reclaimed trail opened in Petoskey with more to follow until 2009.

Beginning at Shanahan Field in Charlevoix, you'll go east for 0.4 mile on the shoulder of Waller Road to reach the trail that runs close by US 31 for the next 16 miles. (At the park, you can also opt to take the Charlevoix Township Bike Path connector into town.) You'll cross a 0.6-mile boardwalk in a nature preserve in the first mile and be gazing out toward a magnificent lake view at a roadside park by mile 3.

The trail rolls inland at about mile 6, but in another 5 miles, you'll arrive at the marina-resort community of Bay Harbor. Descending through East Park, you'll view Little Traverse Bay from a bluff for about 1.5 miles before arriving at the Magnus Park public campground.

In a mile you arrive at a marina and Bayfront Park in Petoskey. This is the path of the original wheelway, marked by the first of three replica arches announcing NO TEAMING OR DRIVING, referring to prohibitions against riding horses or horse-drawn carriages on the original trail. The town's history is remembered at the Little Traverse History Museum, located in a circa-1892 railway depot at the park. A touristy shopping area is accessible through a US 31 underpass near the foot of Bay Street.

Leaving Petoskey, you'll pass a fishing pond left over from an old limestone quarry. It's only a few steps away from Little Traverse Bay, where the exposed cobble on the shoreline is a good place to look for Petoskey stones, pebbles containing designs from fossilized coral.

Soon after leaving the park, salmon-colored sidewalks signal your entry into the historic Bay View neighborhood. This community, dominated by Victorian homes, has long been a summer getaway for prominent Michigan families. The trail leaves the side of US 31 at Division Street and, in 1.4 miles, passes a trail entrance to Petoskey State Park, where you can find sweeping sand dunes and a swimming beach. Along this stretch you will also pass a short spur that crosses on the right over MI 119 and connects with the southern endpoint of the North Western State Trail, which heads north to Mackinaw City.

The wheelway continues for 2.5 miles parallel to busy MI 119 before cutting away to follow the northeast edge of the Harbor Springs Airport. From the airport, a 3-mile section of trail continues west along MI 119 to a trailhead at Kosequat Park near the heart of Harbor Springs, a deep moorage at the head of the bay.

CONTACT: trailscouncil.org

DIRECTIONS

To reach the trailhead near Shanahan Field in Charlevoix from the intersection of US 131 and MI 66 in Mancelona, go 31 miles north on MI 66, and turn right onto US 31. Drive 2.8 miles east through Charlevoix, and turn left onto Martin Road. Go 0.3 mile, and turn right onto Waller Road. Turn left into the trailhead parking lot. After parking, walk east on Waller Road for 0.4 mile; the trailhead is on the left, just before you reach US 31.

To reach the trailhead at Kosequat Park in Harbor Springs from I-75, take Exit 310 onto westbound MI 68. In 0.3 mile, turn left onto MI 68/S. Sturgeon St./S. Straits Hwy. In 0.9 mile, turn right to continue on MI 68, heading west-northwest. Go 9.2 miles, and turn left onto US 31/Burr Ave. After 0.7 mile, turn right onto Powers Road. Go 7.5 miles—Powers becomes Hathaway Road and then Hedrick Road—and turn right onto MI 119/Harbor-Petoskey Road. Go about 1.4 miles, and turn right onto Park Ln. Look for trail parking 0.1 mile ahead on the right (you'll actually cross over the Little Traverse Wheelway).

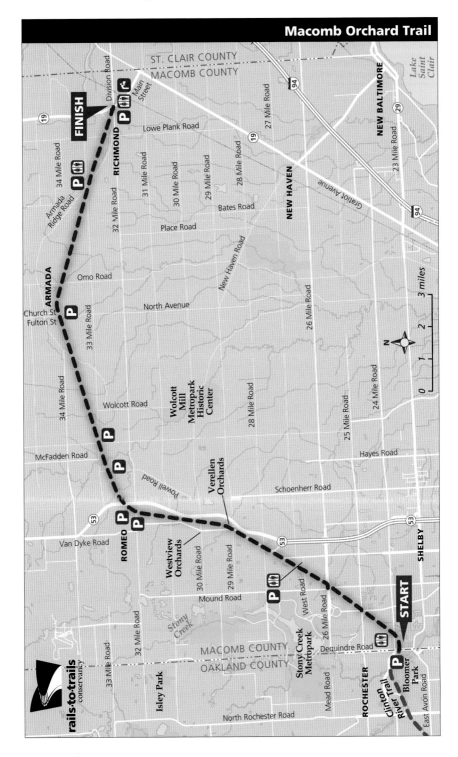

Macomb Orchard Trail

The automotive industry has the most impact on Macomb County's economy, but it's the freshly picked apples and squeezed cider that leave lasting impressions on visitors to the Macomb Orchard Trail. Named for southeastern Michigan's heritage of bountiful apple and peach production, the 24-mile paved trail runs from Rochester's suburbs in metro Detroit to farms and forestland surrounding Richmond.

The trail follows the path of the Michigan Air Line Railroad, which connected Romeo with Richmond by rail in 1871 in an attempt to build a cross-state railroad. The Grand Trunk Western Railroad took control in 1881 and held on to it as a subsidiary of Canadian National Railway in 1971. Trail supporters urged Macomb County elected officials to buy the rail bed when the Canadian National put it up for sale in 1998.

Beginning on the outskirts of Rochester, you'll start at the junction of the Clinton River Trail and the Macomb Orchard Trail on Dequindre Road, where a barn roof–shaped gateway arch is emblazoned with the trail's name. The trail heads northeast through suburban sprawl for about 7 miles on a paved trail and multiuse paths/wide sidewalks until it reaches orchard country.

County
Macomb

Endpoints
Clinton River Trail/
Dequindre Road between
24 Mile Road and
23 Mile Road (Rochester)
to Division Road at
Main St. (Richmond)

Mileage
23.5

Type
Rail-Trail

Roughness Index
1

Surface
Asphalt, Concrete

The trail bridge in Armada offers a chance to take in rural surroundings.

Your first orchard stand—Verellen Orchards—is 0.1 mile north from the trail crossing with Van Dyke Road. Another mile up the trail at 30 Mile Road crossing, you'll find the sixth-generation Westview Orchards by taking a 0.3-mile side trip west. Pick-yourself apples, peaches, cherries, and strawberries are available in season, and a cider mill operates in the fall.

At mile 10, you arrive at the trailhead in Romeo, settled in 1822, and a stop on the Underground Railroad. A half mile east is the town's Main Street historic district, where you'll find antiques shops and cafés in buildings that represent a mix of nine architectural styles.

Leaving town, the trail passes a Ford Motor engine factory. Then, for the next 6 miles to Armada, the trail is surrounded by farmland. The brush and tree cover around the trail gets thicker too, as the utility lines above your head since Rochester leave the trail for another corridor. Food is available in Armada about a half mile north of the trail via Church Street. One of the houses you'll pass is an old railroad depot erected in 1924 and relocated to Church Street after passenger and mail service ended.

If there seems to be a lot of activity for such a small town, you might have arrived in August during the Armada Fair, an annual event since 1872, or the Lions Club Cider Dayze, also in August, or the Apple Fest in October.

Back on the trail, you'll resume a route through woodlots and farmland for 6.7 miles to the gazebo at the trailhead in Richmond. This town, included in the Detroit metro area, also celebrates its agricultural roots at the Good Old Days Festival.

CONTACT: macomborchardtrail.macombgov.org
/macomborchardtrail-trailguidemap

DIRECTIONS

Parking for the Rochester trailhead is available at the Onyx Rochester Ice Arena. From I-75, take Exit 72 to northbound Crooks Road. Go 3.7 miles, and turn right onto MI 150/W. Hamlin Road; then go 3.1 miles, and turn left onto John R Road. Go 1 mile, and turn right onto E. Avon Road, which becomes Dequindre Road. Go 1.7 miles, and look for the entrance to Onyx Rochester Ice Arena, on the left. After parking, take the path to the Clinton River Trail/Macomb Orchard Trail crossing at Dequindre Road.

To reach parking for the Richmond trailhead from I-94, take Exit 248 to eastbound 26 Mile Road. Go 1 mile, and turn left onto County Line Road. Go 5.1 miles, and turn left onto 31 Mile Road/St. Clair Hwy. After 1 mile, turn right onto MI 19/Gratiot Ave.; then go 0.1 mile, and turn left onto Main St. Follow Main for 1.4 miles, and turn right into a parking lot just before Division Road, just past the Village Cafe. The Macomb Orchard Trail is across the Main St.–Division Road intersection on the left.

The Musketawa Trail is one of the best places to get away from it all if you live and work in the western Michigan population centers of Muskegon or Grand Rapids. The 25-mile paved rail-trail rolls between the outskirts of both cities through the peaceful agricultural countryside.

The trail got its start as the Muskegon, Grand Rapids and Indiana Railroad in 1886. Muskegon and Grand Rapids were in the midst of a lumber production boom, and Grand Rapids was gaining a reputation as a furniture-making center. A series of business deals over the years resulted in several railroads—the Pennsylvania, the Penn Central, and the Grand Trunk Western—using the tracks. The last owner, Central Michigan Railroad, discontinued service in 1989 and pulled the tracks the following year.

Part of the rail-trail leads you through greenery.

Counties
Muskegon, Ottawa

Endpoints
Eighth Ave./Fred Meijer Pioneer Trail between E. Garfield St. and Arthur St. (Marne) to Black Creek Road between E. Sherman Blvd. and Olthoff Dr. (Muskegon)

Mileage
25.0

Type
Rail-Trail

Roughness Index
1

Surface
Asphalt

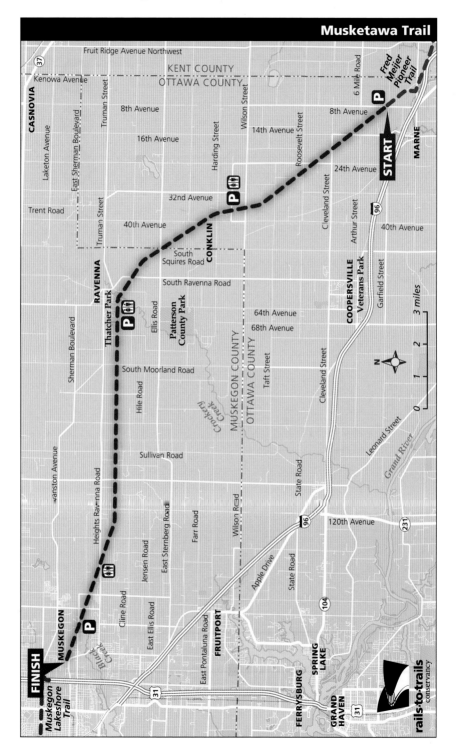

Get away from it all on the Musketawa Trail.

The Musketawa Trail earned its name in a contest; the winning entry combined the two counties through which it passes: Muskegon and Ottawa. By 1997, the town of Ravenna had paved the first mile, and by 2000 the entire trail was paved.

Now trail advocates are looking for connections to other parts of western Michigan's trail network. The trail already connects to the Fred Meijer Pioneer Trail in the east, which brings it closer to Grand Rapids and the 90-mile Fred Meijer White Pine Trail (Trail 6, page 27). In the west in Muskegon, bike lanes bridge the gap between the Musketawa Trail and the Muskegon Lakeshore Trail.

Starting about 10 miles from downtown Grand Rapids in Marne, you'll leave from a 40-car parking area. The village of Marne sits about a mile south of the trailhead. If you stop there for coffee, you might notice that the fairgrounds and some buildings carry the former name, Berlin. The residents changed the name during World War I to Marne to commemorate an Allied victory.

The trail sets off in a northwest direction through cropland and pastures, a common scene for the next 25 miles. Trailside growth gives partial shade in the east, while overhead utility lines in the corridor closer to Muskegon create a less sheltered border.

In about 7 miles you'll reach the old whistlestop of Conklin, which has a small market. In another 5 miles you'll cross Crockery Creek on a 216-foot trestle—the longest of 13 trestles on the trail—and enter Ravenna. The trailhead features an old Grand Trunk Western caboose sitting next to a restored 100-year-old railroad water tower. The business district for the town, settled in the 1840s, has markets, cafés, and pubs located less than a half mile to the right on Crockery Creek Road.

The next 12.6 miles are a straight shot, except for a slight bearing change midway, to the outskirts of Muskegon. Sprawling farm fields and occasional woodlots dominate the landscape. Closer to Muskegon, the farms disappear and housing subdivisions and business parks take their place. At the trail's end, a 5-mile bike route heads into town to the Muskegon Lakeshore Trail and Pere Marquette Park on Lake Michigan.

If you'd like to explore the Musketawa Trail by bicycle with ride support, the Gold Spike Trail Tour is held in the late spring every year. Check out the Friends of the Musketawa Trail (see website) for details.

CONTACT: musketawatrail.com

DIRECTIONS

To reach the Marne trailhead from westbound I-96, take Exit 25 to northbound Eighth Ave. Turn right onto Eighth Ave. and then left onto Hayes St., which becomes Eighth Ave. again. Go 1.4 miles, and turn left into the parking lot immediately after crossing the trail.

To reach the Marne trailhead from eastbound I-96, take Exit 23 toward Marne. Turn right onto Jackson St. and then right onto 16th Ave. Go 0.7 mile, and turn right onto Garfield St. Go 1 mile, and turn left onto Eighth Ave. Go 0.1 mile, and turn left into the parking lot immediately after you cross the trail.

To reach parking for the trailhead in Muskegon from I-96, take Exit 1B onto northbound US 31. Go 2.3 miles, and take Exit 112 to E. Sherman Blvd., heading right (east). Go 1 mile—Sherman bears right at the intersection and becomes Black Creek Road—and turn left onto E. Broadway Ave. Go 0.9 mile and look for parking on the left. The western trail endpoint is 1 mile west of the parking lot.

The 62-mile North Central State Trail offers a multiuse trail adventure into the hills, agricultural areas, woods, and waterways of Michigan, with connections to well-established tourist towns at both ends. For those seeking a longer adventure, the trail helps to make up the developing 2,000-plus-mile Iron Belle Trail, which stretches from Ironwood in the Upper Peninsula to Detroit.

From the northern end, the trail starts just south of the famed Mackinac Bridge spanning 5 miles across the Straits of Mackinac (pronounced "Mackinaw") to join the Lower and Upper Peninsulas of Michigan. The trailhead offers parking, restrooms, and water and also serves as the northeast terminus for the 32-mile North Western State Trail to Petoskey.

Starting in Mackinaw and heading south, the trail is paved and well used for the first half mile, after which its

The trail offers a family-friendly adventure into Michigan's North Woods.

Counties
Cheboygan, Otsego

Endpoints
North Western State
Trail/Mackinaw Crossings
Dr. east of S. Nicolet St.
(Mackinaw City)
to Fairview Road near
N. Ohio Ave./Morgan
Road (Gaylord)

Mileage
62.0

Type
Rail-Trail

Roughness Index
2

Surface
Crushed Stone, Asphalt
(only half mile)

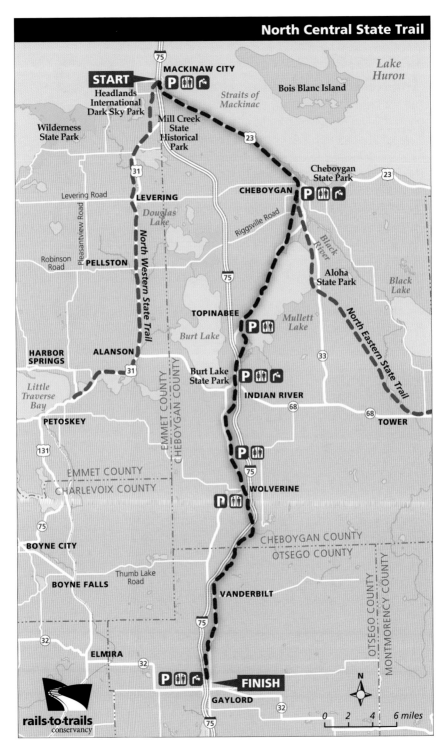

surface turns to well-maintained crushed stone, and usage declines. The trail's route is mostly flat throughout its length, even where there are rolling vistas.

Although the route parallels US 23 for the first 15 miles, it boasts the beautiful northern woods as its backdrop, where you'll get to spot interesting birds as well as an occasional view of Lake Huron, to the east. Rail buffs may be interested in the remaining railroad tracks and historical markers along the trail, chronicling old rail towns. Snowmobiles use the trail in season, and trailside businesses cater to them.

Usage increases again as the trail reaches Cheboygan, at about mile 16. The Cheboygan trailhead offers parking, restrooms, water, picnic facilities, and an option to head southeast on the North Eastern State Trail (see next profile) just south of Lincoln Avenue. You can also detour off the trail here for food and beverage options. Those planning to continue south should fill their water bottles at the trailhead, as water is scarce between Cheboygan and Gaylord.

Continuing south from Cheboygan, you'll pass through a popular section of trail that skirts Mullett Lake, a beautiful, 15-mile-long inland lake that stretches to Indian River. A highlight of this segment is the town of Topinabee, which has a public beach, park and playground, parking, and restrooms, as well as a library inside an old railroad depot. Nearby Indian River has restrooms, a market, covered picnic tables, a playground, and a train depot repurposed into a boutique.

Trail users should be extra-vigilant when crossing busy MI 68, south of Indian River, as the trail is located near an entrance ramp from I-75. South of Indian River, the trail feels more solitary and wildlife sightings increase; be on the lookout for turkey, deer, snakes, and frogs.

As you near the trail's southern endpoint, you'll pass a state forest campground and then a train depot in Wolverine. You'll parallel I-75 between Wolverine and Vanderbilt, the final town along the route, after which the remote feel of the trail continues until its terminus in Gaylord.

CONTACT: northcentraltrail.org

DIRECTIONS

To reach the northern trailhead in Mackinaw City from I-75 heading north, take Exit 338, and turn left onto S. Nicolet St. Take the first right onto Mackinaw Crossings Dr., and then turn left into the trailhead parking lot after you pass the North Central State Trail.

To reach the southern trailhead in Gaylord from I-75, take Exit 282 for MI 32 toward Gaylord/Alpena. Head east on MI 32/W. Main St., and then take the second left onto N. Ohio Ave. Go 1 mile, and turn right onto Fairview Road. Look for parking immediately to your right at the soccer fields. The trail endpoint starts just farther east.

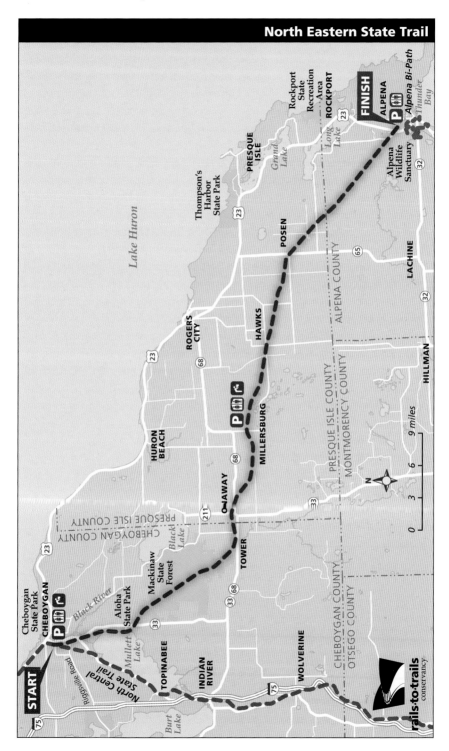

North Eastern State Trail

The 71-mile North Eastern State Trail, along the former Detroit and Mackinac Railway, provides a mostly solitary and meditative experience as you travel through wetlands, farmland, forests, and a few small towns. Starting from the Cheboygan trailhead, which intersects the 62-mile North Central State Trail (see previous profile), people on bikes may find the riding fairly slow given the not-so-compacted crushed limestone surface. Mountain bikes are recommended.

Located along the trail are several places with picnic tables, sometimes shaded, where you can take a break and soak in the natural beauty of northeastern Michigan. Given the isolated nature of the corridor, trail users should carry plenty of water, and cyclists should be prepared to fix a flat tire. In many segments of the trail, access to amenities requires backtracking either on or off the trail.

Long rural stretches allow trail users to soak up the region's natural beauty.

Counties
Alpena, Cheboygan, Presque Isle

Endpoints
North Central State Trail/ S. Western Ave. and Taylor St. (Cheboygan) to Woodward Ave. north of Johnson St. (Alpena)

Mileage
71.0

Type
Rail-Trail

Roughness Index
2–3

Surface
Crushed Stone

You will enjoy inspiring vistas as you make your way to Aloha State Park (8 miles from Cheboygan), with several areas to stop and take in the many small lakes along the trail. You are periodically surrounded by woodlands reminiscent of Michigan's logging era, and it is not unusual for a chicken, goat, or horse to cross your path.

Individuals who are traveling the entire route may wish to stop at the Millersburg trailhead (about halfway through the trail at mile 33); here, you'll find a few restaurants near the pathway as well as a railroad depot museum highlighting the railroad heritage of the region. Another 19 miles takes you to Posen, the next village, where you'll find a few family-owned restaurants and businesses off the trail.

The final stretch of the trail from Posen to Alpena is another 19 miles, and there is no easy access to water or restrooms in the few small towns you pass along the way. Upon reaching the eastern endpoint, you can head south a short distance on Woodward Avenue to Johnston Street, where you can pick up the 14-mile Alpena Bi-Path, which skirts the Alpena Wildlife Sanctuary and extends in various directions through the town.

CONTACT: trailsmichigan.com/North-Eastern-State-Trail-9.php

DIRECTIONS

A large public parking lot for the trail is available at the Cheboygan trailhead. To reach the trailhead from I-75, take Exit 322 toward Cheboygan, and head east on County Road 64/Riggsville Road for 5.9 miles. Turn left to continue on Riggsville Road. In 1.4 miles, bear right to merge onto Woiderski Road; go 0.5 mile, and continue onto W. Lincoln Ave. After another 0.5 mile, turn left onto S. Western Ave., and go 0.2 mile. Turn right onto Taylor St., and make an immediate right into the trailhead parking lot.

To reach the southern trailhead in Alpena from the intersection of MI 65 N. and MI 32 in Lachine, head east on MI 32 and go 13.7 miles. Turn left onto N. Bagley St., and go 1.2 miles, crossing the Thunder Bay River. Turn right onto Long Rapids Road, go 1 mile, and, just past the intersection with US 23 N., continue straight onto Johnson St. for 0.6 mile. Turn left onto Woodward Ave. and, after 0.5 mile, look for the trailhead parking lot and restrooms, to your right.

Even though the Paint Creek Trail is Michigan's oldest nonmotorized rail-trail, the occasional face-lifts and renovations keep it looking as young as ever. Established in 1983, the crushed-limestone trail runs for 8.9 miles between Rochester and Lake Orion through a mostly wooded corridor alongside Paint Creek. It is also part of the developing 2,000-plus-mile Iron Belle Trail, comprising separate routes for hiking and biking from Detroit to Ironwood in the Upper Peninsula.

The trail's many charms include a variety of wildlife, historical sites, rest stops, and a trout-filled creek that the route crosses 12 times. Maps and announcements are posted at the trailheads, where you can also pick up folding maps. Mileage markers, left over from the days when this path was a railway, announce the distance to Detroit. Free bike fix-it stations are installed at the Rochester, Tienken Road, and Goodison trailheads.

County
Oakland

Endpoints
Atwater St. and Atwater Commons Dr. (Lake Orion) to the Rochester River Walk just north of Pine St. and Civic Center Dr. (Rochester)

Mileage
8.9

Type
Rail-Trail

Roughness Index
1

Surface
Crushed Stone

This bridge over Paint Creek is just one of this rail-trail's many charms.

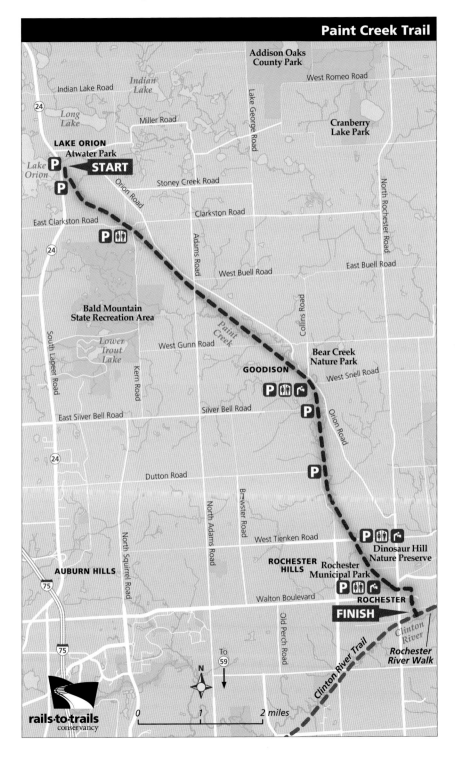

Paint Creek Trail

The trail follows a former segment of the Detroit and Bay City Railroad that launched service in 1872. The Michigan Central and the New York Central Railroads became subsequent operators, running trains between Detroit and Mackinaw City, and the Penn Central took over in 1968. Emerging from bankruptcy, the railroad in 1983 sold the rail bed to a commission comprised of trail advocates and local communities. The commission surfaced the 8-foot-wide trail with crushed limestone, rather than asphalt, in the early 1990s to maintain a rural experience.

Beginning at Lake Orion, you'll follow a barely perceptible downhill slope to Rochester. Lake Orion originally grew up around a sawmill built in 1825 but later became a resort destination. Two miles south, a historical marker notes the site of the water-powered Carpenter Rudd Mill that stood here until 1926. This is also where you can connect to the Bald Mountain State Recreation Area for fishing, swimming, and mountain biking.

For the next couple of miles, Paint Creek meanders alongside and crosses the trail, presenting many opportunities for fishing. If you want to try your hand with a bow and arrow, there's an archery range at mile 2.5. Use caution to cross at busy Adams Road in 0.5 mile.

You'll pass some open prairie and woods before you reach the Gallagher Road trailhead at mile 5. A short side trip leads to good eats in Goodison—home of the Paint Creek Trailways Commission—at the Paint Creek Cider Mill and Goodison Cider Mill. Just before arriving at the Silver Bell Road trailhead in 0.6 mile, you'll pass the Paint Creek Heritage Area–Wet Prairie on the right, where land managers perform spot burning to remove invasive plants and restore a prairie.

As you enter the suburban sprawl of Rochester Hills (horseback riding is prohibited south of here) after crossing Tienken Road at mile 7.8, you'll pass several trail entrances to the 16-acre Dinosaur Hill Nature Preserve, which has nature paths and a visitor center. The trail ends in about a half mile at Rochester Municipal Park, where you'll find parking, restrooms, and drinking water, as well as the annual Art & Apples Festival in the fall.

The Paint Creek Trail seamlessly joins the Rochester River Walk at the park. The river walk follows Paint Creek for another 0.8 mile through Rochester to a junction with the Clinton River Trail, which joins the Macomb Orchard Trail 2 miles to the east.

CONTACT: paintcreektrail.org/wordpress

DIRECTIONS

To reach the trailhead in Lake Orion from I-75, take Exit 81 to northbound MI 24/Lapeer Road (it's a long exit extending 0.8 mile). Go 6.2 miles—Lapeer Road becomes S. Broadway St.—and turn right into a restaurant parking lot just past Converse Court. Signed parking for the trail is behind the shopping center.

To reach the trailhead in Rochester at the Municipal Park from MI 59, take Exit 42 for Adams Road. Head north on S. Adams Road, and go 2.6 miles. Turn right onto Walton Blvd., go 2.3 miles, and continue onto W. University Drive for 0.6 mile. Turn left onto Pine St., and turn right into the parking lot for the park, adjacent to a pond on the left. The Rochester River Walk, in the back of the lot, heads west over Paint Creek to join the Paint Creek Trail.

Many factors contribute to the Pere Marquette Rail-Trail's popularity. It runs for 30 miles on smooth asphalt that is well maintained and, at 14 feet, wide enough to ride or walk side-by-side. At either end, Midland and Clare offer convenient services for weary travelers, as do small towns along the route. Forests, parks, bridges, and historical sites provide diversions and opportunities for reflection along the way.

The trail traces the Flint and Pere Marquette Railroad's segment between Midland and Clare that opened in 1870. The line served a railroad car service across Lake Michigan and timber companies that were clear-cutting the state's old-growth forests. The Pere Marquette Railroad acquired the railway in 1899 and operated it until the Chesapeake and Ohio Railway took over in 1947.

The trail offers a serene journey through nature, but small towns are within easy reach—by bike or by foot.

Counties
Clare, Isabella, Midland

Endpoints
Chippewa Trail near Ashman St. and Ann St. at the confluence of the Chippewa and Tittabawassee Rivers (Midland) to E. Fourth St. and Pine St. (Clare)

Mileage
30.0

Type
Rail-Trail

Roughness Index
1

Surface
Asphalt

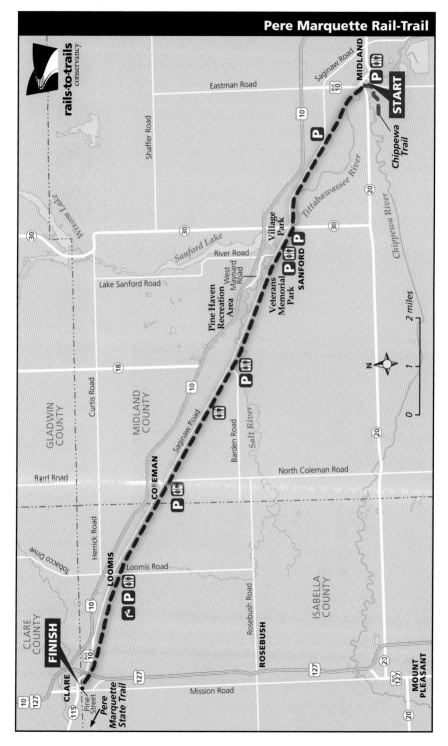

Pere Marquette Rail-Trail

Travelers will experience rural central Michigan along this route.

Traffic continued to dwindle, and the C&O stopped using the line in the 1980s. The trail opened in 1993.

Starting at the Midland Area Farmers Market (open in season on Wednesdays and Saturdays), you can take a quick side trip over the confluence of the Chippewa and Tittabawassee Rivers on a three-span bridge called The Tridge. The Chippewa Trail heads south and west for 4 miles. You'll return to the market and head north on the Pere Marquette Rail-Trail.

Riverside parks and cultural attractions border the trail as you leave town. You'll find covered picnic spots at Emerson Park, statues and blooming flowers at Dahlia Hill, and local history exhibits at Herbert D. Doan Midland County History Center or the Herbert Dow Museum (Dow Chemical got its start in Midland). Another attraction located just off the trail is Bradley House. This restored 1874 home offers visitors a glimpse into the everyday life of an early Midland family.

After passing through woods for about 8.4 miles, you'll arrive in Sanford. There's plenty to explore here, such as restaurants and shops or the riverside park. Just across the steel trestle you'll find the Sanford Centennial Museum, complete with a relocated circa-1870 railroad depot and railroad cars. About a mile ahead is Veterans Memorial Park, which features 200-year-old red and white pines. Hiking, mountain biking, and cross-country skiing trails at Pine Haven Recreation Area are 2.7 miles off the Pere Marquette Rail-Trail via Saginaw Road to Northwest River Road and then West Maynard Road.

The forest opens to farmland in a few miles, and Coleman comes into view about 11 miles past Sanford. Meals are available right next to the trail, or you can explore town for shops and more cafés. The old railroad depot has been renovated, and you can visit the library about two blocks away at Railway and First Streets, or the bike shop at Railway and Seventh Streets.

In another 4.7 miles you'll arrive at Loomis. Like other towns along the route, Loomis also started with a sawmill during the timber boom and benefited from the railroad. A general store and a few homes are all that remain today.

The Pere Marquette Rail-Trail ends in Clare in another 5.4 miles. An on-road bike lane on Pine, Fifth, and Main Streets ushers you through town to the Pere Marquette State Trail. The 53-mile crushed-stone pathway goes all the way to Baldwin.

CONTACT: peremarquetterailtrail.org

DIRECTIONS

To reach the trailhead at the Midland Area Farmers Market from I-75, take Exit 162B toward Midland on US 10 W. Continue west on US 10 for 11.2 miles, and exit left onto Bus. US 10/MI 20. Go 2.6 miles, and take the second right off the roundabout onto Patrick Road, heading west. Go 1.6 miles—Patrick Road becomes E. Indian St.—and turn left onto Ashman St. Go 0.4 mile into the parking for the farmers market. The trail leaves from the circle behind the farmers market.

To reach the trailhead in Clare from US 127 heading north, take Exit 156 left to E. Bus. US 127 toward Clare. Go 0.9 mile, and bear right around the traffic circle: the road joins N. Mission Road and then becomes N. McEwan St. In 0.7 mile, turn right onto E. Fourth St. Just before the end of the block, find a multiuse trail on your right and on-street or municipal parking on your left, behind the public library at E. Fourth St. and Pine St. The trail begins as a multiuse trail just across E. Third St.

The Portland Riverwalk ushers visitors around the charming town of Portland on 9 miles of paved trail. Also known as the Rivertrail Linear Park, the trail connects a handful of parks, scenic views overlooking the Grand and Looking Glass Rivers, and a renovated downtown that features restaurants, an ice-cream shop, and bakeries.

The trail's backbone is a 3.5-mile rail-trail conversion that follows the route of the Ionia and Lansing Railroad, which launched operations in 1869. A series of acquisitions and mergers put it under control of the Pere Marquette Railroad in 1899 and the Chesapeake and Ohio Railway in 1947. CSX took over C&O in 1987 and subsequently stopped using this section of rail bed.

Near Thompson Field stands a statue honoring Verlen Kruger, a record-setting canoeist and proponent of clean waterways.

County
Ionia

Endpoints
Loop from Portland High School at Ionia Road between Juniper Lane and Rosmond St. to to Cutler Road to I-96 to Market and Canal Sts. to Water St./Lyons Road and back to Portland High School (Portland)

Mileage
9.0

Type
Rail-Trail

Roughness Index
1

Surface
Asphalt

Portland Riverwalk

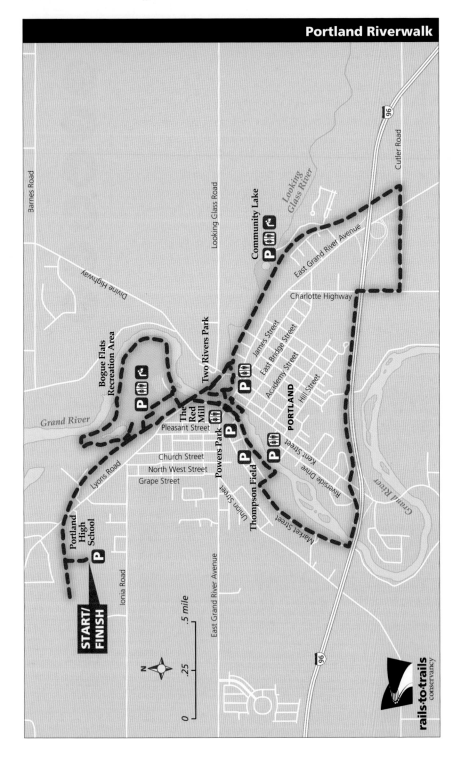

Barnes Road

I-96

Cutler Road

Looking Glass Road

Looking Glass River

Community Lake

East Grand River Avenue

Charlotte Highway

Divine Highway

Two Rivers Park

James Street

East Bridge Street

Academy Street

Hill Street

PORTLAND

Bogue Flats
Recreation Area

Grand River

The Red Mill

Pleasant Street

Powers Park

Kent Street

Grand River

Church Street

North West Street

Grape Street

Lyons Road

Union Street

Thompson Field

Riverside Drive

Market Street

I-96

Portland
High
School

START/
FINISH

Ionia Road

East Grand River Avenue

N

.5 mile

.25

0

rails·to·trails
conservancy

Beginning at Portland High School north of town, you'll head east on the trail and pass beneath a canopy of maples and pines on the old rail corridor until you reach a junction at 0.9 mile. Take the left fork that follows the Grand River for 1.6 miles through the Bogue Flats Recreation Area, where you'll find sports fields, restrooms, and turnouts overlooking the river.

Turn left as the trail returns to the railroad grade and cross the Grand River on a vintage 1899 railroad bridge, the first of three historic bridges that you'll cross. Fishing is allowed on all of them, and you will likely see anglers casting for smallmouth bass, perch, or trout. After crossing the bridge, a spur trail on the right loops through Two Rivers Park, which fronts the Grand and Looking Glass Rivers and passes a band shell for concerts. Another side trip from the park crosses a pedestrian bridge into historic downtown Portland on a boardwalk.

Returning to the main trail, you'll immediately cross Looking Glass River on the so-called Burroughs Street Bridge that was relocated here from its original location in Kent County, Michigan, in 1995. For the next 1.4 miles, you'll follow the river and pass through the woodsy Community Lake park and a short tunnel beneath I-96 before making a hard right onto a multiuse path that runs along Cutler Road, Charlotte Highway, and I-96 to another Grand River bridge. Known as the Kent Street Bridge, it was built in 1907 and relocated here.

The trail rolls between Market Street and the river for 0.6 mile to Thompson Field, where it runs along the shoreline. Look here for the memorial statue of Verlen Kruger, a proponent of clean waterways who set canoeing records.

The trail hugs the Grand River shoreline for 0.7 mile until it veers left and rejoins the former rail bed at the old railroad bridge you crossed earlier (you won't cross this time). Just past here you'll see the historic grainery for the Portland Cooperative; the multistory building is now called the Old Red Mill and is home to a farmers market on Saturday mornings in season. From the mill, you're 1.1 miles from Portland High School.

CONTACT: portland-michigan.org/251/rivertrail-linear-park

DIRECTIONS

To reach the northern trailhead at Portland High School from I-96, take Exit 77 onto E. Grand River Ave., heading northwest. Go 1.3 miles, crossing the Grand River, and turn right (north) onto Water St. Go 1.1 miles—Water St. becomes Lyons Road—and turn left into the driveway for Portland High School. Follow the driveway for 0.2 mile, and make the first right. Look for parking near the football stadium.

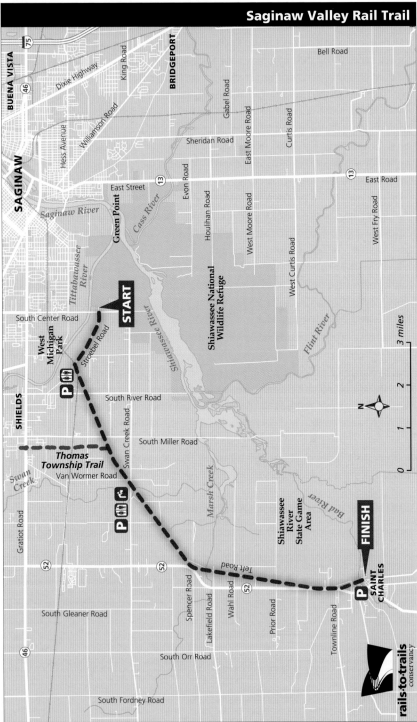

The Saginaw Valley Rail Trail offers a year-round rural retreat from the urban confines of Saginaw. Rolling through a continuous woodsy border past farms, fields, and game areas for 11 miles, the paved trail connects the manufacturing center of Saginaw with the former coal-mining town of St. Charles.

The trail follows a rail bed first used by the Jackson, Lansing and Saginaw Railroad in the late 1860s. By 1881, it extended north all the way to Mackinaw City and was under the control of the Michigan Central Railroad, a subsidiary of the New York Central Railroad. Ownership changes put the line under the Penn Central in 1968, Conrail in 1976, and the Tuscola and Saginaw Bay Railway in 1982.

Advocates pressed for a trail after the railway became inactive. Work began on the Saginaw Valley Rail Trail in 1999, and it was completed in 2009. The trail's builders

The Saginaw Valley Rail Trail is a year-round rural retreat.

County
Saginaw

Endpoints
S. Center Road and
Stroebel Road (Saginaw)
to Lumberjack Park at
E. Water St. and N. Miami
St. (St. Charles)

Mileage
11.0

Type
Rail-Trail

Roughness Index
1

Surface
Asphalt

The route ends with a beautiful bridge over the Bad River in St. Charles.

preserved much of the tree canopy to provide shade in the summer and color in the fall. Bird watchers use viewing platforms and the trails seven bridges to spot a share of the 100 species documented through the year. An equestrian trail parallels the paved trail for 8 miles.

Beginning at the Stroebel Road trailhead, you'll head southwest on the old railroad grade to get to St. Charles in 9.6 miles. In the other direction, a newer 1.4-mile trail addition alongside Stroebel Road intersects a sidewalk for South Center Road that crosses the Tittabawassee River for access to southern Saginaw.

Luscious displays of Queen Anne's lace and other wildflowers cluster along the route, and interpretive signs identify many of these species. A thick growth of vegetation flanks much of the trail, and the intact canopy of trees makes you feel as if you are in a large forest.

About 2 miles from the Stroebel Road trailhead, you'll come to a junction with the Thomas Township Trail. The right fork heads due north through farmland for 2.3 miles to chain grocery stores and restaurants. Back on the Saginaw

Valley Rail Trail, at mile 3 you'll come to a trailhead at Swan Creek and Van Wormer Roads that has restrooms, soda machines, drinking fountains, and parking. Crossing Swan Creek, there's a fishing platform where you may see anglers hoping to snag trout, perch, or smallmouth bass.

There are three pocket parks, complete with wooden gazebos and benches, along the trail. The first is located between Stroebel Road and River Road, the second between Spencer Road and Lakefield Road, and the third between Teft Road and Prior Road.

After crossing Marsh Creek just before mile 6, you'll skirt the Shiawassee River State Game Area. A viewing platform south of Wolf Creek at about mile 8 is a good place to watch for geese, ducks, swans, and white-tailed deer throughout the year. Approaching St. Charles, the trail crosses the Bad River on a scenic restored bridge and enters the southern trailhead at Lumberjack Park.

CONTACT: saginawcounty.com/parks/saginawvalleyrailtrail.aspx

DIRECTIONS

To reach the northern trailhead on Stroebel Road from I-75, take Exit 149B west onto MI 46/ E. Holland Road. Go 1.2 miles, veer right onto MI 46/E. Remington St., follow for 1.1 miles, and then turn left onto Sheridan Ave. Go 0.4 mile, and turn right onto MI 46/Rust Ave. Go 1.8 miles—Rust becomes Williams St. across the Saginaw River—and, in 0.2 mile, turn left onto S. Michigan Ave. Go 1.2 miles, and veer right onto W. Michigan Ave. Go 1.5 miles, and turn left onto S. Center Road, crossing the Tittabawassee River. After 0.7 mile, turn right onto Stroebel Road. Look for parking on the left in 1.4 miles, just before the railroad tracks. The trail endpoint is located about 1.4 miles southeast along the trail, which parallels Stroebel Road.

To reach the trailhead at Lumberjack Park in St. Charles from I-75, take Exit 136 onto westbound MI 83/Main St./Birch Run Rd. Go 10 miles, and turn right onto Bueche Road. Go 0.5 mile, and turn left onto Fergus Road. After 6.9 miles, turn right onto Sharon Road just after you cross the Shiawassee River. Go 3.3 miles—Sharon Road becomes Chesaning St.—and veer left onto S. Saginaw St. After 0.3 mile, turn right onto E. Water St. Go 0.2 mile and look for parking on the left in Lumberjack Park.

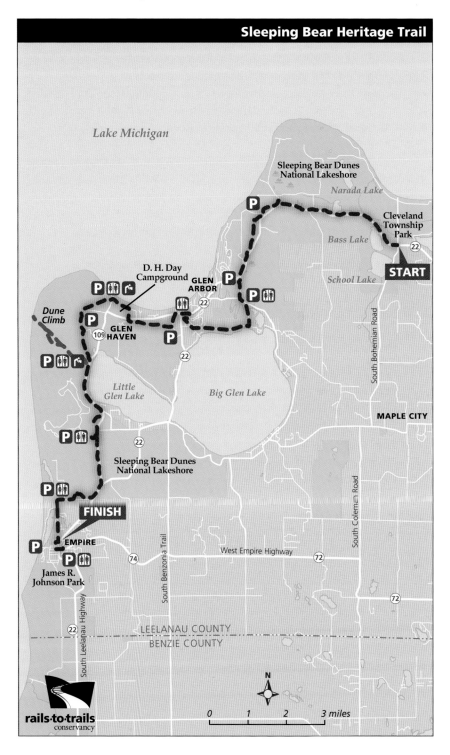

Sleeping Bear Heritage Trail

When completed, the Sleeping Bear Heritage Trail will wind for 27 miles through the stunning Sleeping Bear Dunes National Lakeshore—a national park on the shores of Lake Michigan in the northwest corner of Michigan's Lower Peninsula. In 2011, *Good Morning America* proclaimed this area "The Most Beautiful Place in America."

The trail is built partially on what once was a narrow-gauge railroad (constructed in 1907) that transported lumber from a sawmill on Glen Lake to the port town of Glen Haven on Sleeping Bear Bay. Most of the trail, however, was not constructed on a former rail bed, and visitors will find steep grades of as much as 12 percent in some parts of the currently 21-mile route.

The northeastern endpoint for the trail is currently located at South Bohemian Road and MI 22/West Harbor Highway in Maple City, between Little Traverse Lake to the east and Bass Lake and School Lake to the west; the southwestern endpoint is located at South Lacore Street and

The Sleeping Bear Heritage Trail winds through a region declared "The Most Beautiful Place in America" in 2011 by Good Morning America.

County
Leelanau

Endpoints
MI 22/W. Harbor Hwy. and County Road 669/ S. Bohemian Road (Maple City) to S. Lacore St. and S. Leelanau Hwy. (Empire)

Mileage
21.2

Type
Rail-Trail

Roughness Index
1

Surface
Asphalt, Gravel

The Port Oneida Rural Historic District along the trail showcases late-19th-century farm life.

South Leelanau Highway in Empire. When the trail is finished, its northeastern terminus will extend to County Road 651/Good Harbor Trail in Good Harbor Bay Beach, and its southwestern terminus will extend to Manning Road in Honor.

Beginning at South Bohemian Road, you'll head northwest to the Port Oneida Rural Historic District, which showcases Midwestern turn-of-the-century farm life. The area preserves a rare collection of more than a hundred buildings and farming sites dating back more than a century. Note that most of the Sleeping Bear Heritage Trail is paved except for the section of hard-packed crushed stone running through this historic district.

After leaving the historic farm area, you'll head south toward Glen Lake and then west into the town of Glen Arbor, where the trail continues on low-traffic roads. Here, you'll find a grocery store, several restaurants, a bike-rental shop, and numerous other stores catering to the tourist trade.

After exiting Glen Arbor, the trail continues west through a wooded area that in 2015 was struck by a storm with winds of up to 100 miles per hour that felled hundreds of trees. The devastation is still visible for a couple of miles, with large trees scattered like matchsticks along the corridor. Continuing west, the trail winds through D. H. Day Campground and the historic town of Glen Haven before arriving at the Dune Climb—the primary point of public access to the Sleeping Bear Dunes and one of Michigan's most famous natural features.

Rising to 260 feet, Dune Climb is a popular climbing point that provides a breathtaking view of Glen Lake below. The climb can be strenuous, however, with a 20 percent grade on loose white sand, but you can choose to walk, run,

or roll back to the bottom. Or you might continue the dune hike for another 1.5 miles to reach Lake Michigan. Those who do so should be prepared with sturdy shoes, a hat, sunscreen, and plenty of water, particularly during the summer, when the sun and sand can be extremely hot.

The trail turns south after the Dune Climb and enters a deeply forested part of the park. This section includes one major hill that is challenging but results in a long descent into the town of Empire. You'll pass a small trailhead on your right at West Voice Road and North Bar Lake Road with a pit toilet and parking, after which the off-road trail ends about 200 feet past where West Voice Road turns south and becomes South Lacore Road. From there, a signed on-road section continues for just under a mile to S. Leelanau Highway where South Lacore Road has become South Lacore Street.

In Empire, you can enjoy a local restaurant or take a quick dip at the town's sandy Lake Michigan beach. You can also access the Philip A. Hart Visitor Center, which provides information and interpretive displays for Sleeping Bear Dunes National Lakeshore.

CONTACT: sleepingbeartrail.org

DIRECTIONS

The best place to park near the northeastern endpoint is at the Bay View Trailhead in Maple City. To reach it from the intersection of MI 72 and Maple City Road, head north on Maple City Road for 8.8 miles. Turn left on MI 22/W. Harbor Hwy., and go 5.3 miles. Turn right (north) onto S. Thoreson Road, go 0.3 mile, and turn left into the trailhead parking lot. The endpoint is approximately 4.3 miles east.

To reach the southern trailhead from the intersection of S. Lacore St. and MI 22 in Empire, head north on S. Lacore St. where MI 22 heads northeast. After 1.1 miles—S. Lacore St. becomes Lacore Road—bear right onto W. Voice Road and, in 0.2 mile, turn left onto N. Bar Lake Road. Look for the parking lot on your right in less than 300 feet. The trail's official endpoint is about 1.3 mile farther down the trail in Empire.

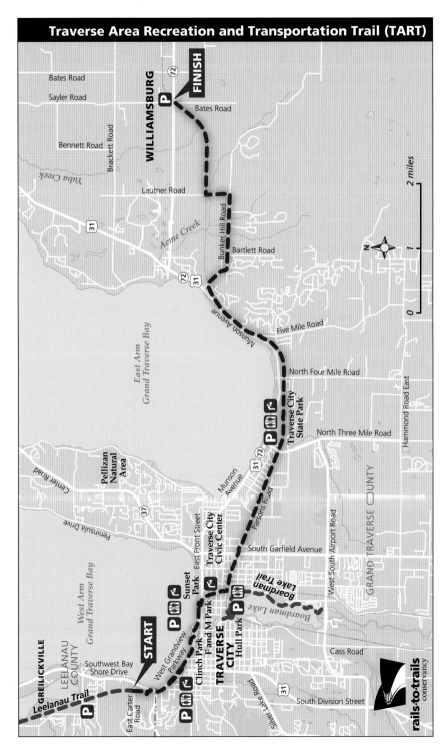

Traverse Area Recreation and Transportation Trail (TART)

The 13-mile Traverse Area Recreation and Transportation (TART) Trail provides trail users with extended waterfront access in Traverse City, the self-proclaimed Cherry Capital of the World, brushing by swimming beaches and a bayfront state park as it weaves through town. The trail then makes its way east through the countryside before terminating in Williamsburg.

Sitting at the head of Lake Michigan's Grand Traverse Bay, Traverse City, founded in 1847, was once the site of a sawmill that processed timber harvested in northern Michigan's old-growth forests. The city grew into a manufacturing center with the arrival of railroads, but in recent years has relied on tourism and agriculture for its livelihood. It hosts the annual National Cherry Festival in July, as well as craft-beer and winemaking events.

The TART Trail connects over the Boardman River and affords users a great view of the water.

Counties
Grand Traverse, Leelanau

Endpoints
E. Carter Road between S. Thorn Creek Dr. and SW Bay Shore Dr./ Leelanau Trail (Greilickville) to MI 72 at Bates Road (Williamsburg)

Mileage
13.0

Type
Rail-with-Trail

Roughness Index
1

Surface
Asphalt, Concrete

A restored caboose along the TART Trail reminds users of railroad days gone by.

The TART Trail—*TART* being an appropriate acronym in light of the area's cherry growing—runs east–west using the rights-of-way of highways and a working railroad. The multiuse trail is paved throughout, marked by red and green TART logo arrows. A partnership of trail volunteers and local governments conducts maintenance, including snow removal in the winter.

Beginning at the junction with Leelanau Trail (Trail 14, page 57), another TART project on East Carter Road, you'll pass through a commercial area and emerge onto a wide sidewalk trail alongside Southwest Bay Shore Drive/MI 22, which becomes West Grandview Parkway as it enters town.

The trail crosses the busy four-lane highway at North Elmwood Avenue and skirts West End Beach (where there's parking) and Clinch Beach, which are big draws for tourists. The Clinch Park Marina sits between the two beaches. You can opt instead to stay on the trail along the south side of the parkway until Division Street, at the end of West End Beach, where there is another crossing. You'll then continue along the north side of the parkway and through Clinch Park, eventually crossing the Boardman River. A bronze sculpture of a parent's attempt to help a child ride a bike may catch your eye before the trail heads south and passes beneath East Grandview Parkway alongside the Boardman River.

A bike lane and sidewalks along Woodmere Avenue lead you to the 2-mile Boardman Lake Trail along the east side of its namesake, which starts at Hull Park and ends at Medalie Park. If you want to make this connection, travel for a few blocks, pass the library, turn right on Hannah Avenue, and proceed 100 yards to the lake.

The trail then wends its way through the hustle and bustle of downtown Traverse City, providing easy access to shops, pubs, and eateries. Just west of Boyd and Railroad Avenues, a restored depot honors the history of railroad days gone by.

You'll travel alongside the tracks of the regional Great Lakes Central Railroad for the next 6 miles from the depot to Bunker Hill Road. Along the way, you'll pass Traverse City State Park, which offers camping, cottages, parking, and beach access to the East Arm Grand Traverse Bay.

The off-road trail ends at Bunker Hill Road, where a 2-mile connector on county roads takes you to an orphaned trail section stretching from Lautner Road to MI 72 in Williamsburg. Future plans call for connecting to that isolated section through a proposed development.

CONTACT: **traversetrails.org/trail/tart-trail**

DIRECTIONS

Parking at the western end of the TART Trail is available at the Leelanau Trail's southern trailhead in Greilickville. To reach the trailhead from US 31, take the highway north into Traverse City, where it becomes Division St. Where Division dead-ends at the intersection with MI 22/ W. Grandview Pkwy., near the waterfront, turn left onto Grandview, go 1.9 miles, and turn left again onto E. Cherry Bend Road. After 0.4 mile, turn right into the trailhead parking lot. The western endpoint for the TART Trail is 0.9 mile south.

To reach the easternmost parking at Traverse City State Park from I-75, take Exit 254 toward Traverse City. Go 0.4 mile off the exit; then go 0.6 mile north on Bus. Loop I-75, and veer left onto MI 72 E./N. James St. in Grayling. Follow for 0.7 mile, turning left to stay on MI 72 W. Go 17.5 miles, and turn right onto County Road 571. After 2 miles, turn left onto Nash Road NE. Follow for 6 miles and, just after the intersection with MI 66/US 131 N. in Kalkaska, continue straight on MI 72 W./W. Mile Road for 15.8 miles. At the traffic circle in Williamsburg, take the second right to stay on MI 72 W. for 0.5 mile. At the next traffic circle, take the first exit to stay on MI 72 W. for 0.8 mile. Turn left onto MI 72/US 31 S. and follow for 3.6 miles. Turn left into the Traverse City State Park parking lot. The trail runs along the southern border of the park. Follow the trail and county-road connector 6.7 miles to reach the eastern endpoint at Bates Road.

Wadhams to Avoca Trail

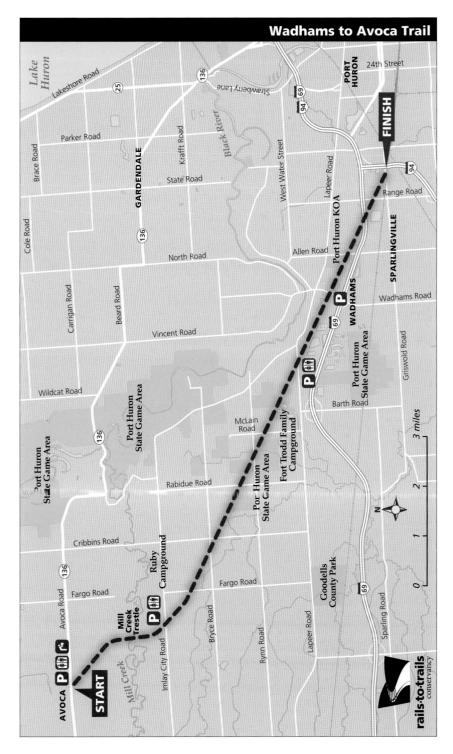

The Wadhams to Avoca Trail passes through 12 miles of woods and farmland in southeastern Michigan, but it's the historic railroad bridge over Mill Creek that's the big draw. Everyone from solo sightseers to participants in charity running events enjoy the breathtaking views 60 feet above the valley in an otherwise flat landscape.

The trail's name reflects its initial endpoints, although the trail now extends from Avoca to the outskirts of Port Huron, about 4 miles from downtown. It follows the route of a railway built by the Flint and Pere Marquette Railroad between Yale and Port Huron in 1890. It subsequently came under control of the Pere Marquette Railroad, the Chesapeake and Ohio Railway, and finally CSX, which sold the rail bed to the county in 1999.

Completed in 2003, the trail is covered in limestone fines for 6.7 miles from Avoca to McLain Road and paved

The historic 60-foot-high Mill Creek Trestle affords breathtaking views of the valley below.

County
St. Clair

Endpoints
MI 136/Avoca Road and Main St. (Avoca) to Griswold Road between Range Road and I-94 (Port Huron)

Mileage
12

Type
Rail-Trail

Roughness Index
1

Surface
Asphalt, Crushed Stone, Gravel

the rest of the way to Griswold Road near Port Huron. Three trailheads offer vault toilets but no drinking water. After Avoca, there are no services for about 10 miles until the residential areas around Wadhams.

Starting in the rural town of Avoca, you'll find the trailhead across the road from an old grain elevator located on the old rail right-of-way. A couple of diners in this rural town date to the 1880s, and the trailhead offers trailer parking, hitching posts, and vault toilets.

You'll come to the Mill Creek Trestle in less than 2 miles. The 640-foot-long railroad bridge has been outfitted with side rails and decking for safety, plus four overlooks where visitors can enjoy the views without blocking passersby. The bridge is the destination of an annual Labor Day event called Trek the Trestle and a half marathon in the spring. A trailhead is located 0.8 mile south of the bridge. Because hardwood trees flank much of the trail, autumn is a spectacular time to visit. In addition to the colorful views from the trestle, numerous small ponds and wetlands next to the trail mirror the bright colors on the trees.

The trail mostly passes through rural farmland for the first 4 miles, making for a beautiful walk or ride during any season and a pleasant cross-country ski route. Passing just south of the Abbotsford crossroads community at 4.4 miles, you'll enter a forest and pass tracts of the Port Huron State Game Area.

The last 5 miles, beyond McLain Road, is paved to the end at Griswold Road. This section of the trail passes through a developing residential area, where you'll find fast-food restaurants and other services at Wadhams Road, the location of the last trailhead.

Three campgrounds are located within 1.5 miles of the trail at various points: on Imlay City Road (Ruby Campground), at McLain and Lapeer Roads (Fort Trodd), and off Lapeer Road between Wadhams and Allen (Port Huron KOA).

CONTACT: stclaircounty.org/offices/parks/wadhams.aspx

DIRECTIONS

To reach the trailhead in Avoca from I-69, take Exit 189 toward Wales Center Road (the exit will last for about 0.5 mile). Head north on Wales Center Road, and go 1.4 miles. Turn left onto Old State Highway 21, and go 0.6 mile. Turn right onto Kilgore Road, and follow for 4.8 miles; then turn right onto MI 136 E./Avoca Road, and go 0.2 mile to Beech St. Turn right into where Beech St. and Main St. meet; at the Y, bear left on Main St., and look for parking immediately to your left.

To reach the closest parking for the eastern endpoint from I-69, take Exit 196 onto northbound Wadhams Road. Look for an overhead street sign for the trail in 0.1 mile; the parking entrance is just past the trail crossing. The trail ends 2.6 miles to the east, at Griswold Road.

T he West Bloomfield Trail sails along for nearly 7 miles through a municipality that claims to be one of the wettest in the nation—not from rainfall but from the sheer number of lakes (28), ponds (150), and wetlands (3,500 acres). You'll stay high and dry on the crushed-limestone trail, however, as you pass the waterways that historically made this a weekend and summer getaway for Detroit and Pontiac.

The trail follows the 1880s route of the Michigan Air Line Railroad, which merged with the Grand Trunk Western Railroad in the 1920s. Beginning in 1899, the Orchard Lake Division of the Detroit Urban Railway paralleled those existing tracks between Orchard Lake and Pine Lake as it carried passengers on electric trolleys between Detroit and Pontiac.

The West Bloomfield Trail opened in 1993, and it has been a work in progress ever since. In the east, it links with the Clinton River Trail that rolls into Pontiac and beyond. In the west, it ends at Haggerty Road, but plans call for a connection to the M-5 Metro Trail. Benches, bike racks, scenic overlooks, and mileage markers (based on rail miles from Richmond) have been added to support users. Travelers curious about the surroundings will enjoy the MotorCities Wayside Exhibits posted along the trail.

County
Oakland

Endpoints
Haggerty Road south of Walnut Lake Road to Woodrow Wilson Blvd. and Depew Dr. at Sylvan Manor Park/ Clinton River Trail (West Bloomfield Township)

Mileage
6.8

Type
Rail-Trail

Roughness Index
1

Surface
Crushed Stone

Take your bike out and enjoy the scenery on the West Bloomfield Trail.

West Bloomfield Trail

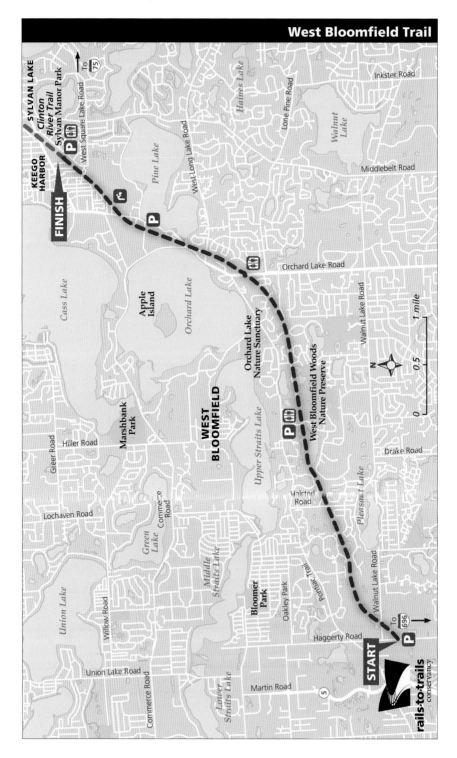

Beginning at the Haggerty Road trailhead, you'll soon discover the trail is steeped in nature, in spite of pockets of development. Don't be alarmed if what appears to be a lawn ornament suddenly turns and bounds toward the forest; one pass on this trail provides sightings of deer, raccoons, and rabbits. Turtles, waterfowl, and assorted frogs populate the ponds and lakes, and the forests are filled with spruce, hickory, oak, and maple trees.

You'll find the greatest concentration of wildlife at the 162-acre West Bloomfield Woods Nature Preserve at mile 2.6. A path winds through the urban wildlife sanctuary to connect overlooks, some with telescopes to aid in spotting the 100 bird species that have been documented here. Red foxes, coyotes, and minks make their homes here.

A narrow strip of land carries the trail between Orchard Lake and Pine Lake at about mile 5. Apples grew in abundance here in the 1800s, resulting in the first lake's name. An island in its midst is called Apple Island, where legend has it that Chief Pontiac held council with neighboring tribes to plan an attack on Fort Detroit in the mid-18th century. Fast forward to the early 20th century, and you can imagine this shoreline was a popular stop for tourists who took the train up from Detroit.

Leaving the lakes behind, the trail brushes the southern border of Keego Harbor before entering Lake Sylvan. The West Bloomfield Trail ends at Sylvan Manor Park, but your travels can continue on the Clinton River Trail that rolls for 16 miles through Pontiac to the east side of Rochester, where it picks up the Macomb Orchard Trail (Trail 16, page 65).

CONTACT: westbloomfieldparks.org/west-bloomfield-trail.html

DIRECTIONS

To reach the Haggerty Road trailhead from I-696, take Exit 10, and merge onto MI 10, heading northwest. Go 5.4 miles, and turn left onto W. 14 Mile Road. In 0.1 mile, round the traffic circle, and take the second right to continue west on 14 Mile Road. In 0.9 mile, bear right at a second traffic circle to head north on Farmington Road; in another 0.9 mile, bear right to round a third traffic circle, and take the second right to continue west on Maple Road. In 2.9 miles, turn right onto Haggerty Road. After 0.8 mile, look for parking on the right.

To reach the Sylvan Manor Park trailhead from I-75, take Exit 75 west onto Bus. I-75 toward Pontiac. In 1.5 miles, merge onto Square Lake Road. Go 3.4 miles, and turn right onto St. Joseph St.; then go 0.2 mile, and turn left onto Empire Drive. Go 0.3 mile, turn left onto Woodrow Wilson Blvd., and, in 0.1 mile, look for the entrance to Sylvan Manor Park on the right.

William Field Memorial Hart-Montague Trail State Park

The name tells the tale of the William Field Memorial Hart-Montague Trail State Park. Rolling for 22 paved miles through the farms, orchards, and forests of western Michigan between Hart and Montague, the trail may never have come into existence if not for the late William Field.

As a fruit grower from Shelby and an Oceana County commissioner in the early 1980s, Mr. Field couldn't raise interest among his fellow commissioners to turn the recently dismantled railroad into a recreational trail. Fearing a lost opportunity, he bought the corridor in 1982 and donated it to the state. Seven years later, the trail's northern half opened as the state's first paved rail-trail, followed in 1991 by the second half. The state legislature honored his

The trail winds through several charming communities in western Michigan.

Counties
Muskegon, Oceana

Endpoints
Spring St. and Water St. near Trailway Campground/Medbery Bike Trail (Montague) to Wood St. at Water St. (Hart)

Mileage
22.7

Type
Rail-Trail

Roughness Index
1

Surface
Asphalt

The depot at the trail's southern end serves as a visitor center.

efforts by naming the trail for him in 2014. In 2016, the state completed a yearlong face-lift for the trail, which included asphalt resurfacing and widening to 10 feet.

The Chicago and Michigan Lake Shore Railroad originally built that rail bed in 1872 as a segment of its route from New Buffalo to Pentwater. It later came under control of the Chicago and West Michigan Railway, the Pere Marquette Railroad (depots still stand in Hart and Shelby), and the Chesapeake and Ohio Railway. CSX Transportation removed the tracks between Hart and Montague in 1982.

Starting in Montague next to a campground on White Lake, a 0.2-mile side trip via the connecting Medbery Bike Trail takes you to the world's largest working weathervane on the corner of Dowling and Water Streets. The 48-foot-tall structure is topped by a replica of the *Ella Ellenwood,* a 19th-century schooner that carried lumber on Lake Michigan. Another trail, the White Lake Pathway, crosses White Lake into Whitehall, where it meets the Fred Meijer Berry Junction Trail, which goes south toward Muskegon.

Heading north on the William Field Memorial Hart-Montague Trail, you'll pass Christmas tree farms, orchards, and the 100-acre Clear Springs Nature Preserve on the way to Rothbury (mile 6.2). Be on the lookout for deer in the fields

and orchards, especially in the morning and evening. A 4-mile section between West Fruitvale Road and Rothbury is open for horseback riders.

The village of New Era (mile 10) is near the halfway point of the trail, and during the summer you can stop for homemade ice cream at the trailside dairy bar. Another 4.3 miles up the trail, the village of Shelby gained renown in 1876 as a hunting center for one of the last mass nestings of now-extinct passenger pigeons.

In 5.8 miles, the trail brushes the southern edge of Mears, another food and water stop. The farmland here gives rise to Oceana County's claim as the Asparagus Capital of the Nation. If you arrive in Hart during June, you might see the National Asparagus Festival, complete with a parade and crowning of an Asparagus Queen. Any other time, you'll find Hart is the gateway to the beaches and giant sand dunes of Silver Lake and Lake Michigan.

CONTACT: michigandnr.com/parksandtrails#list (choose "William Field Memorial Hart-Montague Trail State Park")

DIRECTIONS

To reach the southern trailhead in Montague from US 31, take the Bus. US 31 exit toward Montague and Whitehall, heading west. Go 1.8 miles on Bus. US 31/E. Colby St., and turn right onto Bus. US 31/Thompson St. Go 0.5 mile—Thompson St. becomes Dowling St. on the other side of White Lake—and turn right onto Bus. US 31/Water St. Go 0.1 mile, and turn right onto Spring St. Parking is at the end of the block on the left, behind Whitehall Products.

To reach the northern trailhead in Hart from US 31, take Exit 149 east toward Hart on W. Polk Road. Go 0.8 mile, and look for parking on the left. The northern terminus is 0.6 mile up the trail.

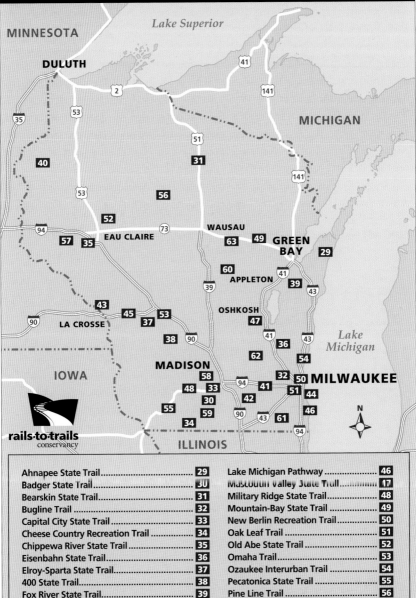

Wisconsin

MINNESOTA

Lake Superior

DULUTH

MICHIGAN

WAUSAU

EAU CLAIRE

GREEN BAY

APPLETON

LA CROSSE

OSHKOSH

Lake Michigan

MADISON

IOWA

MILWAUKEE

rails·to·trails
conservancy

ILLINOIS

N

Wisconsin

The Elroy-Sparta State Trail (Trail 37, page 141) is arguably the oldest rail-trail in the United States.

The Ahnapee State Trail in northeast Wisconsin provides a scenic 45-mile journey between Sturgeon Bay and Kewaunee, featuring a tour of water bodies along the Door Peninsula.

The trail follows the former corridor of the Ahnapee and Western Railway, which once served as an industrial link between Door, Brown, and Kewaunee Counties. The steam- and diesel-powered locomotives hauled dairy goods, cherry crops, and lumber until the early 1970s.

Start your journey at Sturgeon Bay, home to a variety of restaurants and cafés. Parking is available at the northernmost trailhead at South Neenah Avenue and Wilson Road, just south of town, as well as at various points throughout the city. The first 11.5 miles to the town of Forestville traverse agricultural fields and forested areas. At Forestville Dam County Park, you'll find parking, restrooms, and your first views of the Ahnapee River through the trees to the west. You'll follow the Ahnapee River south another 6.1 miles to the town of Algoma, where the river flows into Lake Michigan.

Counties
Door, Kewaunee

Endpoints
S. Lansing Ave. and
Green Bay Road
(Sturgeon Bay) to
Main St. and Willow St.
(Luxemburg) or
Miller St. and Milwaukee
St. (Kewaunee)

Mileage
44.9

Type
Rail-Trail

Roughness Index
2

Surface
Asphalt, Crushed Stone

A beautiful view of Lake Michigan from the Ahnapee State Trail

The route detours briefly in Algoma to Navarino Street, where you can opt to continue for several blocks on-road to the lakefront. Crescent Beach and its attractive boardwalk are located just farther south, along Lake Street. To bypass Algoma, make a sharp right turn to stay on the trail, just past Birch Street.

About 10.5 miles past Algoma, just beyond Casco, trail users can detour west to the town of Luxemburg or head east along the Kewaunee River, which playfully disappears and reappears along the remaining 12.3 miles of trail. Along this segment, you'll find fields of sunflowers and apple orchards that sometimes shed their bounty on the trail (a favorite of horses).

Bruemmer Park, located just outside of Kewaunee, offers shady spots to rest and a small zoo, which is open from 7 a.m. to sunset year-round and offers free admission. As you reach the southern end of the trail, it curves north and splits, with one prong leading to Main Street, just above two marinas, and the other leading to the trail's southern terminus where the Kewaunee River empties into Lake Michigan.

Here, you'll find an old train depot that has been converted into a public pavilion with parking. Explore the old clock tower on the depot for a piece of history, or enjoy the lake and the various shops and restaurants that Kewaunee has to offer.

NOTE: *Snowmobilers and ATV/UTV users must display either a Wisconsin registration or an ATV/UTV or snowmobile State Trail Pass. For more information, go to dnr.wi.gov/topic/parks/trailpass.html.*

CONTACT: ahnapeestatetrail.com

DIRECTIONS

To access the northern trailhead and parking at Sturgeon Bay from WI 42, turn south off WI 42 onto S. Neenah Ave. Go 1.2 miles and, with a cornfield and a brown AHNAPEE STATE TRAIL sign on your right, turn left to reach the parking area (0.2 mile north of Wilson Road). Parking is also available at various locations toward Sturgeon Bay, such as Cherry Blossom Park on S. Lansing Ave. and various on-street spots.

To access the southern trailhead in Kewaunee from I-43, take Exit 171 for Depere Road toward Greenleaf/Denmark, heading east, and follow Depere for 0.9 mile—Depere Road turns into Main St. along the way. Veer right onto Wisconsin Ave. and continue for 0.2 mile. Bear left to continue on County Road KB for 2.3 miles, crossing the Neshota River, and then turn left onto County Road P. After 6 miles, turn right onto WI 29 E./WI 29 Trunk E. Go 14.4 miles and turn left onto Milwaukee St., noting the AHNAPEE STATE TRAIL sign on your right at the intersection of Milwaukee and Harrison Sts. In 0.1 mile, turn left into the trailhead parking lot, located across the street from Harbor Park and a restaurant parking lot.

Rail-trail fans know that Wisconsin's Elroy-Sparta State Trail is famous for its three tunnels. The Badger State Trail, which heads south from Madison to the Illinois state line (where it connects with the Jane Addams Trail), boasts its own 1,200-foot Stewart Tunnel—with a twist: the Stewart Tunnel is built on a curve, so riders cannot see the other end as they enter the tunnel.

The trail starts in Madison just south of Lovell Lane, where it intersects the Southwest Commuter Path (Trail 58, page 219), which heads 5.6 miles from Madison to Fitchburg. Heading south on the Badger State Trail, you'll quickly cross over an intersection of the Capital City State Trail (Trail 33, page 127), a 17-mile route that stretches from Fitchburg to Madison, and the Cannonball Path, a 3.9-mile route from the University of Wisconsin–Madison Arboretum to the Military Ridge State Trail (Trail 48, page 183) in Fitchburg.

Counties
Dane, Green

Endpoints
Southwest Commuter Path just southeast of Lovell Ln. and Carling Dr. (Madison) to Jane Addams Trail just north of Wuetrich Road and east of Clarno Road (Orangeville, IL)

Mileage
40.0

Type
Rail-Trail

Roughness Index
1–2

Surface
Asphalt, Crushed Stone

A wooded area greets trail users near the Illinois–Wisconsin state line.

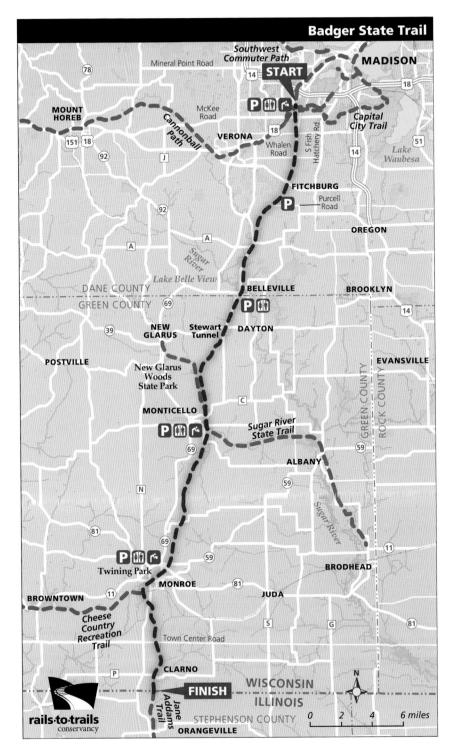

Badger State Trail

The Badger State Trail affords beautiful views of the Wisconsin countryside.

The first 6 miles of the Badger State Trail are paved to Purcell Road, after which the surface gives way to crushed stone. (*Note:* Snowmobiling is permitted from Purcell Road to the Illinois state line. Winter ATV use is permitted, but UTVs are prohibited.) The small town of Belleville will greet riders just shy of the 13-mile mark. It's a quaint historical town where one can see remnants of how the railroad used to go right through the heart of the community.

Approximately 4 miles south of Belleville, riders will find the Stewart Tunnel. The Wisconsin Department of Natural Resources recommends that all riders walk their bikes through the entirety of the tunnel. Flashlights and light jackets to guard against the dampness are also recommended.

Once you clear the tunnel, it's only 5 more miles to Monticello. Parking can be found a couple hundred yards to the right of the trail on Pratt Road. Here the trail also connects to the Sugar River State Trail (Trail 59, page 223).

The next 5 miles run through wooded areas and farm fields—with rolling hills and several nice creeks and bridges along the way—to the small farming town of Stearns, after which it's only a few more miles to Monroe. The seat of Green

County (population 10,000), Monroe is home to the famous Swiss Colony gourmet food company and is also known as the "Swiss Cheese Capital of the USA."

Just a few blocks west of Badger State Trail, on West 21st Street, you'll find the eastern terminus for the Cheese Country Recreation Trail (Trail 34, page 131), a 47-mile route that heads west and then north to Mineral Point.

The final few miles of trail takes you to Clarno, the last town in the state of Wisconsin, where you'll find a few businesses. From there, it's just a short ride to the Illinois state line and Wuetrich Road, where you can pick up the 14.8-mile Jane Addams Trail to Freeport, Illinois.

NOTE: A State Trail Pass ($25 annually/$5 daily) is required for bicyclists and in-line skaters ages 16 and older. Snowmobilers and ATV/UTV users must display either a Wisconsin registration or an ATV/UTV or snowmobile State Trail Pass. For information, go to dnr.wi.gov/topic/parks/trailpass.html.

CONTACT: dnr.wi.gov/topic/parks/name/badger

DIRECTIONS

Parking near the northern endpoint is available at Dawley Conservancy in Fitchburg—which also serves as the western trailhead for the Capital City State Trail. To reach the Fitchburg trailhead from the intersection of US 18/US 151/Verona Road and McKee Road, take McKee Road east. Go 0.9 mile to S. Seminole Hwy., turn left, and then go 0.4 mile and turn left into the parking lot for Dawley Conservancy. Take the short path in back of the parking lot north for 0.1 mile to the Capital City State Trail, which you'll then take left (northwest) less than a quarter mile to where it meets the Cannonball Path and the Southwest Commuter Path. Head north on the Southwest Commuter Path a short ways to where it meets the Badger State Trail.

To reach the southern trailhead in Monroe from WI 11/WI Trunk Hwy. 11, take the WI 69 N. (Monticello/New Glarus) exit, and head south on 18th Ave. Drive about 0.3 mile, and turn right onto Mansion Dr. After 0.2 mile, turn left onto 14th Ave. After about 0.3 mile, turn right onto Park Dr. Look for parking immediately to your right. The southern endpoint is just over 8 miles south along the trail at Wuetrich Road and the Wisconsin–Illinois state line, which is also the northern terminus for the Jane Addams Trail.

The Bearskin State Trail follows a route blazed into the heart of the great North Woods, first by pioneers and loggers, and then by passengers and outdoors enthusiasts on trains with such names as the *Hiawatha* and *Fisherman's Special*. Now it's bicyclists, hikers, and snowboarders who disappear into the woods on a mostly crushed-gravel trail that runs for some 26 miles between Minocqua and Heafford Junction.

The trail follows an old spur of the Chicago, Milwaukee, St. Paul and Pacific Railroad (the Milwaukee Road) built from New Lisbon to Minocqua in 1887 to haul logs and lumber. As the timber industry declined, residents of big cities escaped to the area, encouraging the Milwaukee Road to run a *Fishermen's Special* on weekends. Later, the streamlined *North Woods Hiawatha* ran vacationers north.

Passenger service ended in 1955 because of slumping ridership, and the Milwaukee Road ceased freight service to Minocqua in 1971. The state of Wisconsin acquired the rail bed and opened a trail in the late 1970s. The state extended the route 8.5 miles, including 4.5 miles on road, in 2016.

The views of changing leaves in autumn are breathtaking on this route.

Counties
Lincoln, Oneida

Endpoints
Front St. and Flambeau St. (Minocqua) to Hiawatha Trail/County Road N between Heafford Road and Beach Road (Heafford Junction)

Mileage
26.5

Type
Rail-Trail

Roughness Index
2

Surface
Crushed Stone

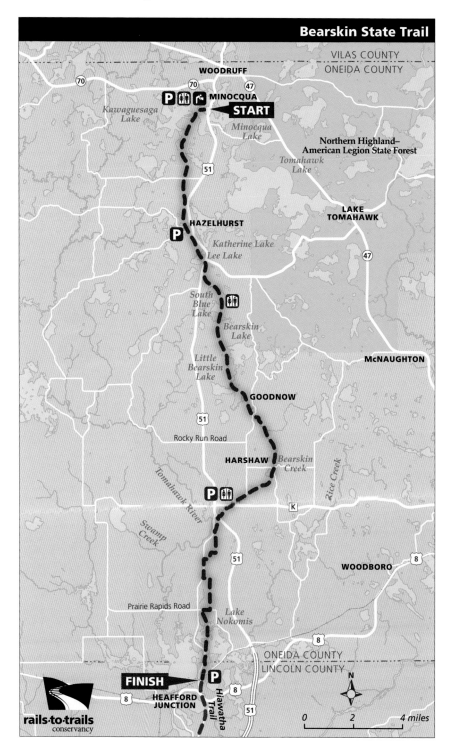

Bearskin State Trail

The trail traverses a sparsely populated area known for dense forests and a proliferation of lakes. Those lakes are a destination for fishermen as well as birders, especially during migratory season. In addition to spotting bald eagles and loons from the lakeside, you might spot deer from the trail. You'll cross 16 converted railroad trestles, 8 alone spanning Bearskin Creek, the trail's namesake.

Beginning in Minocqua, you'll cross the longest of those trestles—375 feet long, to be exact—spanning Minocqua Lake. Although occasional clearings can be found next to marshes or lakes, the trail is mostly forested. Tree branches arching over the trail give the impression of passing through a tunnel.

Restrooms, drinking water, and food are scarce. Hazelhurst, at 5.1 miles, is the last town with full services until the end. A pit toilet and pump water are available at a picnic spot next to South Blue Lake (8.9 miles), and Goodnow (13.6 miles) has a restaurant.

You'll gain insight into the former backwoods life from interpretive signs posted along the trail. A century-old railroad line shed, about 9.5 miles from Minocqua, attests to the rustic living conditions of some railroad workers. Elsewhere, you can read about the flora and fauna.

A rest stop is located on Old Highway K at 18 miles, and 1 mile later you'll arrive at a 4.5-mile on-road segment. The final 2.5 miles of off-road gravel trail start again on Lake Nokomis Road and cross the lake on two trestles, one which completes a 0.3-mile causeway. The trail ends in Heafford Junction, which has food and lodging, where you join the Hiawatha Trail.

NOTE: A State Trail Pass ($25 annually/$5 daily) is required for bicyclists ages 16 and older. Snowmobilers must display either a Wisconsin registration or a snowmobile State Trail Pass. For information, go to dnr.wi.gov/topic/parks/trailpass.html.

CONTACT: dnr.wi.gov/topic/parks/name/bearskin

DIRECTIONS

To reach the trailhead in Minocqua from US 51, turn westbound onto Front St. in Minocqua (about 2 miles south of Woodruff or 0.3 mile after crossing Minocqua Lake heading north). Turn right into the trailhead parking lot (behind the post office) 1 block after you pass Flambeau St. The trail starts at the west end of the parking lot.

To reach the trailhead in Heafford Junction from US 51, take Exit 234 westbound to US 8. Go 2.5 miles, and turn right onto County Road L. Go 1.6 miles, cross a bridge, and look for parking on the right, just past an ice-cream shop. The southern trail end is about a 1 mile south, at County Road N.

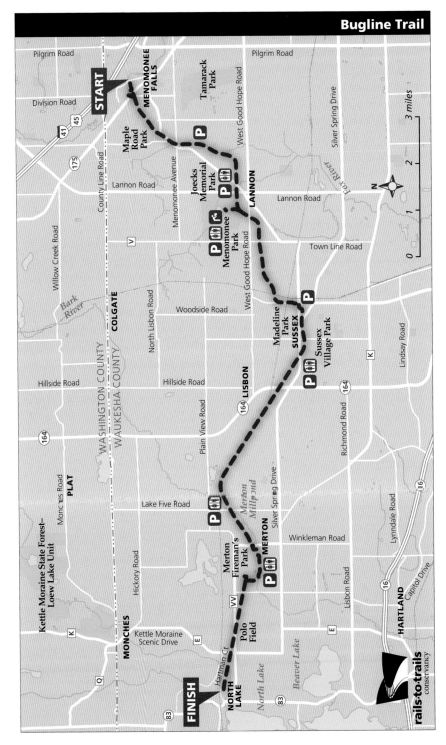

Wisconsin might have 56 species of mosquitoes, but that's not how the 15.6-mile Bugline Trail got its name. Tradition has it that an early train passenger compared the curvy railroad route now followed by the rail-trail to a bug crawling on a grapevine.

Local residents adopted "Bugline" as the nickname for the Milwaukee, Menomonee Falls and Western Railway trains that in 1890 began hauling limestone from the quarries near Lannon, as well as ice, milk, and sugar beets. The Chicago, Milwaukee, St. Paul and Pacific Railroad later bought it but stopped using the line in 1978.

Located roughly 20 miles from Milwaukee, the trail runs, though not in a straight line, through several suburban communities, starting in Menomonee Falls in the

The Bugline Trail in autumn

County
Waukesha

Endpoints
Just south of Grand
Ave. and Laurel Ln.
(Menomonee Falls)
to Hartman Court just
south of Kilbourne Road
(Hartland)

Mileage
15.6

Type
Rail-Trail

Roughness Index
1

Surface
Asphalt

Stop for a gorgeous view of the quarry lake.

east and traveling through Lannon, Sussex, and Lisbon to North Lake in the west. In 2015, Waukesha County completed a three-year asphalt-paving and trail-extension project.

Before you begin in Menomonee Falls, you might want to check out Old Falls Village, where many historic cabins and buildings were moved to avoid demolition. The town's vintage 1890 railroad station stands at the park's entrance at the corner of County Line and Pilgrim Roads, about 2 miles from the trailhead.

Beginning in Menomonee Falls, you'll follow the railroad corridor west through a commercial and residential area where homeowners have fashioned makeshift trail entrances. The trail dips into a forest of bur oak and linden until a clearing opens up to a working limestone quarry. The sheer sides of the excavation site dwarf vehicles inside.

About 4 miles from the trailhead is a short rail-trail spur to Menomonee Park, the former site of a 19th-century quarry that has been transformed into a 16-acre swimming hole surrounded by a 464-acre park. The stone mined here, and at several more quarries you'll pass, is called Lannon limestone. Mined since the 1850s,

the high-grade limestone has been used in buildings and public works projects in Milwaukee and Chicago. An example can be found at St. John's Lutheran Church, one block south of Good Hope Road on Main Street in Lannon.

Passing through Lannon and Sussex, the trail runs alongside a railroad through farmlands and wetlands to Lisbon Community Park at about mile 11. After a long mill pond, the trail leaves the railway grade and rolls through Pollworth and Merton Fireman's Parks on the Bark River. Winding through a neighborhood, the trail then regains the railroad grade and shares the last 2-mile leg to North Lake with the Ice Age Trail.

Along the trail, signs are posted explaining allowable uses. Snowmobiles are allowed between Main Street in Menomonee Falls and the railroad underpass on the east side of Sussex, between Pewaukee Road in Sussex to Pollworth Park in Merton, and from County Road VV to Hartman Court in Hartland. Horseback riding is allowed between Main Street in Menomomee Falls and Menomonee Park in Lannon.

CONTACT: waukeshacounty.gov/bugline

DIRECTIONS

A large parking lot near the eastern end of the trail is available at Menomonee Park, about 4.5 miles from the endpoint. To reach Menomonee Park from I-41, take Exit 54 for WI 167/County Road Y/Lannon Road/Mequon Road. Head southwest on Lannon Road, and go 4.4 miles. Turn right into the park access road, go 0.3 mile, and turn left onto Park Dr. Make a right into the parking lot.

On-street parking is also available about 0.3 mile from the trail's eastern endpoint in Menomonee Falls. From I-41, take Exit 52 onto County Line Road, heading west. Go 0.7 mile, and turn left onto Appleton Ave. Go 0.8 mile to St. Francis Dr., turn right, and look for on-street parking on St. Francis Dr. or 3 blocks southwest on Roosevelt Dr. The eastern endpoint of the trail begins about 0.3 mile east at Grand Ave, which is east of WI 175.

To reach the Merton trailhead from I-41, take Exit 52 onto County Line Road, heading west. Go 8.5 miles to Lake Five Road, and turn left. Go 2.1 miles to Plainview Road, and turn right. After 0.4 mile, turn left onto Center Oak Road, go 0.8 mile, and then turn right onto County Road VV. Go 0.2 mile to Bark River Road, and turn left; then go 0.4 mile, and turn left onto White Tail Run. You can find parking in Pollworth Park or Merton Fireman's Park. The western endpoint is about 2 miles west.

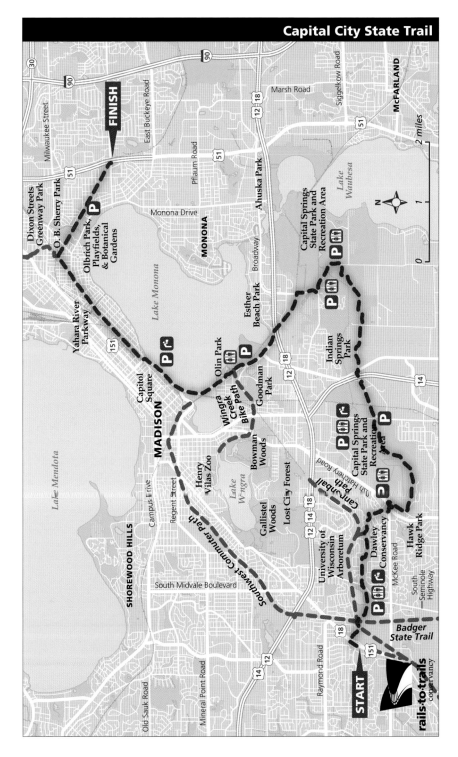

Capital City State Trail

The Capital City State Trail contributes to the impression that you're never far from a bike path in the Madison area. The paved trail meanders for 17 miles from the suburb of Fitchburg in the southwest, through downtown Madison, to the eastern neighborhoods. It demonstrates why this area always ranks among the top bicycle-friendly communities.

Less than half the trail is on former rail lines: the Chicago, Milwaukee, St. Paul and Pacific Railroad along western Lake Monona, and the Chicago and North Western Railway in the east. Most of the trail comprises a collection of paths (the Nine Springs E-Way, the John Nolen Lakeshore Path, and the Isthmus and East Side Bike Paths) that were renamed into a single trail.

Beginning in Fitchburg, you'll take a tunnel beneath US 18/US 151 (Verona Road) and, in less than a mile, arrive at a "bike trail interchange" where you'll cross the Southwest

Approaching Madison, the trail provides beautiful views of Madison and the Lake Monona shoreline.

County
Dane

Endpoints
Williamsburg Way at Verona Road/US 18/ US 151 (Fitchburg) to Cottage Grove Road at US 51/S. Stoughton Road (Madison)

Mileage
17.0

Type
Rail-with-Trail

Roughness Index
1

Surface
Asphalt

The Capital City State Trail contributes to Madison's reputation as a bike-friendly city.

Commuter Path (Trail 58, page 219; heads north to Madison), the Badger State Trail (Trail 30, page 115; heads south to Illinois), and the Cannonball Path (connects with Military Ridge State Trail, Trail 48, page 183). You'll pass through a forest and enter a prairie planted by Fitchburg's Dawley Conservancy, where you'll find restrooms, parking, and a bike-repair station.

You'll alternate in and out of wooded park settings for the next 2 miles to a pedestrian crossing over Fish Hatchery Road and a trail interruption at Glacier Valley Road (turn right on this street, and look for the trail on the left in 0.4 mile). For roughly the next 6 miles, you'll pass through the 2,500-acre Capital Springs State Park and Recreation Area, which features marshes, creeks, and lakes across a rolling golden terrain sparsely dotted with trees. You can learn about local American Indian culture and pioneer settlement patterns at the Lussier Family Heritage Center at mile 8.3, next to a campground.

Look for Olin Park at mile 12 for breathtaking views of downtown Madison across Lake Monona. The Wingra Creek Bike Path on the left goes 2.2 miles to

Henry Vilas Zoo, beaches at Vilas Park, and, farther on, a shady ride through the University of Wisconsin–Madison Arboretum. Continuing north, the Capital City State Trail runs alongside John Nolen Drive on a causeway that crosses the lake with exceptional views of the State Capitol dome.

The trail hugs the shoreline for a few blocks, and you'll pass the visually striking Monona Terrace Community and Convention Center designed by architect Frank Lloyd Wright. Farther on, the trail travels through historical Madison neighborhoods, including Schenk-Atwood-Starkweather-Yahara at mile 16, where the trail is flanked by community garden plots, bungalow-style homes, and shops. Here you can pick up a bite to eat or a cup of joe.

The trail takes a southeasterly tack where you'll pass Olbrich Botanical Gardens, with 16 acres of plants, paths, and a tropical paradise in the conservatory. You'll also see a Thai pavilion easily recognizable from the trail.

The trail ends 1.4 miles past the gardens, but there are plans to connect with the 53-mile Glacial Drumlin State Trail (Trail 41), which begins about 6 miles away in Cottage Grove.

NOTE: A State Trail Pass ($25 annually/$5 daily) is required for bicyclists and in-line skaters ages 16 and older for the 9 miles between Verona Road and Nob Hill Road near Industrial Drive. For information, go to dnr.wi.gov/topic/parks /trailpass.html. Regular commuters can get a fee-waiver sticker by filling out a form supplied by the Dane County Department of Land & Water Resources/Parks Division; download a printable form at parks-lwrd.countyofdane.com/documents/pdf /capitalstatetrail-380-162.pdf.

CONTACT: dnr.wi.gov/topic/parks/name/capcity

DIRECTIONS

Parking near the western endpoint is available at Dawley Conservancy in Fitchburg. To reach the Fitchburg trailhead from the intersection of US 18/US 151/Verona Road and County Road PD/McKee Road, take McKee Road east. Go 0.9 mile to S. Seminole Hwy., turn left, and then go 0.4 mile and turn left into the parking lot for Dawley Conservancy. Take the short path in back of the parking lot north for 0.1 mile to the Capital City State Trail. Left goes to the western endpoint in 1 mile, while right goes to Madison.

To reach the parking near the eastern endpoint in Madison from WI 30/Aberg Ave., take the Fair Oaks Ave. exit, heading south. Go 0.5 mile, and turn left at Milwaukee St.; then, in 0.3 mile, turn right onto Walter St. Go 0.6 mile to parking for Olbrich Playfields on the right (Johns St. is on the left). To get on the trail, head back to Walter St., and walk north (left) about 500 feet to the street, crossing for Capital City State Trail. Right goes 1 mile to the endpoint at Cottage Grove Road, and left goes toward downtown Madison.

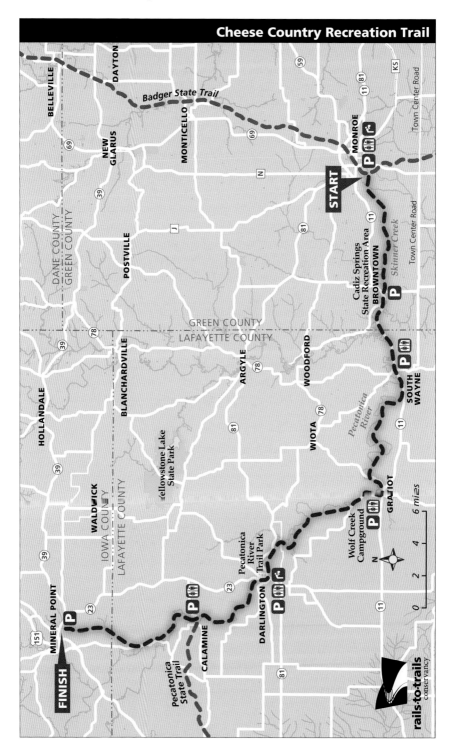

Cheese Country Recreation Trail

I f you're looking for an invigorating motorized-trail experience, the Cheese Country Recreation Trail (aka the Tri-County Trail) won't disappoint. If you're on foot, hoof, or self-propelled two wheels, however, the trail is a challenge. ATVers, trail bikers, and snowmobile riders primarily use the trail, leaving some areas in deep mud or dust while other sections are rutted or deeply graveled. Motorized traffic is heaviest on weekends.

The 47-mile trail meanders through the heart of southwest Wisconsin's Driftless Area, noted for its rolling hills and rocky outcroppings left untouched by glaciers. It follows the corridor of the Chicago, Milwaukee, St. Paul and Pacific Railroad, which stopped using it in 1980. In addition to the graded route between Monroe and Mineral Point, the railroad left behind dozens of bridges, including the 440-foot Browntown trestle, whose stone supports date to the 1880s, as it followed the Pecatonica River drainage.

Beginning in Monroe just a few blocks west of the Badger State Trail, the Cheese Country Recreation Trail's southern terminus, you'll find yourself in a town that calls itself the "Swiss Cheese Capital of the USA." The trailhead is

Dozens of bridges left over from this rail-trail's railroad past still grace its corridor.

Counties
Green, Iowa, Lafayette

Endpoints
W. 21st St. and Fourth Ave. W. (Monroe) to Commerce St. and Old Darlington Road (Mineral Point)

Mileage
47.0

Type
Rail-Trail

Roughness Index
3

Surface
Crushed Stone

just 0.2 mile from the Badger State Trail and 0.7 mile from the National Historic Cheesemaking Center, both east on 21st Street.

Heading west from Monroe, you'll pass the lakes of the Cadiz Springs State Recreation Area and in 7.4 miles arrive in Browntown. Rolling within sight of WI 11, you'll notice the countryside is primarily cropland and dairy farms.

The trail veers away from the highway just past South Wayne, 4.9 miles from Browntown, and in 9.3 miles arrives in the old mining town of Gratiot, a good place for a break at the local restaurants and shops. From here, the trail continues northwest along stretches of farmland and wooded ridges for 10 miles to Darlington. You'll pass through the historic downtown on city streets, giving you an opportunity to explore or to stop for refreshments or supplies.

Another 5.8 miles on the trail brings you to Calamine. You'll pass a junction for the Pecatonica State Trail (Trail 55, page 209), another ATV/snowmobile trail that rolls 10 miles west to Belmont. From Calamine, the Cheese Country Recreation Trail heads north 9.3 miles to the northern trailhead in Mineral Point at the old Railroad Depot Museum, built in 1856 and the oldest in the state. Mineral Point, a historic mining village, is rich with artists' studios and galleries, restored homes, restaurants, and bed-and-breakfasts.

NOTE: Cheese Country Recreation Trail stickers are required for motorcycles, mopeds, golf carts, and dirt bikes, as well as bicyclists and horseback riders ages 18 and older. ATVs and UTVs are not required to have a Cheese Country sticker, although they do need an in-state DNR registration sticker. For information, go to tricountytrails.com/trail_stickers.iml.

CONTACT: tricountytrails.com

DIRECTIONS

To reach the Monroe trailhead from I-39/I-90, take Exit 142A onto US 12/US 14/US 18/Beltline Hwy., heading west. In 8 miles, take Exit 258 and, in 0.7 mile, turn left (south) to continue on US 18. Go 9.6 miles on US 18, and take Exit 77 to WI 69 toward Monroe, heading south. Go 8.9 miles, and turn right onto WI 69/WI 92/W. Main St. in Belleville, heading west. In 3.6 miles, bear left at the Y to continue south on WI 69. In 19.3 miles, bear right (west) at the exit for WI 11 W./WI 81 W./WI 69 S. toward Dubuque. In 0.3 mile, bear right at the exit for WI 81 W./WI 69 S. toward Argyle and Freeport. In another 0.3 mile, turn right (north) onto WI 81 and, in 0.4 mile, make a U-turn south onto WI 81/WI 69/Seventh Ave. In 1.9 miles, turn right onto W. 21st St. in Monroe. The trailhead is 0.7 mile ahead on the right.

To reach the Mineral Point trailhead, follow the directions above through the second sentence. Follow US 18/US 151 west-southwest for 43.9 miles. Take Exit 40 onto WI 23 toward Mineral Point, go 1.5 miles, and turn left onto Commerce St. Go 0.8 mile, turn left onto Old Darlington Road, and turn left immediately into parking for the Mineral Point trailhead.

The 30.4-mile Chippewa River State Trail kicks off at the confluence of the Eau Claire and Chippewa Rivers in downtown Eau Claire's Phoenix Park, where visitors can access a walking labyrinth, amphitheater, farmers market, restrooms, parking, and the southwestern endpoint of the 28-mile Old Abe State Trail (Trail 52, page 197), which heads to Cornell. Heading southeast, your journey begins over a 500-foot-long trestle that used to carry train cars of the Chicago, Milwaukee, St. Paul and Pacific Railroad.

The trail hugs the shoreline of the Chippewa River as it winds south to Owen Park, which features the Sarge Boyd Bandshell, listed on the National Register of Historic Places. Riding past, you may witness an Eau Claire Municipal Band concert, wedding, play, or other lively public events.

Long, straight stretches of trail await as you leave the city and enter farm country; enjoy the fresh air and the

A beautiful view at Old Tyrone, a ghost town along the path

Counties
Dunn, Eau Claire, Pepin

Endpoints
Riverfront Terrace south of Wisconsin St./Old Abe State Trail in Phoenix Park (Eau Claire) to E. Main St. just north of US 10/WI 25 (Durand)

Mileage
30.4

Type
Rail-Trail

Roughness Index
1

Surface
Asphalt, Asphalt Emulsion (Caryville–Red Cedar State Trail junction)

Chippewa River State Trail

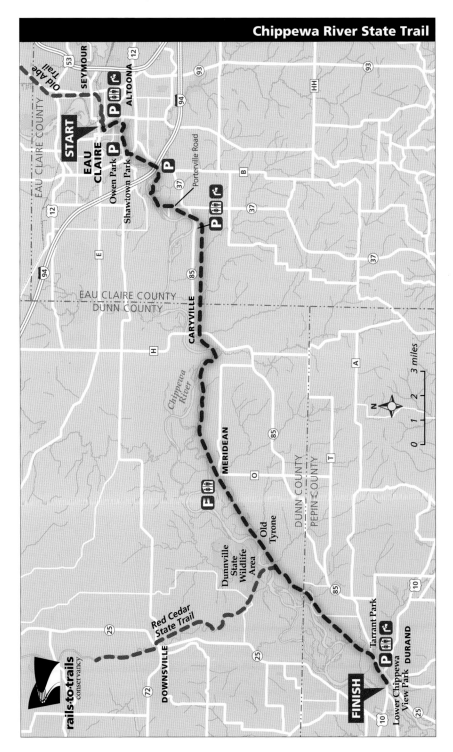

fragrant aroma of the many wildflowers that dot the region. Near the trail's half-way point you'll reach the Caryville trailhead, just off WI 85, which provides restrooms, drinking fountains, and ample parking. The route then winds along the banks of the river in a deciduous forest until you reach Meridean, an unincorporated community in the town of Peru.

At about 22 miles, after passing two trestles over the snaking Cranberry Creek, you'll enter Old Tyrone, a ghost town marked by an interpretive plaque. A shelter perched above the trail, just a few steps up the cliffside, offers picturesque views of the nearby river bend.

The trail terminates at the Tarrant Park trailhead in Durand, approximately 6.5 miles past the junction of the Red Cedar State Trail (Trail 57, page 215). Here, you'll find ample parking as well as a registration office for purchasing State Trail Passes. About a mile and a half farther west of Tarrant Park, Lower Chippewa View Park provides beautiful waterside views. Snowmobiles are permitted between Porterville Road and Durand.

NOTE: A State Trail Pass ($25 annually/$5 daily) is required between Eau Claire and the Pepin County line for bicyclists and in-line skaters ages 16 and older. Snowmobilers must display either a Wisconsin registration or a snowmobile State Trail Pass. For information, go to dnr.wi.gov/topic/parks/trailpass.html.

CONTACT: dnr.wi.gov/topic/parks/name/chiprivertrail or **chippewa-river-trail.com**

DIRECTIONS

In Eau Claire, metered parking is available in a municipal lot just east of the trailhead off N. Farwell St. From I-94, take Exit 70 onto northbound US 53. In 3.8 miles, take Exit 89 toward River Prairie Dr. Head west on River Prairie Dr. for 0.6 mile, and turn left onto Galloway St. just after crossing the Eau Claire River. In 1.8 miles, turn left onto N. Farwell St. The Railroad Street parking area is located midblock to your right.

The eastern end of the trail is located about a block west in Phoenix Park. Additional on-street parking is available here on Riverfront Terrace (2-hour parking from 9 a.m. to 5 p.m., Monday–Friday) by following the directions to the Farwell St. lot above and continuing on Galloway St. for an additional block. Turn left onto N. Barstow St. and then right onto Riverfront Terrace. Look for parking on the left. The trailhead is on the left, just after you pass the Royal Credit Union.

To reach the Tarrant Park trailhead in Durand from I-94, take Exit 88 onto US 10 in Osseo, heading west. Drive 38.8 miles, and turn right onto E. Prospect St. After 0.3 mile, turn left onto 14th Ave. E. The parking lot is 0.1 mile ahead on your right, just past where the trail intersects 14th Ave. The endpoint is located 0.8 mile southwest along the trail.

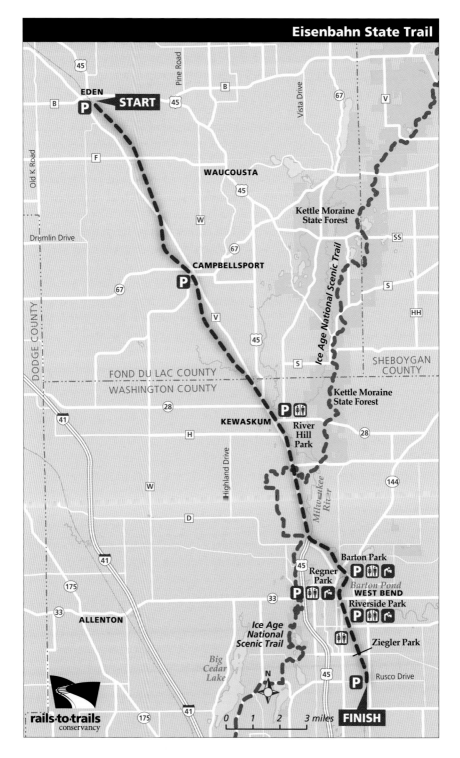

Eisenbahn State Trail

The Eisenbahn State Trail gives a nod to Wisconsin's German heritage in its name—*Eisenbahn* is German for "railway." The strict translation, "iron road," refers to the iron rails originally used as tracks in the old country. A more apt name today might be *Velobahn*, as the trail is popular for cyclists pedaling the 25 miles between Eden and West Bend. In the winter, most of the trail north of West Bend is open to snowmobiles; winter ATV use is permitted between December 15 and March 15, when the ground is frozen and the temperature is 28°F or lower.

The trail follows the original route of the Milwaukee and Fond du Lac Air Line, a branch of the Milwaukee and Superior Railroad built in the 1850s. It later came under control of the Chicago and North Western Railway in the 1880s. The Fox River Valley Railroad took over in 1988

The Eisenbahn's flat, easy route is popular with cyclists and provides good views of the surrounding countryside.

Counties
Fond du Lac, Washington

Endpoints
Pine St. just south of
US 45/E. Main St. (Eden)
to Rusco Dr. between
E. Progress Dr. and S.
River Road (West Bend)

Mileage
25.0

Type
Rail-Trail

Roughness Index
1–2

Surface
Asphalt, Crushed Stone

The Eisenbahn State Trail runs for 25 miles between Eden and West Bend.

and operated the line until it stopped using the section from Eden to Rusco Drive in West Bend in 1999. The trail opened in 2006, but the Canadian National Railway runs trains in the corridor from Rusco Drive south to Milwaukee.

Beginning at the Eden Community Park, you'll head south through Fond du Lac County on a crushed-stone trail that typifies this route until West Bend. The trail passes through farmland along a slightly elevated ridge for good views of the countryside. Only occasional trees shade your passage. In 7.5 miles, you'll arrive in Campbellsport, where Main Street eateries are only a block away.

Another 4.5 miles brings you to the Washington County line and the village of Kewaskum, named for a chief of the Potawatomi tribe. You also can find refreshments in cafés and grocery stores within one or two blocks of the trail. The Ice Age National Scenic Trail, a hiking trail that stretches for 1,000 miles around Wisconsin, crosses the Eisenbahn State Trail near County Road H on its way to Kettle Moraine State Forest to the east.

Leaving Kewaskum, the trail runs alongside US 45 for 4.5 miles until you reach northern West Bend. Shortly after crossing the Milwaukee River, you'll find the trail paved from Barton Park south. A side trail, less than a mile from Barton Park, heads to the 136-acre Lac Lawrann Conservancy. More than 200 bird species have been recorded in the nature preserve's mix of open prairie and hardwood forests. Deer, mink, and muskrat also live here.

Continuing south, the lake on your right is Barton Pond, which powered gristmills and sawmills below the dam in West Bend's early days. Today the pond is a fishing destination (including ice fishing). After passing the lake, watch for the old railroad depot, built in 1900 and renovated in 2009, about 0.2 mile south of Washington Street.

At the southern end of West Bend, after crossing Decorah Road, Ziegler Park is off a path to the right and has picnic tables, restrooms, and drinking fountains. The trail again becomes rural in its last mile from Paradise Road to Rusco Drive.

NOTE: Snowmobilers and ATV users must display either a Wisconsin registration or an ATV or snowmobile State Trail Pass. For information, go to dnr.wi .gov/topic/parks/trailpass.html.

CONTACT: dnr.wi.gov/topic/parks/name/eisenbahn

DIRECTIONS

To reach the northern trailhead at Eden Community Park from I-41, take Exit 92 onto County Road B toward Eden, heading east. Go 3.7 miles, and turn right onto County Road V. Go 0.6 mile, and turn left onto Shady Ln. Take an immediate left onto Seybold Dr; then go 0.1 mile, and turn right onto Reagan Dr. Turn left into the parking lot. The trail starts just north of Reagan Dr., about 400 feet south of the parking lot.

To reach parking for the trail in West Bend from I-43, take Exit 96 onto WI 33 (E. Green Bay Ave.) toward Saukville, heading west across the Milwaukee River. Go 0.5 mile, and bear right to continue east on WI 33/E. Dekora St. Go 13.3 miles—WI 33 becomes E. Washington St. in Newburg—and turn left onto N. Forest Ave. in West Bend. Go 0.1 mile, and turn right onto Willow Lane; then go 0.1 mile, crossing Wisconsin St. Just after the road curves left, look for parking on your left at the depot and the trail. More parking is available a block south of Willow Lane on the left, at the corner of Wisconsin St. and Water St. The trail endpoint is 3 miles south.

A trailhead at the southern endpoint on Rusco Dr. is planned for the spring of 2017. To reach it from I-43, follow the directions above through the second sentence. Follow WI 33 for 7.5 miles, and turn left onto Decorah Road. Go 5.7 miles, and turn left onto S. River Road. Go 2 miles, and turn right onto Rusco Dr. The trailhead is 0.1 mile ahead on your right.

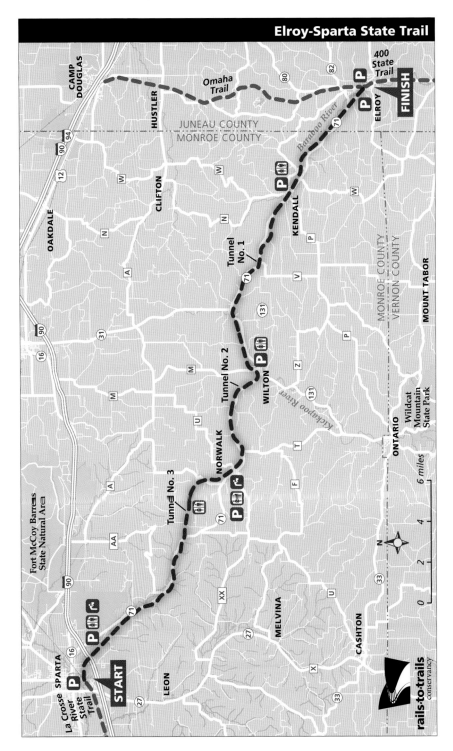

Elroy-Sparta State Trail

Utter darkness is as much a part of the scenery along the Elroy-Sparta State Trail as the views of the rolling hills and farmland. That's because visitors pass through three hand-dug railroad tunnels on their 33-mile journey from Sparta to Elroy on what is widely acknowledged to be the oldest rail-trail conversion in the United States.

Those tunnels—two at 1,600 feet and the other at 3,800 feet—have long been a big draw for the trail, which opened in 1967. They are unlit, and water drips down the walls and pools at your feet. The temperature in the tunnels is a cool 50–60 degrees, regardless of the outside temperature.

Work crews had to chip through solid rock in those shafts before the Chicago and North Western Railway could open a direct route between St. Paul and Chicago in

The Elroy-Sparta Rail-Trail's three tunnels date back to the 1870s. Because of Wisconsin's harsh winters, each tunnel was fitted with large doors that are still in place today.

Counties
Juneau, Monroe

Endpoints
S. Water St. and Milwaukee St./La Crosse River State Trail (Sparta) to WI 82 at WI 71 (Elroy)

Mileage
33.8

Type
Rail-Trail

Roughness Index
2

Surface
Crushed Stone

At the Elroy Commons Trail Shop, you can pick up trail information and rent bikes.

1873. In its prime, the route carried 6 passenger trains and 40–50 freight trains daily. The railroad discontinued passenger service in 1953 and freight in 1964. A state agency bought the right-of-way soon after and began developing the trail.

It's a less strenuous trek between Sparta and Elroy because of those tunnels, although you'll be climbing a grade to each one, followed by a downhill run to the town on the other side. The trail's hard-packed crushed limestone base is comfortable for walking and running, and it's suitable for wider bicycle tires. Even so, bicyclists must dismount to pass through the tunnels.

There are rest areas, restrooms, drinking fountains, camping areas, and snack concessions at the endpoint towns and in between at Norwalk, Wilton, and Kendall. You can pick up the La Crosse River State Trail (Trail 45, page 171) in Sparta or the 400 State Trail (Trail 38, page 145) and Omaha Trail (Trail 53, page 201) in Elroy. The trail is a middle leg of the Bike 4 Trails route that runs for 100 miles from the Mississippi River through Wisconsin's rugged Driftless Area.

Beginning in Sparta at the trailhead tourist center, you might first want to check on "Ben Bikin," a large statue of a mustachioed 19th-century sportsman atop a Victorian-style "penny-farthing" high-wheel bicycle, about a half mile north on South Water Street. Returning to the trail, you'll head east for 8.9 miles to the first and longest tunnel, Number 3, which is 3,810 feet long. Seasonal kiosks

at both ends sell flashlights among other goods. Just past the tunnel is the Summit Rest Area, where you'll find a reconstructed watchman's shack and, with a little searching, an 8-foot-deep stone flume to divert water away from the rails.

Leaving the tunnel, it's 3.2 miles through forest and farmland to the trailhead and services in Norwalk. Another 3.2 miles takes you to Tunnel Number 2, which is 1,694 feet long. Like the others, this tunnel has 20-foot-tall double doors at the entrances that the watchmen opened and closed for passing trains to prevent winter temperatures from damaging walls inside the portals. These wooden doors are closed all winter now; snowmobilers take a detour around them.

You'll travel 2.2 miles to services in Wilton, and then another 5.4 miles to Tunnel Number 1, which is 1,649 feet long and the driest of the three. You'll make a 3.3-mile downhill run to the trail headquarters in Kendall at a restored depot that also serves as a museum and bike rental. You also can contact the trail headquarters for shuttles between any points on the trail. The last segment consists of 6 miles of mostly flat, open farm country to the end of the trail in Elroy.

NOTE: A State Trail Pass ($25 annually/$5 daily) is required for bicyclists ages 16 and older. Snowmobilers must display either a Wisconsin registration or a snowmobile State Trail Pass. For information, go to dnr.wi.gov/topic/parks/trailpass .html. Camping is available in Elroy, Kendall, Sparta, and Wilton.

CONTACT: **dnr.wi.gov/topic/parks/name/elroysparta** or **elroy-sparta-trail.com**

DIRECTIONS

To reach the western trailhead in Sparta from I-90, take Exit 28 toward Sparta onto WI 16, heading west. Go 2.3 miles, and turn left onto S. Water St. Go 0.5 mile, and turn left onto Milwaukee St. Turn immediately right into the trailhead parking lot. The trailhead is at the old railroad depot at 111 Milwaukee St.

To reach the southern trailhead in Elroy from I-90/94, take Exit 69 toward Mauston on WI 82/Gateway Ave., heading west. In 0.6 mile, bear left on WI 82/N. Union St. to head south across the Lemonweir River. In 0.2 mile, turn right on E. State St., go 0.3 mile (4 blocks), and turn left to head south on WI 82/Division St. In 0.6 mile, bear right around the traffic circle, and take the first right to continue east on WI 82/Grayside Ave. In 10.5 miles, turn left to continue south on WI 82. In 1.6 miles, turn left onto Franklin St. in Elroy. Take the first left into the parking lot, located behind the Elroy Commons Trail Shop on Railroad St. After you park, look for the 400 State Trail in front of the trail shop. Head north (left) on the trail about 0.2 mile to Cedar St., turn left, and look for the Elroy-Sparta State Trail, which heads northwest just north of where Cedar St. intersects Main St.

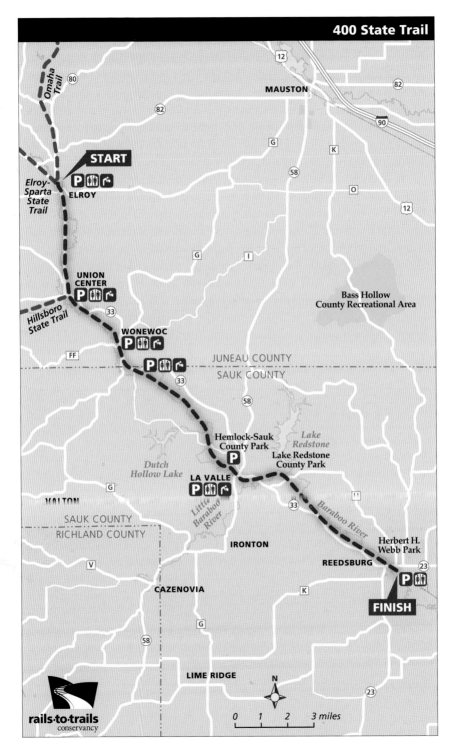

400 State Trail

Omaha Trail

80

12

MAUSTON

82

82

90

G

K

58

START

P

Elroy-Sparta State Trail

ELROY

O

12

G

I

Bass Hollow County Recreational Area

UNION CENTER

P

Hillsboro State Trail

33

WONEWOC

P

FF

JUNEAU COUNTY

SAUK COUNTY

33

58

Hemlock-Sauk County Park

P

Lake Redstone

Dutch Hollow Lake

Lake Redstone County Park

LA VALLE

P

G

WALTON

SAUK COUNTY

RICHLAND COUNTY

Little Baraboo River

Baraboo River

IRONTON

33

Herbert H. Webb Park

REEDSBURG

23

V

P

K

CAZENOVIA

FINISH

G

58

LIME RIDGE

N

23

0   1   2   3 miles

rails·to·trails
conservancy

Traveling the 400 State Trail is a numbers game. The trail's name refers to the old Chicago and North Western Railway's "No. 400" passenger train that zoomed through here between Chicago and St. Paul—a distance of 400 miles accomplished in 400 minutes. Other numbers related to the trail might interest you: 22, the number of miles between trailheads in Elroy and Reedsburg; 10, the number of times you'll cross the Baraboo River; 7, the miles of parallel horseback-riding trail; 3, the number of junctions with other trails.

The Chicago and North Western Railway started running trains here in 1873 after completing three tunnels on the Elroy-to-Sparta section. The railroad discontinued the line, and the state acquired it in 1988 and opened the trail in 1993. It's the eastern link in the state's Bike 4 Trails adventure that combines four state trails—the Great River

The packed-limestone trail showcases the rural beauty of central Wisconsin.

Counties
Juneau, Sauk

Endpoints
Cedar St. between Main
St. and Second St. (Elroy)
to S. Walnut St. between
Railroad St. and South
Ave. (Reedsburg)

Mileage
22.3

Type
Rail-Trail

Roughness Index
2

Surface
Crushed Stone

Interesting rock formations are common sights along the 400 State Trail.

(Trail 43, page 165), the La Crosse River (Trail 45, page 171), the Elroy-Sparta (Trail 37, page 141), and the 400—into a 100-plus-mile bicycle trek.

Beginning in the historic railroad hub of Elroy, you'll start a couple of blocks from the Elroy-Sparta State Trail and a mile south of the Omaha Trail (Trail 53, page 201), which runs 12.5 miles north to Camp Douglas.

In the first mile heading south, you'll cross the first of nearly a dozen bridges or trestles spanning the Baraboo River. The valley provides a level ride to Reedsburg, but you'll readily see hilltops, cliffs, and dramatic rock formations common to the so-called Driftless Area that wasn't scraped flat by Ice Age glaciers.

You'll arrive at a park and restrooms in Union Center in 4 miles, followed by a junction with the Hillsboro State Trail (it goes 4.1 miles west to Hillsboro). Another 3 miles puts you in Wonewoc, a narrow part of the valley that's a tourist destination for trail pedalers as well as river paddlers. Wonewoc has two campgrounds (Baker's Field is on the trail) and numerous restaurants, taverns, and grocery stores.

The horseback-riding trail runs from here to La Valle. The old railroad grade passes through woodlots and wetlands in this section where you might spy deer, raccoons, and skunks, as well as a variety of songbirds and waterfowl. Two public recreation areas, Hemlock-Sauk County Park and Dutch Hollow Lake, offer waterside recreation close to the trail 5.4 miles past Wonewoc on Dutch Hollow Road.

You'll find more refreshments in La Valle. About 2 miles past the La Valle business district, County Road V takes you on a 1-mile side trip to Lake Redstone, a reservoir nestled in the hills.

About 7.7 miles past La Valle, you'll arrive in Reedsburg. While its early history involved growing hops and brewing beer, now it's the home to the annual 10-day Fermentation Fest that celebrates all things fermented. The trail ends at a restored railroad depot that serves as an information center. By far the trail's largest town, there are antiques shops and a selection of restaurants, as well as bed-and-breakfasts and a campground.

NOTE: *A State Trail Pass ($25 annually/$5 daily) is required for bicyclists and horseback riders ages 16 and older. Snowmobilers must display either a Wisconsin registration or a snowmobile State Trail Pass. For information, go to dnr.wi.gov /topic/parks/trailpass.html.*

CONTACT: dnr.wi.gov/topic/parks/name/400

DIRECTIONS

To reach the northern trailhead in Elroy, about 0.3 mile south of the trail's start point, from I-90/94, take Exit 69 toward Mauston on WI 82/Gateway Ave., heading west. In 0.6 mile, bear left on WI 82/N. Union St. to head south across the Lemonweir River. In 0.2 mile, turn right on E. State St., go 0.3 mile (4 blocks), and turn left to head south on WI 82/Division St. In 0.6 mile, bear right around the traffic circle, and take the first right to continue east on WI 82/Grayside Ave. In 10.5 miles, turn left to continue south on WI 82. In 1.6 miles, turn left onto Franklin St. in Elroy. Take the first left into the parking lot, located behind the Elroy Commons Trail Shop on Railroad St. The endpoint is about 0.3 mile north along the trail.

To reach the southern trailhead in Reedsburg from I-90, take Exit 89 for WI 23 toward Lake Delton/Reedsburg, heading south. In 0.1 mile, turn right onto County Road P, and head west 4.9 miles. At the T, turn left onto County Road H, and follow for 6.8 miles. In Reedsburg, turn right onto Main St., and go a little more than 1.1 miles. Turn left onto S. Walnut St., and go 0.2 mile. The parking lot is to the left, just before South Ave. and behind the Reedsburg Area Chamber of Commerce.

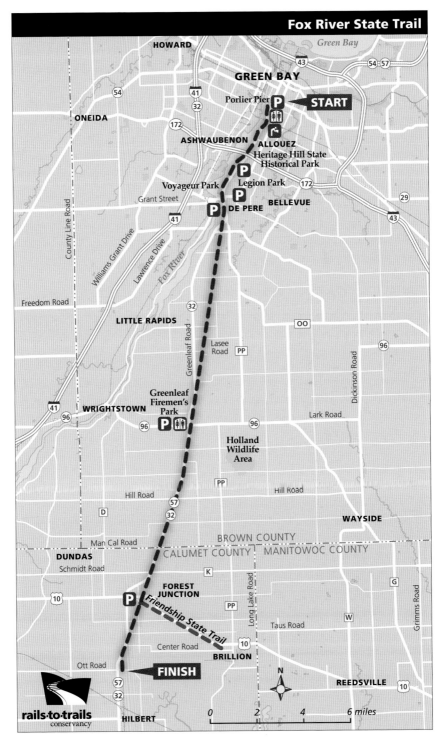

The Fox River State Trail connects Packerland with pastureland as it rolls for 25 miles from the hometown of NFL's Green Bay Packers to farming communities south. Named for the river that spawned the city's industrial heritage, the trail veers from the Fox River after about 5 miles and heads across the eastern Wisconsin countryside.

Early settlers used the Fox River for trade, but entrepreneurs in the mid-1800s harnessed the river to power flour and paper mills. The development of one particular paper product in 1901 earned Green Bay the nickname "Toilet Paper Capital of the World." Heavy industry still has an impact on the city's economy.

The trail has been well traveled: first by Native Americans, then French explorers and traders, and later by the Milwaukee and Northern Railroad. The Chicago, Milwaukee, St. Paul and Pacific Railroad took over and ran the

The Fox River State Trail connects Packerland with beautiful Wisconsin countryside.

Counties
Brown, Calumet

Endpoints
S. Adams St. at Porlier St. (Green Bay) to Ott Road west of Irish Road (north of Hilbert)

Mileage
24.5

Type
Rail-Trail

Roughness Index
1

Surface
Asphalt, Crushed Stone

The trail's northern segment is paved for about 10 miles, after which the surface switches to crushed stone.

line until it sold it to the Soo Line in 1985. Fragments of the route were used until the tracks were removed in 1999 and work began on a trail in 2001.

Officially the Fox River State Trail starts at the corner of South Adams and Porlier Streets. It joins a busy riverfront trail that runs northward for 1.7 miles, where you'll pass restaurants, pubs, and a bicycle shop. One block north of the Mason Street Bridge is the old railroad passenger depot (now home to a private business) built of brick and stone in 1090.

Beginning at an old railroad trestle that has been converted into the Porlier Pier for fishing, you'll head south through the old Porlier neighborhood, where the Victorian-era Hazelwood House has been turned into a museum for the Brown County Historical Society. In another 2 miles, the 54-acre Heritage Hill State Historical Park interprets the state's bygone days in period buildings and displays.

At mile 4.3 you can explore the dam, locks, and lock tenders' island at Voyageur Park in De Pere, and then say goodbye to the Fox River as the trail turns away. While the northern part of the trail can be busy, trail users thin out as you head south. By mile 7, you're out of the suburbs and warehouse districts and entering farmland.

After riding on asphalt for 10 miles, your trail becomes crushed stone at Lasee Road, although there are asphalt sections farther south. Four miles later you'll enter Greenleaf, which offers convenience stores and cafés, as well as the

southernmost trailhead at Follett and Klaus Streets. Horses are allowed on gravel portions of the trail south of WI 96, which passes through town.

More services are available in 7.5 miles in Forest Junction, where you'll pass the junction for the eastern segment of the Friendship State Trail, which runs 4 miles to Brillion. The Fox River State Trail ends in 2.9 miles at Ott Road.

Snowmobilers are permitted on the limestone portion of the trail in Calumet County and from Man Cal Road north to Fair Road in Brown County.

NOTE: A State Trail Pass ($25 annually/$5 daily) is required for bicyclists, in-line skaters, and horseback riders ages 16 and older. Snowmobilers must display either a Wisconsin registration or a snowmobile State Trail Pass. For information, go to dnr.wi.gov/topic/parks/trailpass.html.

CONTACT: dnr.wi.gov/topic/parks/name/foxriver

DIRECTIONS

To reach the trailhead in Green Bay from I-43, take Exit 180 onto WI 172, heading west. Go 3.8 miles, and take the Webster Ave. exit. Turn right onto WI 57/Riverside Dr., go 2.2 miles, and turn left onto Porlier St., which curves right and turns into S. Adams St. Look for on-street parking on S. Adams St., on your left.

To reach the southern trailhead in Greenleaf from I-43, take Exit 164 toward Maribel, and turn left (west) onto County Road Z. Go 9.8 miles, and turn right onto County Road W. Go 2.6 miles, and turn left onto WI 96; then go 4.2 miles, and turn right onto Follett St. Go 0.2 mile to the trailhead, just past Klaus St. on the right. The trail's southern endpoint is 10.7 miles south.

To reach parking in Forest Junction from I-43, take Exit 154 toward Reedsville on US 10/WI 310. Go 22.1 miles, and turn left onto Church St. Go 0.2 mile, and turn left onto Campground Road, which becomes Main St. and bears right (south). In 0.1 mile, look for parking on the left side of the street. The trail's southern endpoint is 2.8 miles south.

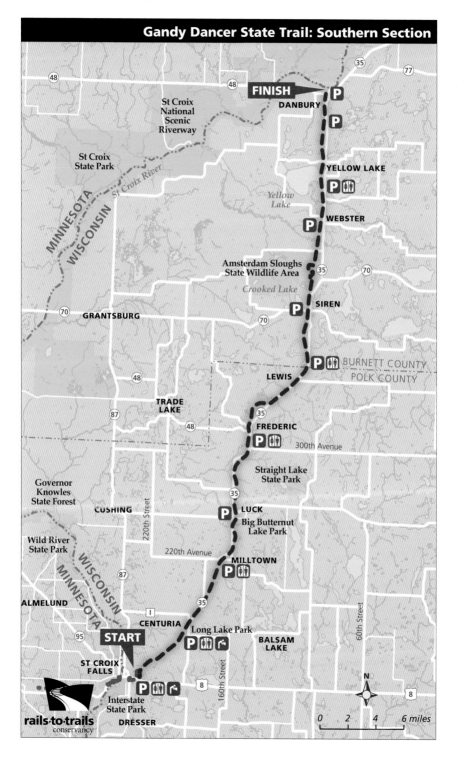

Gandy Dancer State Trail: Southern Section

The 47-mile Gandy Dancer State Trail: Southern Section, between St. Croix Falls and Danbury, commemorates gandy dancers, those hardworking section crews who manually restored the railroad tracks in alignment to prevent train derailments. While *dancer* probably referred to their rhythmic motion of working in unison to tamp down ties or adjust rails, *gandy* comes from the fact that the tools were made by the Gandy Tool Company of Chicago (according to the website for the Wisconsin Department of Natural Resources).

The northern and southern sections of the rail-trail roll for 98 miles from St. Croix Falls north to Superior. Along the way, it crosses into Minnesota for 32 miles and then returns to Wisconsin.

The southern portion of the Gandy Dancer passes through forests and farmland for most of its journey.

Counties
Burnett, Polk

Endpoints
Pine St. near Lincoln Dr.,
south of Riegel Park
(St. Croix Falls)
to WI 77 just west of
WI 35 (Danbury)

Mileage
47.0

Type
Rail-Trail

Roughness Index
1

Surface
Crushed Stone

The Gandy Dancer State Trail emanates pastoral Wisconsin charm.

The crushed-limestone trail follows an old route of the Minneapolis, St. Paul and Sault Ste. Marie Railroad, which became the Soo Line Railroad after a 1961 merger. Wisconsin Central Ltd. gained control in the late 1980s, disusing this branch. The states of Wisconsin and Minnesota acquired the right-of-way, and Wisconsin surfaced the southern section with limestone in 1995.

Beginning in St. Croix, you can set off on the Interlink Trail that leaves the Polk County Information Center. With 15 trails for hiking, biking, and cross-country skiing, the town on the St. Croix River has earned its nickname of "City of Trails." Meeting up with the Gandy Dancer Trail as you leave Riegel Park, you'll be passing through forests and farmland for the rest of your journey.

This area is sparsely populated, but you'll find small towns with services every 4–8 miles. The first of these is Centuria, which you'll reach in less than 5 miles, where the trailhead has a library.

Another 10 miles up the trail, after passing through Milltown, you'll arrive in Luck. The town earned the title "Yo-Yo Capital of the World" after Duncan Toys opened a yo-yo factory here in 1946 to take advantage of the area's hard maple forests. You'll find Frederic in another 6 miles where the circa-1901 Soo Line Railroad Depot has been renovated and serves as a museum.

After visiting Lewis, in another 5 miles you'll arrive in Siren, named for the (misspelled) Swedish word for "lilac." The town also has a vintage railroad depot,

privately owned, and a park on the shores of Crooked Lake next to the trail just north of town. ATVs and UTVs are permitted on the trail from Siren to the northern terminus. North of Crooked Lake, the trail passes the Amsterdam Sloughs State Wildlife Area, where bald eagles and blue herons make their homes.

More services are available in Webster in 6 miles, after which the final leg to the trailhead in Danbury is the longest, about 10 miles. The trail crosses the St. Croix River on a 520-foot trestle into Minnesota here.

Snowmobiles are allowed the entire length of the trail under snow conditions, and ATVs and UTVs are allowed in the winter (check local conditions) north of Tewalt Road in Burnett County, just south of Siren.

NOTE: A State Trail Pass ($25 annually/$5 daily) is required for bicyclists ages 16 and older. Snowmobilers and ATV/UTV users must display either a Wisconsin registration or an ATV/UTV or snowmobile State Trail Pass. For information, go to dnr.wi.gov/topic/parks/trailpass.html.

CONTACT: dnr.wi.gov/topic/parks/name/gandydancer

DIRECTIONS

St. Croix Falls is about 25 miles east of Minneapolis–St. Paul. To find parking at the Polk County Information Center from US 8 in town, exit onto southbound WI 35/S. Vincent St. In 0.5 mile, with the entrance to Wisconsin Interstate State Park on your right, make a U-turn to return north on WI 35. In 0.4 mile, turn right at the sign for the information center into the parking lot.

A connector trail that leaves the information center heading southeast meets and then follows little-used Old Highway 8 for a short distance to Industrial Parkway. Turn left at Industrial Parkway and then, with a fast-food restaurant on your left, veer right onto the pathway to head southeast underneath WI 35 and then north to Pine St. Turn right onto Pine St., and go 2 blocks to where the rail-trail begins, curving left and heading north.

To reach the northern trailhead in Danbury from I-35, take Exit 183 eastbound on MN 48 in Hinckley, Minnesota. Go 27.2 miles—the road becomes WI 77 at the state line, across the St. Croix River—and look for parking on the right about 300 feet past Glass St., immediately after you pass the trail.

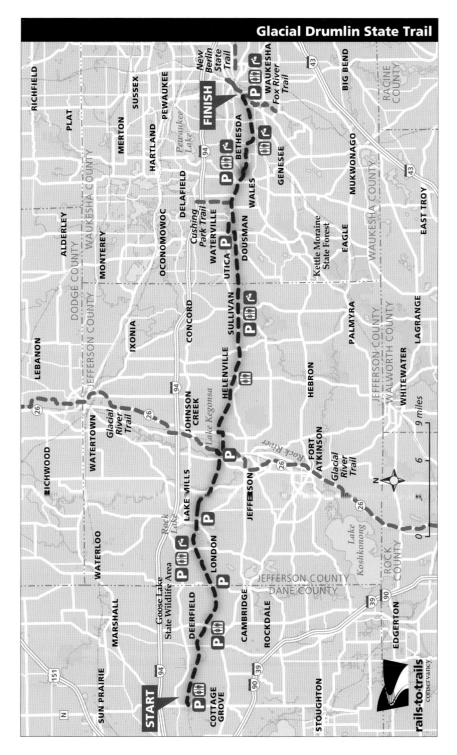

Glacial Drumlin State Trail

The 53-mile Glacial Drumlin State Trail between Cottage Grove and Waukesha provides a glimpse into the past when glaciers bore down on southeastern Wisconsin in the last Ice Age. Those gigantic sheets of ice created wetlands, ponds, and rivers, as well as hundreds of low, cigar-shaped hills called drumlins.

The landscape challenged the Chicago and North Western Railway's builders as they established the rail line between Madison and Milwaukee in the 1880s. The wooden pilings that supported bridges sank in the deep muck of extensive wetlands, creating dangerous passages for trains. Declining rail traffic forced the railroad to stop using the route in 1983, and it was transformed into a rail-trail in 1986.

Those wood-planked bridges now provide popular features on the trail as viewpoints for the wetlands, where a host of wildlife thrives. You may spot large sandhill

The path offers views of the southern Wisconsin countryside.

Counties
Dane, Jefferson, Waukesha

Endpoints
S. Main St./County Road N and Clark St. (Cottage Grove) to the Fox River Sanctuary at W. College Ave. and Sentry Dr. (Waukesha)

Mileage
53.4

Type
Rail-with-Trail

Roughness Index
2

Surface
Asphalt, Crushed Stone, Gravel

The flavor of the Glacial Drumlin is distinctly rural.

cranes, graceful birds with bright red caps on their heads, or hear spring peepers and a chorus of frogs. Deer, wild turkeys, foxes, and other critters are often seen. Although the trail stops short of the railroad's original destinations, plans are afoot to link with Madison via the Capital City State Trail (Trail 33, page 127) and with Milwaukee via the New Berlin Recreation Trail (Trail 50, page 191).

Snowmobiles are permitted on the limestone section of trail—but not the paved asphalt section—between Waukesha and Dousman.

Beginning in Cottage Grove, you'll head east for about 40 miles on a crushed-stone surface until you hit pavement in Dousman, one of many small towns along the trail providing rest, refreshment, and exploration. After leaving Cottage Grove, you'll pass through miles of open country before reaching Deerfield and London. At around mile 14, you'll sail over a 0.25-mile-long bridge that separates upper and lower Rock Lake, just before you reach Lake Mills. A restored 1895 train depot provides exhibits on local nature and railroad history, as well as other visitor services. Camping is available at Sandhill Station State Campground, 1.3 miles south of the depot on Mud Lake Road.

In the 5-mile stretch between Lake Mills and Jefferson, the trail tunnels under a thick tree canopy in the summer and crosses Crawfish River and Rock River (a fishing haven for locals). In Jefferson, at about 22 miles, signs guide you

through a 1.5-mile on-road section before reconnecting with the trail. While you journey through small towns and the communities of Helenville, Sullivan, Dousman, and Wales, you'll find nearby restaurants and grocery stores.

Before reaching Sullivan, the trail parallels US 18 for a couple of miles, and then a stream and wetland populated with yellow finches and purple thistles. Outside of Dousman, the crushed-stone surface ends, and the final 13 miles to Waukesha are smooth pavement. Even with the smoother surface, you might notice the grade increase as you pass south of the Lapham Peak Unit of the Kettle Moraine State Forest. The Cushing Park Road Recreation Trail, 4 miles past Dousman, will take you there. It's a well-deserved downhill after Wales for the last 7 miles to the Fox River and the trail's end at the E. B. Shurts Environmental Learning Center at the Fox River Sanctuary in Waukesha.

NOTE: A State Trail Pass ($25 annually/$5 daily) is required for bicyclists and in-line skaters ages 16 and older. Snowmobilers must display either a Wisconsin registration or a snowmobile State Trail Pass. For information, go to dnr .wi.gov/topic/parks/trailpass.html. State campgrounds are located in Lake Mills, Dousman, and Delafield.

CONTACT: **dnr.wi.gov/topic/parks/name/glacialdrumlin** or **glacialdrumlin.com**

DIRECTIONS

To reach the Cottage Grove trailhead from I-94, take Exit 244 onto southbound County Road N/ N. Main St. Go 2.2 miles, and then turn left at Clark St. into the parking lot for the Glacial Drumlin State Trail.

To reach the Fox River Sanctuary trailhead in Waukesha from I-94, take Exit 293 toward Waukesha onto southbound County Road T/N. Grandview Blvd. Go 1.6 miles, and turn left onto US 18/Summit Ave.; then go 0.3 mile, and turn right onto N. Moreland Blvd., which becomes S. Moreland Blvd. Go 1.3 miles, and turn left onto W. St. Paul Ave. Go 0.5 mile, and turn right at N. Prairie Ave. Go 0.3 mile, and turn right onto W. College Ave. Parking is the first driveway on the right, at the E. B. Shurts Environmental Learning Center in the Fox River Sanctuary. After parking, take the Fox River Trail west 0.2 mile to the Glacial Drumlin State Trail, on the right.

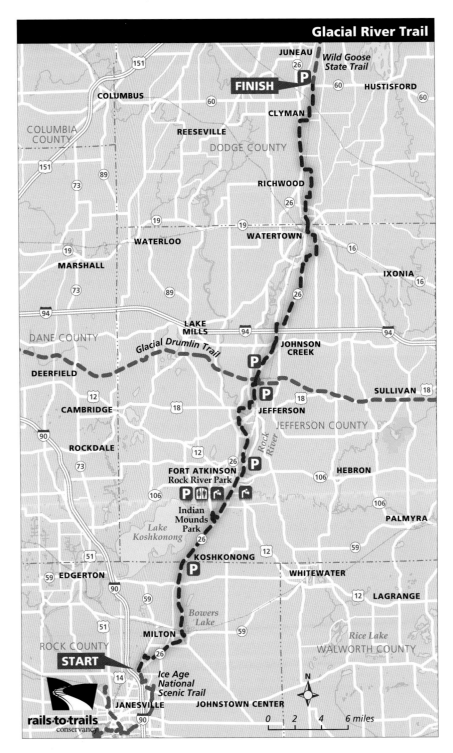

The Glacial River Trail provides bikers, pedestrians, and in-line skaters with a 55.8-mile off-road/on-road rural route winding through farmland, prairie, wetlands, and woodlands as it passes through three counties in southeastern Wisconsin.

Technically, the southern endpoint begins in Janesville at Milton Avenue, where you can also pick up a segment of the 1,200-mile, hiking-centric Ice Age National Scenic Trail. Note that the closest dedicated trail parking is about 10 miles farther down the trail in Koshkonong. Heading north from Janesville on the Glacial River Trail, you'll travel through Milton and rural countryside to Koshkonong, where you'll leave Rock County and head into Jefferson County. A quaint covered bridge greets you just after this crossing.

A quaint covered bridge marks the Glacial River Trail's crossing from Jefferson County into Rock County.

Counties
Dodge, Jefferson, Rock

Endpoints
County Road Y and Milton Ave./Ice Age National Scenic Trail (Janesville) to WI 60 and Junction Road/Wild Goose State Trail (Juneau)

Mileage
55.8

Type
Rail-Trail

Roughness Index
1

Surface
Asphalt

The rail-trail passes through three counties in southeastern Wisconsin.

Open areas and woods serve as pleasant companions as you travel north along WI 26. Take a worthy side trip by heading west (left) at Koshkonong Mounds Road to Indian Mounds Park, which features 11 Native American effigy mounds and an ancient Indian trail. The mounds, large earthworks with religious or ceremonial origins, can be seen from the trail. Look closely to see the turtle and bird shapes identified by experts. The mounds are thought to have survived about 1,500 years.

About 16 miles into your journey you'll reach Fort Atkinson. Note that just before reaching Fort Atkinson, the trail detours from the railroad corridor for about 1.5 miles, heading northwest and then east on Schwemmer Lane (under WI 26), and then right on Groeler Road, which meets up with the off-road trail again on the northern side of where WI 26 and WI 26 Trunk meet. Nearing busy Janesville Avenue, a low stone wall next to the path marks the Glacial River Rotary Depot, which offers a drinking fountain and covered picnic area.

You might detour three blocks east onto South Third Street West (where the trail crosses Janesville Avenue), turn right (south) onto South Main Street, and then head a block and a half (veering left) onto Whitewater Avenue to the Hoard Historical Museum. The museum is named after the Hoard family, who are behind the nationally distributed dairy farm magazine *Hoard's Dairyman.*

Exhibits of tools, textiles, and American Indian artifacts will get you up to speed on the area's early fort history, European settlers, and American Indian culture.

At Lorman Bicentennial Park, you can access the Riverwalk, which takes you through the park and underneath the bridge across the Rock River. Head right along the Riverwalk to find quaint shops and restaurants.

Back on Glacial River Trail, continue north over the Rock River and through a beautiful metal archway. The paved pathway unwinds along the east side of WI 26 through Wisconsin countryside and over the Crawfish and Rock Rivers in Jefferson. After you go under the Jefferson bypass, look for a connection to the 53.4-mile Glacial Drumlin State Trail (see previous profile), which heads west to Cottage Grove and east to Waukesha.

The trail then continues to Watertown and into Dodge County, using on-street and off-street sections, and ends at the southern terminus of the Wild Goose State Trail at WI 60 in Juneau.

CONTACT: jeffersoncountywi.gov/departments/departments_f-r/bike_trails.php

DIRECTIONS

The closest parking to the southern endpoint is in Koshkonong, about 10 miles north. From I-90, take Exit 163 toward WI 59 E., and head south, then east on WI 59, crossing the Rock River. After 2.8 miles, bear left at the Y onto County Hwy. N; go 3 miles, and then turn left to merge onto northbound WI 26/WI 26 Trunk. Go 1.7 miles, and then turn left onto County Line Road. Turn left onto Old Hwy. 26, and then make the first left into the parking lot.

To reach the northern endpoint from I-94, take Exit 267 to WI 26 toward Watertown, heading north. Go 18.9 miles, and take Exit 52 to WI 60, heading east. Go 1.7 miles, and turn left into the parking lot just past where the trail begins, with Junction Road on your right.

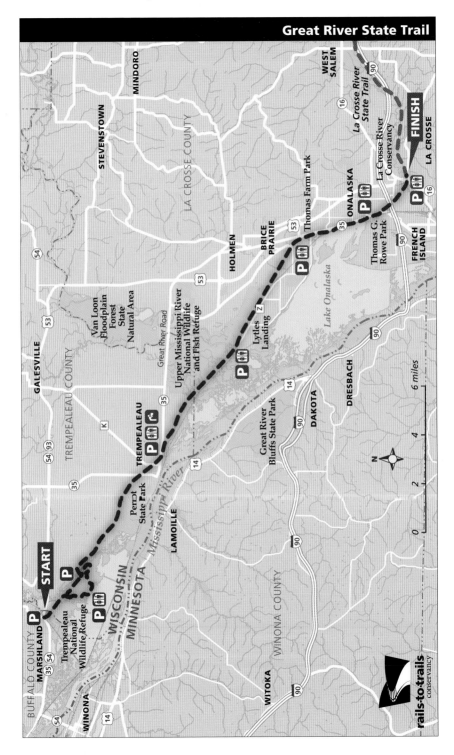

Great River State Trail

The Great River State Trail is named for the Mississippi River, but Ol' Man River stays mostly out of sight if you follow this 24-mile trail through river marshes, wildlife preserves, hardwood forests, and old river towns on its eastern shoreline.

The trail traces the old Chicago and North Western Railway, which opened a route between the Twin Cities and Chicago in the 1870s. It became disused in the 1970s and was acquired for use as a trail in 1984. A 100-mile length of that former rail route is preserved by Bike 4 Trails, a combination of four state rail-trails—Great River, La Crosse River (Trail 45, page 171), Elroy-Sparta (Trail 37, page 141), and 400 (Trail 38, page 145)—that roll from the Mississippi River and across the rugged Driftless Area. The Great River State Trail is also part of a designated 3,000-mile bicycle

This bridge over the water makes for a great sightseeing tour on the Great River State Trail.

Counties
Buffalo, La Crosse, Trempealeau

Endpoints
Great River Road/WI 54/ WI 35 at County Road P (Marshland) to County Road B/La Crosse River State Trail, east of WI 16 (La Crosse)

Mileage
24.0

Type
Rail-Trail

Roughness Index
2

Surface
Crushed Stone

Brilliant fall colors pop along the Great River State Trail.

route, called the Mississippi River Trail, that runs from the headwaters of Itasca, Minnesota, to the Gulf of Mexico.

Beginning in Marshland on Great River Road, you'll immediately enter the Trempealeau National Wildlife Refuge. The 6,500-acre refuge is on the Mississippi Flyway, so if you time your visit right, you'll be in the company of a vast assortment of waterfowl, wading birds, and migratory songbirds. Watch for off-shoot trails that explore the refuge. You'll pick up the railroad grade as you leave the preserve on Refuge Road. About 2.3 miles after leaving the refuge, you'll pass the entrance to a campground for Perrot State Park, which features more wildlife viewing in its rugged terrain of hills, ridges, and bluffs.

Less than 3 miles past the campground, you'll enter the small town of Trempealeau, which provides a nice break with its cafés and parks. Earthen mounds in the vicinity are evidence of civilizations that date back 1,000 years. For the next 10 miles, you'll pass through peaceful wooded areas that provide shade on a warm summer day, and then a series of bridges that span several small tributaries within the Upper Mississippi River National Wildlife and Fish Refuge. Six miles past Trempealeau is Lytles Landing, a boat launch park that provides parking and trail access, as well as a 1,200-foot-long railroad trestle spanning the river.

Continuing south, the trail passes small neighborhoods and pockets of woods. You'll ride alongside Lake Onalaska, an impoundment of the Black and Mississippi Rivers, for a couple of miles before arriving in the heart of Onalaska about 8 miles past Lytles Landing. There are restaurants and pubs here. A 0.7-mile trail gap requires that you follow signs on side streets to Hilltopper and Oak Forest Drives, where the trail resumes.

You'll pass through a warehouse zone and some woods with a bridge over the La Crosse River before you arrive, in 1.9 miles, at the trailhead for the La Crosse River State Trail. This marks the end of the Great River State Trail, but more adventures await if you choose to continue ahead to Sparta.

Snowmobiling and cross-country skiing are permitted based on local county announcements. Hunting is allowed, in season, about 3 miles north and 10 miles south of the village of Trempealeau.

NOTE: A State Trail Pass ($25 annually/$5 daily) is required for bicyclists ages 16 and older. For information, go to dnr.wi.gov/topic/parks/trailpass.html. Snowmobilers must display either a Wisconsin registration or a snowmobile State Trail Pass, and hunters must have a license.

CONTACT: dnr.wi.gov/topic/parks/name/greatriver

DIRECTIONS

To reach the Marshland trailhead from I-90, take Exit 4 onto US 53 headed north. Go 19.1 miles on US 53 to Galesville, and follow WI 54/WI 93 straight as US 53 goes right. Go 5.2 miles, and stay straight on WI 54 as WI 93 turns right and WI 35 enters from the left. In 5.2 miles, just before the railroad tracks in Marshland, turn left at the brown MARSHLAND ACCESS sign. Parking is a short distance down this road in the Trempealeau National Wildlife Refuge.

To reach the southern trailhead from I-90, take Exit 5 south toward La Crosse on WI 16. Go 1.8 miles, and turn left onto County Road B. Go 0.4 mile, and turn left into the parking lot for the La Crosse River State Trail. The Great River State Trail heads northwest from here.

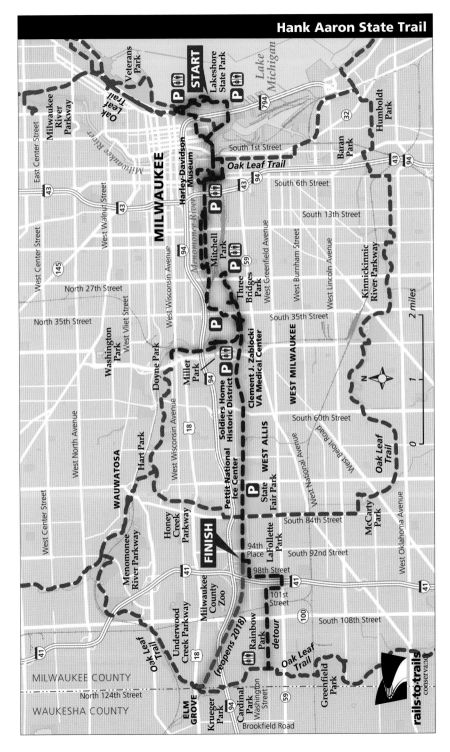

Hank Aaron State Trail

In 1957, baseball legend Hank "The Hammer" Aaron led the Milwaukee Braves to the first of two consecutive World Series appearances and a championship over the usually dominant New York Yankees. In 2004, the State of Wisconsin opened the first segment of the Hank Aaron State Trail, commemorating his many accomplishments as a ballplayer. Aaron's baseball successors, the Milwaukee Brewers, now play at Miller Park, within sight of the trail.

The trail, which spans the breadth of Milwaukee County, begins at Lakeshore State Park in Milwaukee, where it overlooks Lake Michigan to the east and provides breathtaking views of the downtown Milwaukee skyline to the north. Ample parking is available under the Hoan Bridge, south of the Summerfest Grounds, which movie buffs may recognize as the site of a famous chase scene from the 1980 movie *The Blues Brothers*.

Riders heading west will make their way through a brief on-street section, passing through the thriving Historic Third Ward, and emerge to pick up the trail again in the Menomonee River Valley. Attractions are numerous

The Hank Aaron State Trail provides beautiful views of and access to the city of Milwaukee.

County
Milwaukee

Endpoints
E. Michigan St. and
N. Art Museum Dr.
(Milwaukee) to
S. 94th Place north
of W. Schlinger Ave.
(West Allis)

Mileage
13.2 (15.2 total)

Type
Rail-Trail

Roughness Index
1

Surface
Asphalt

in this resurgent part of town; fans of another form of two-wheeled transport might stop by the Harley-Davidson Museum off North Sixth Street.

Continuing west, riders can take the Valley Passage across the Menomonee River to visit the Urban Ecology Center, Three Bridges Park, and the historic Mitchell Park Horticultural Conservatory ("The Domes"). Returning to the main trail, fans will recognize Miller Park baseball stadium with its retractable roof.

The Soldiers Home Historic District lies between Miller Park to the north and the Clement J. Zablocki VA Medical Center to the south, providing a historic contrast with its modern neighbors; this was a place for veterans of the Civil War to recuperate before reentering society. Emerging west of the Soldiers Home, the path straightens and stays level for most of the way to the trail's western endpoint. At South 84th Street, the trail connects to the Oak Leaf Trail (Trail 51, page 195), which traces a messy figure eight throughout the Milwaukee metro area.

The trail terminates just farther west at its currently truncated end at South 94th Place, where trail-closure signs and on-street detours greet trail users. The detour route leads to the southern end of Rainbow Park and stops at 120th Street and a short north–south connector route to the to the Oak Leaf Trail. The Hank Aaron Trail used to extend to US 18/West Blue Mound Road in Elm Grove; this section, however, is closed until at least 2018, the earliest predicted completion date for the state's Zoo Interchange highway-construction project.

CONTACT: dnr.wi.gov/topic/parks/name/hankaaron

DIRECTIONS

To reach the eastern trailhead at Lakeshore State Park from I-43, take Exit 72B toward Lakefront. After 0.8 mile, merge onto I-794 E., and keep right to stay on I-794 E. After 0.2 mile, take the exit on the left toward N. Lincoln Memorial Dr., and go 0.3 mile. Turn right onto N. Lincoln Memorial Dr., and go 0.4 mile. Turn left onto E. Polk St., and then make an immediate right on an unnamed road. Go 0.2 mile, and then turn left to cross under I-794—note that this road may be closed at certain times or on certain days. In another 0.2 mile, look for parking on your right after the crossing.

Parking and trail access are also at Mitchell Park Horticultural Conservatory, south of the trail at 524 S. Layton Blvd. in Milwaukee. From I-94 heading north, take Exit 311 toward WI 59/National Ave., following the exit about 0.5 mile north and then west. Turn right onto S. Ninth St.—look for the signs for WI 59/National Ave./Harley-Davidson Museum. Turn left at the first cross street onto W. National Ave. Go 1.3 miles, and turn right (north) onto S. Layton Blvd. In 0.3 mile, turn right into the parking lot for Mitchell Park Horticultural Conservatory. You can access a trail spur on the left side of The Domes (if you're facing the complex) that heads north and west through Three Bridges Park, then south to the trail spur at the Urban Ecology Center.

The La Crosse River valley provides level terrain through a rugged area of western Wisconsin for the La Crosse River State Trail. This screened-limestone rail-with-trail passes through farmland, marshes, and tracts of surviving prairie as it rolls for 21 miles between the Mississippi River town of La Crosse and Sparta.

Railway builders chose this route in the 1870s for the Chicago and North Western Railway (CNW) to carry freight and passengers between St. Paul and Chicago. A century later the railroad discontinued the route, and the state acquired it for a recreational trail that opened in the 1980s. The tracks of CNW's rival during that time, the Chicago, Milwaukee, St. Paul and Pacific Railroad (the Milwaukee Road), still parallel the trail and carry Canadian Pacific Railway trains and Amtrak's *Empire Builder*.

The trail provides a level route as it passes through a rugged part of western Wisconsin.

Counties
La Crosse, Monroe

Endpoints
County Road B east of WI 16/Great River State Trail (La Crosse) to S. Water St./Elroy-Sparta State Trail at Hemstock Dr. (Sparta)

Mileage
21.0

Type
Rail-with-Trail

Roughness Index
2

Surface
Crushed Stone

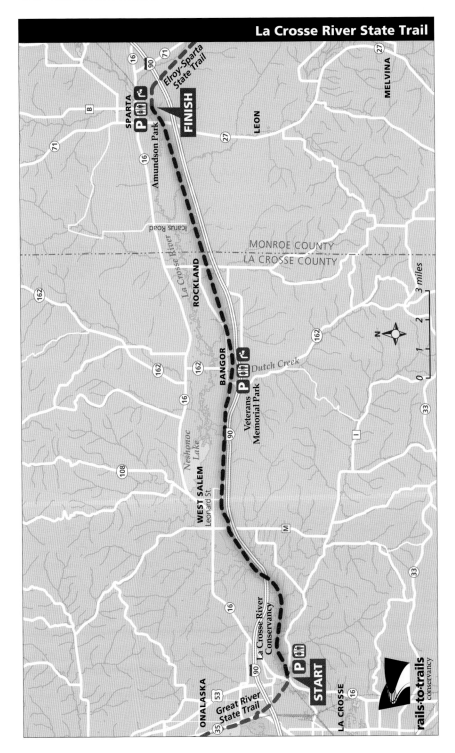

La Crosse River State Trail

The screened-limestone trail rolls for 21 miles between the towns of La Crosse and Sparta.

The La Crosse River State Trail passes through the old whistlestops of West Salem, Bangor, and Rockland and serves as a middle leg of Wisconsin's Bike 4 Trails route. That course comprises the Great River State Trail (Trail 43, page 165), La Crosse River State Trail, Elroy-Sparta State Trail (Trail 37, page 141), and 400 State Trail (Trail 38, page 145) as it rolls along the Mississippi River and through the state's Driftless Area. Snowmobiling is permitted in season.

You'll begin at the Medary trailhead, shared with the Great River State Trail just east of La Crosse. For about the next 3 miles, you're passing through the La Crosse River Conservancy, a privately funded refuge surrounding the marshes bordering the river. Migrating waterfowl frequent the area, which is home to beaver, red foxes, and river otters.

In 7 miles you'll arrive at West Salem, founded in the 1850s. You can find cafés, taverns, and food stores on Leonard Street, which intersects the trail. Farmland borders the trail for the next 5 miles to Bangor, which offers restrooms and a drinking fountain at Veterans Memorial Park, just off the trail at Park Drive and James Street. More services are available in town.

Leaving Bangor, you travel through the La Crosse River Trail Prairies for the next 9 miles, with a brief interruption for the small town of Rockland. Although

farms cover large areas, pockets of prairie along the trail represent the extensive grasslands that once covered this part of the state. Looking across this landscape of marshes and grasslands sprinkled with bur oaks, you can see the hilltops, bluffs, and ridges left unscathed in the last Ice Age.

The trail ends in Sparta at a renovated railroad depot, which also serves as the start of the Elroy-Sparta State Trail, widely considered to be the oldest rail-trail in the United States. To understand what bicycling means to this town, head up Water Street for a couple of blocks to "Ben Bikin'," a large statue of a man astride an old-fashioned high-wheeler bicycle.

NOTE: A State Trail Pass ($25 annually/$5 daily) is required for bicyclists ages 16 and older. Snowmobilers must display either a Wisconsin registration or a snow-mobile State Trail Pass. For information, go to dnr.wi.gov/topic/parks/trailpass .html. Camping is offered at Veterans Memorial Campground via a 0.5-mile trail at mile 5.2, and at a Department of Natural Resources walk-in campground that's 1.2 miles east of Sparta on the Elroy-Sparta State Trail (9890 Imac Ave.).

CONTACT: dnr.wi.gov/topic/parks/name/lacrosseriv

DIRECTIONS

To reach the western trailhead in La Crosse from I-90, take Exit 5 south toward La Crosse on WI 16. Go 1.8 miles and turn left onto County Road B. Go 0.4 mile, and turn left into the trailhead parking lot. The La Crosse River State Trail heads east from here.

To reach the eastern trailhead in Sparta from I-90, take Exit 28 toward Sparta onto WI 16, heading west. Go 2.3 miles, and turn left onto S. Water St. Go 0.5 mile, and turn left onto Milwaukee St. Turn immediately right into the trailhead parking lot. The trailhead is at the old railroad depot at 111 Milwaukee St.

The 13.5-mile Lake Michigan Pathway keeps you in close touch with the sixth-largest freshwater lake in the world as it links rail-trails north and south of the port city of Racine. Along the way, the trail visits such attractions as beaches, marinas, parks, the zoo, and museums, as well as the revitalized downtown district.

The Root River splits the Lake Michigan Pathway where it empties into the lake, marking the location of a settlement that came to be known as Racine, French for "root," in 1841. Danish immigrants who began arriving after the Civil War influenced the city's culture and cuisine, specifically in its bakeries serving fruit- and nut-filled pastries called *kringle*.

Using the paved path alongside the lake as well as city streets, the Lake Michigan Pathway serves commuters as well as sightseers. In the north, it connects to the MRK Trail (named for the Milwaukee-Racine-Kenosha Electric

Highlights of the trail include this 3.3-mile off-street paved segment along Lake Michigan.

County
Racine

Endpoints
3 Mile Road/MRK Trail and Douglas Ave. to Chicory Road/North Shore Trail between Lathrop Ave. and S. Memorial Dr. (Racine)

Mileage
14.0

Type
Greenway/Non Rail Trail/ Sidewalks

Roughness Index
1

Surface
Asphalt, Concrete, Crushed Stone

Lake Michigan Pathway

A leisurely stroll along the pathway

Railway) at South Street and 3 Mile Road. In the south it connects to the North Shore Trail at Chicory Road.

The highlight for visitors is the 3.3 miles of off-street paved trail that runs alongside Lake Michigan. Beginning at Samuel Myers Park (parking is available here and along the lakeshore), you can hop on the pathway and follow it north toward downtown, passing Pershing Park on the left. In 0.6 mile, you'll pass the Civic Centre and Festival Park concert and event venues. Together with the 900-slip marina, they make up part of the harbor revitalization project that got under way in the 1980s.

The pathway heads up Root River to the Main Street bridge. A left turn onto Main Street leads to a four-block side trip to the Racine Art Museum. A right turn crosses the bridge, where you can take another side trip upstream on the 4-mile Root River Pathway to a bird sanctuary. To stay on the Lake Michigan Pathway, follow the signs. Back on the off-road trail, you'll pass a 0.5-mile gravel trail atop a breakwater that juts into the lake.

The white sands of North Beach, a popular spot for swimming, sunbathing, and trout and salmon fishing, stretch for a half mile along the lakefront north of the breakwater. The beach ends at the entrance to the Racine Zoo. About 0.3 mile north, the off-road portion of the pathway ends and continues as an on-street or sidewalk route marked by LAKE MICHIGAN PATHWAY signs.

To explore southern Racine from Samuel Myers Park, take the Lake Michigan Pathway west as it becomes an on-street and sidewalk route on 11th Street. Turn left onto Main Street to head south. (About 0.3 mile south, you can take

a side trip west on 14th Street for 0.4 mile to see the SC Johnson headquarters designed by Frank Lloyd Wright.) In 1 mile, you'll arrive at the picturesque DeKoven Center, a church-affiliated conference center that was founded as Racine College in 1852.

The pathway splits at DeKoven Avenue for two mostly on-street routes to the North Shore Trail. The left pathway, built in 2016, heads south on the east side of Wisconsin Avenue through Dodge Park to a connection with Roosevelt Park Drive and Durand Avenue. The right pathway takes DeKoven Avenue west, and then left on Case Avenue, right on Gilson Street, left on Drexel Avenue, right on Maryland Avenue, and left on Knoll Place to a right on Chicory Road.

CONTACT: racinecounty.com/visiting/biking

DIRECTIONS

To find trail parking at Samuel Myers Park from I-94/I-41, take Exit 333 toward Racine onto WI 20. Go 8.1 miles—WI 20 becomes Washington Ave.—and bear right onto 14th St. Go 0.7 mile, and turn left onto Main St. After 0.3 mile, turn right onto 11th St. Parking is on the right in Samuel Myers Park or on the left along the lakefront. The trail's southern endpoint is located about 4.4 miles south, following the easternmost section of the trail.

To find parking near the north end at Lake View Park/Racine Zoo from I-94/I-41, take Exit 329 east onto Northwestern Ave. Go 7.3 miles, and turn left onto Rapids Dr. Go 0.9 mile, and turn left onto Mt. Pleasant St.; then take the first right onto Goold St. Go 1.1 miles, and turn left onto N. Wisconsin St. Look for parking on the right in about 500 feet. The trail's northern endpoint is located about 2.7 miles northwest along the trail.

The Mascoutin Valley State Trail is divided into two segments along a former corridor of the Chicago and North Western Railway. The eastern section runs 10 miles between Fond du Lac and Rosendale. The western and more well-used section runs for 11 miles between Ripon and Berlin.

Note that the section of corridor between Rosendale and Ripon is privately owned, so trail users wishing to travel both sections in one journey must use roads for access. Horseback riding is available only in Winnebago and Fond du Lac Counties between May and October;

The western portion of the trail passes through the countryside near Rush Lake.

Counties
Fond du Lac, Green Lake, Winnebago

Endpoints
Rolling Meadows Dr. north of W. Scott St. (Fond du Lac) to WI 26 and W. Rose-Eld Road (Rosendale); Eureka St./ County Road E north of West View Dr. (Ripon) to S. Church St. north of South St. (Berlin)

Mileage
21.0

Type
Rail-Trail

Roughness Index
2

Surface
Crushed Stone

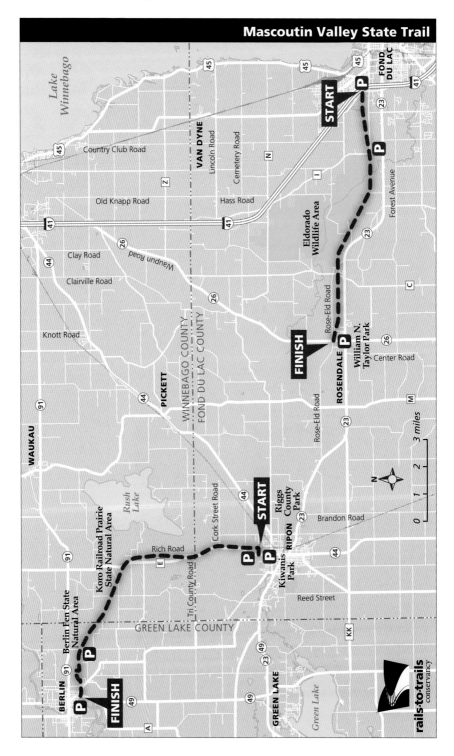

Mascoutin Valley State Trail

it is not allowed on the Green Lake County portion of the trail (from Berlin to about 2.6 miles east). Snowmobiling is permitted on both segments of the trail when other snowmobile trails in the counties are open. The trail, though nongroomed, is open to cross-country skiing and snowshoeing. Hybrid bikes are recommended.

Fond du Lac to Rosendale: 10 miles

Starting at the eastern end of the trail in Fond du Lac, you head west on a gently rolling grade while passing farms, prairies, and the Eldorado Marsh wetland. Here, it's not uncommon to see geese and heron making themselves comfortable at the marsh. The approach to Rosendale includes a peaceful wooded area, and summer and fall afternoon visitors should not be surprised to see members of the nearby Laconia High School boys' and girls' cross-country teams on the trail.

CONTACT: **dnr.wi.gov/topic/parks/name/mascoutin**

DIRECTIONS

To reach the eastern endpoint in Fond du Lac from I-41, take Exit 99 for WI 23 W./Johnson St., and head west on WI 23. After 0.2 mile, turn right onto N. Rolling Meadows Drive, and go 0.8 mile. Turn left into the trailhead parking lot.

At the western end of this segment, parking is available along city streets and at Taylor Park in Rosendale. To reach Taylor Park from I-41, follow the directions above through the first sentence. Drive west 10.4 miles on WI 23, and turn left onto S. Main St. Take the first right onto Taylor Park St. Look for parking on your left. The trailhead endpoint is accessible by heading north on Main St. for just over a half mile.

Ripon to Berlin: 11 miles

The western section travels between Ripon and Berlin. Beginning on the northern edge of Ripon, with access at Eureka Street, you'll encounter a straight, flat grade. After about 1 mile, you'll come across a parking lot for the trail at Locust Road; proper signage and a shelter with picnic tables await you here.

The trail heads north to the western shores of Rush Lake, where a winery is accessible along the trail just past Rich Road. Heading northwest, you'll pass Koro Railroad Prairie State Natural Area, which provides many opportunities to view wildlife and a variety of native prairie plants, as well as the Berlin Fen State Natural Area.

On the approach to Berlin, riders are treated to a boardwalk section that traverses yet another wetland. Several "bump-outs" allow for photographs, or just the opportunity to take in the scenery while others pass by.

CONTACT: dnr.wi.gov/topic/parks/name/mascoutin

DIRECTIONS

To reach parking near the Ripon endpoint from the intersection of WI 23/E. Fond du Lac St. and WI 44 N./Douglas St, head north on WI 44 for 2 miles. Turn left onto Locust Road, and look for the trailhead parking lot 0.5 mile ahead on the right, just after you cross the Mascoutin Valley State Trail. The endpoint is about 0.8 mile south and then west along the trail.

To reach parking at the Berlin endpoint from WI 91 heading west, take Spring St. south for 0.1 mile. Continue on Ripon Road for 0.2 mile, and then continue on S. Church St. for 0.2 mile. Turn right into the parking lot just before the intersection with South St.

The Military Ridge State Trail finds the high ground as it rolls across 40 miles of idyllic farmland from the outskirts of Madison to the historic mining town of Dodgeville. It follows an American Indian footpath later used by pioneers and railroaders. Travelers will pass the base of the highest point in southern Wisconsin and find opportunities to explore small towns, state parks, and natural areas.

The trail was built on a branch of the Chicago and North Western Railway, which started service on the line in 1881 but stopped using it by 1982. Work on the trail started in 1983.

Beginning in the Madison suburb of Fitchburg, you'll start on a paved trail that parallels the busy US 18/151 for the first few miles. Just south of McKee Road, you'll find the junction for the Cannonball Path, which heads 3.9 miles northeast toward the University of Wisconsin–Madison

The route of the Military Ridge Trail follows what was once an American Indian footpath.

Counties
Dane, Iowa

Endpoints
Verona Frontage Road
east of US 18/US 151/
Verona Road (Fitchburg)
to County Road YZ at
WI 23 (Dodgeville)

Mileage
40.0

Type
Rail-Trail

Roughness Index
2

Surface
Asphalt, Crushed Stone

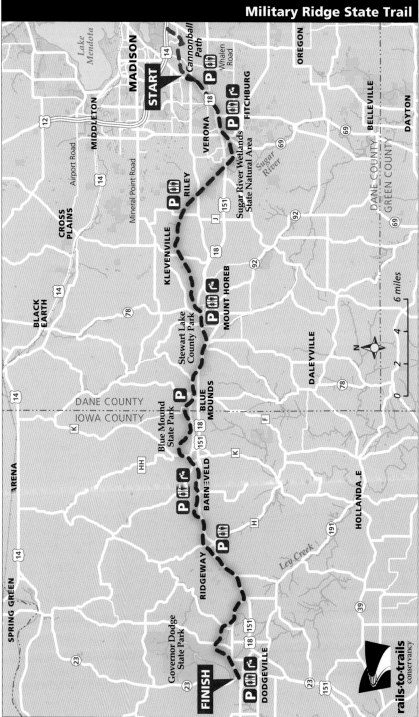

Military Ridge State Trail

The Military Ridge State Trail boasts idyllic farm landscapes.

Arboretum. After you cross the first of nearly 50 bridges on the route, that paved trail becomes screened limestone as you leave behind the noisy highway and enter the town of Verona. A park, coffeehouse, and brewpub are all within a block of the trail here.

The trail crosses the Sugar River Wetlands as it leaves town, and then enters farmland on its way to Riley. In a couple of miles, you'll pass through Klevenville and notice that the grade increases on the way to Mount Horeb, which celebrates its Norwegian settlers' heritage as the self-described "Troll Capital of the World." Located at about the trail's halfway point, the town offers plenty of cafés, bakeries, and brewpubs just a block or two north of the trail's visitor center.

From Mount Horeb, the trail traverses the top of Military Ridge, whose name comes from its use by the US Army and militias during the Black Hawk War in 1832. Local militia built a fort at the nearby town of Moundville (now

Blue Mounds) during that war, sparked when American Indian followers of Sauk war chief Black Hawk attempted to resettle lands lost in a disputed treaty.

The entrance road to Cave of the Mounds is about 3.8 miles past Mount Horeb. The limestone caverns are known for colorful patterns left by minerals underground. Another 1.5 miles past the road to the cave is the town of Blue Mounds and Blue Mound State Park. The trail passes the southern border of the park, but you can hike 435 feet to the summit at 1,716 feet. Observation towers provide views of the surrounding Driftless Area. Camping also is available.

The trail heads downhill as you leave Blue Mounds. Tidy dairy farms populate the views across the final 15 miles, and you're often sheltered by tree canopies. About 9 miles past Blue Mounds you'll enter Ridgeway, home to a restored 1913 railroad depot (and museum) that replaced an 1883 station lost in a fire that consumed most of downtown.

The trail ends in Dodgeville (settled in 1827 by the first governor of the Wisconsin Territory), an old lead mining town that has plenty for tired and hungry travelers. Nearby, Governor Dodge State Park offers camping, as well as miles of hiking, mountain biking, and horseback trails through the park's prairies and forests.

Snowmobiling is permitted on the limestone section of trail but not on the paved section between Fitchburg and Verona.

NOTE: A State Trail Pass ($25 annually/$5 daily) is required for bicyclists and in-line skaters ages 16 and older. Snowmobilers must display either a Wisconsin registration or a snowmobile State Trail Pass. For information, go to dnr.wi.gov/topic/parks/trailpass.html.

CONTACT: dnr.wi.gov/topic/parks/name/militaryridge or
friendsofmilitaryridgetrail.org

DIRECTIONS

To reach the trailhead in Fitchburg from the intersection of US 18/US 151/Verona Road and County Road PD/McKee Road, go 0.1 mile west on McKee Road, and turn left onto Nesbitt Road. Go 0.9 mile, and turn left onto Fitchrona Road; then go 0.2 mile, and turn left into the parking area at Quarry Ridge Recreation Area. A short path from the parking lot leads north to Military Ridge State Trail—go right for 0.8 mile to the eastern endpoint, or go left to Dodgeville.

To reach the trailhead in Dodgeville from the intersection of US 18 and WI 23 N./N. Bequette St., go north 0.2 mile on WI 23, and turn right onto County Road YZ. Go 0.3 mile, and turn left on Johns Street into the DNR Dodgeville Service Center, on your left just after you cross the Military Ridge State Trail. The endpoint is 0.4 mile west.

The 83-mile Mountain-Bay State Trail, one of the longest trails in the state, travels a mostly scenic, wooded route through three counties—Marathon, Shawano, and Brown—as it makes its way from Weston in central Wisconsin to Howard in the east. In spite of its length, numerous parking facilities are located along the length of the trail, and restrooms are frequent.

Bikers, take note: mountain bikes or tires measuring 25 centimeters or wider are necessary to negotiate the trail's surfaces and conditions, which vary but are generally passable. Snowmobiling is permitted on the trail in Marathon and Shawano Counties—and for 6 miles in Brown County—and snowmobiling clubs along its length help keep it open for users year-round. Horseback riding is also permitted in Shawano County.

Historical remnants of Eland's railroad days

Counties
Brown, Marathon, Shawano

Endpoints
Mesker St. and Corozalla Dr. (Weston) to Lakeview Dr. just north of Glendale Ave. and Howard Memorial Park (Howard)

Mileage
83.4

Type
Rail-Trail

Roughness Index
2

Surface
Asphalt, Dirt, Crushed Stone, Grass, Gravel

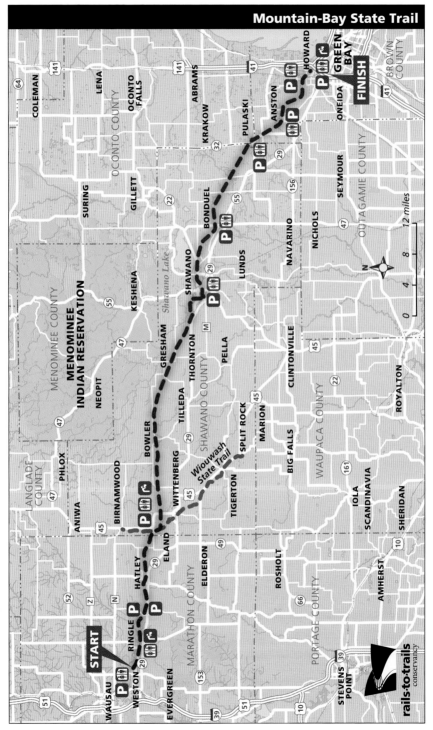

Though long and rural, the Mountain-Bay State Trail offers many places for amenities and respite.

Starting in Weston, you'll head southeast for a little more than 18 miles to Eland. Here, just past Fourth Street and before Cedar Street, you can head north 4 miles on the Wiouwash State Trail to the Village of Birnamwood. Continuing south on the Mountain-Bay State Trail, you'll share the route briefly with the Wiouwash State Trail (Trail 63, page 237) for about 0.7 mile, at which point the Wiouwash State Trail breaks off and heads another 36 miles south to Split Rock; to continue east on the Mountain-Bay State Trail, stay left at this break.

The multiple bridges along the route can become slippery when wet, so be careful when crossing. About 12 miles from Eland, you'll reach Bowler and a highlight of the trail: a covered bridge that crosses over the North Branch Embarrass River. Here, you can access the bank of the river for a dramatic picture of the covered bridge above.

After another 20 miles, the trail approaches a gap before you reach the city of Shawano at Maple Avenue. Signs direct you along several lightly traveled

roads until the route meets up again with the off-road trail at County Road M and heads into the city, paralleling West Oshkosh Street. Here, you'll find many restaurants, shops, stores, a former train depot turned bicycle-and-outfitters shop, and Twig's Beverage (South Washington Street), a soda factory and museum that offers tours.

After leaving Shawano, you'll travel a long stretch through mainly woods and farmland to the Village of Pulaski; at Pulaski Community Park you'll find a trailhead with restrooms and parking; ice cream and snacks are available for purchase nearby.

The trail ends 12 miles farther south near Howard Memorial Park on Lakeview Drive. You can access a variety of restaurants and bars just south of the trail in Howard by heading left on Glendale Avenue and right onto Riverview Drive.

NOTE: A State Trail Pass ($25 annually/$5 daily) is required for bicyclists ages 16 and older. Snowmobilers must display either a Wisconsin registration or a snowmobile State Trail Pass. For information, go to dnr.wi.gov/topic/parks/trailpass.html.

CONTACT: dnr.wi.gov/topic/parks/name/mountainbay or **mountain-baytrail.org**

DIRECTIONS

To reach the western trailhead in Weston from US 51/I-39, take Exit 187 for WI 29 E. toward Weston/Green Bay, and go 0.9 mile east across the Wisconsin River. Continue on WI 29 E./WI 29 Trunk E. for 2.5 miles. Take Exit 173 for County Road X/Camp Phillips Road toward Weston. After 0.3 mile, take a sharp left off the exit ramp onto northbound County Road X/Camp Phillips Road—note the signs for US 51—and go 0.8 mile. Turn right onto Schofield Ave., go 1.1 miles, and turn left onto Municipal St. In 0.1 mile, bear right at the Y, and take the first right into the short driveway to the trailhead, on your right. (Restrooms are available here.) You can also access a small parking lot 0.3 mile farther, near the trail endpoint, by heading left where Municipal St. meets Sternberg Ave. and then turning right onto Mesker St. The parking lot will be on your right, just before Corozalla Dr.

There are multiple places you can park and access the trail in Shawano County, including the communities of Eland, Bowler, Shawano, and Bonduel. The trail roughly follows WI 29 to its north but is generally separated from the highway by 1 or 2 miles.

To reach the eastern trailhead in Howard from I-41, take Exit 170 for US 141 S./Velp Ave. Head west about 0.3 mile on Velp Ave. across Duck Creek to Riverview Dr., and turn right. After 0.3 mile, turn left onto Glendale Ave. and then right onto Lakeview Dr. Go 0.2 mile, and turn right into the trailhead. The trail endpoint is just across (west of) Lakeview Dr., just before the railroad tracks and trailhead parking.

The paved New Berlin Recreation Trail runs straight as an east–west compass bearing for 7 miles through the western Milwaukee suburbs, from New Berlin to Waukesha. While it is void of trestles, tunnels, and trees as it passes beneath the power lines of We Energies, many residents find it a fast and convenient commuter route, with a few distractions along the way.

This rail-with-trail follows the former interurban railway route of the Milwaukee Electric Railway & Light Company, which started running trains and providing electricity in the 1890s. Waukesha, New Berlin, and West Allis were sleepy outposts at the time, but a critical turning point came in 1892 when Wisconsin chose West Allis as the official location of the annual state fair. The electric railway launched trolley service toward the west in 1898, and the communities began to thrive. Railway business

County
Waukesha

Endpoints
S. 124th St. between W. Honey Ln. and W. Forest Dr. (New Berlin) to dead end of Lincoln Ave., 0.3 mile east of Frederick St./ Perkins Ave. (Waukesha)

Mileage
7

Type
Rail-with-Trail

Roughness Index
1

Surface
Asphalt

Sod farms on the north side of the trail before Waukesha

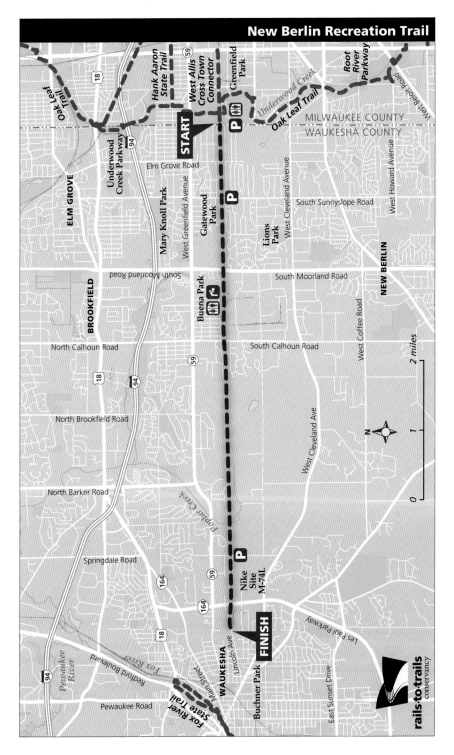

New Berlin Recreation Trail

declined, however, as car and truck use expanded in the 20th century. The Waukesha line, taken over by the Milwaukee Rapid Transit and Speedrail Co., was shut down in 1951, leaving only the utility corridor.

The New Berlin Recreation Trail begins in the east at the Waukesha–Milwaukee county line on South 124th Street. Here, it connects in Greenfield Park with the Oak Leaf Trail (see next profile) and West Allis Cross Town Connector Trail. Two miles north is the Hank Aaron State Trail (Trail 44, page 169), which runs nearly all the way into downtown Milwaukee. In the west, the trail ends within 2 miles of both the Fox River State Trail (Trail 39, page 149) and the Glacial Drumlin State Trail (Trail 41, page 157), which travels cross-country to within 6 miles of Madison's bike path network.

Beginning at the 282-acre Greenfield Park, you'll head west on a pedestrian bridge over South 124th Street and enter Waukesha County and the city of New Berlin. Railroad tracks run alongside the trail on the wide right-of-way, and trees screen leafy, established neighborhoods.

After 1.2 miles, you'll pass the entrance to the shady Gatewood Park, and at 2.4 miles you'll find Buena Park, which has restrooms. A bike shop sits at the corner of Calhoun Road at mile 3, with a couple of cafés nearby. The electric railway stopped at the Calhoun crossroads in the old days, and the Pabst Farms grew hops in a nearby field.

The trail takes on a more rural character as you begin a 3-mile stretch without any street crossings until Springdale Road. Two miles later, you're waiting at the unsignaled crossing of six-lane Les Paul Parkway, named for the famous guitar player and designer. Waukesha has its share of restaurants, brewpubs, and a Saturday farmers market that make it a close-by getaway from Milwaukee via the trail.

CONTACT: waukeshacounty.gov/newberlin

DIRECTIONS

To reach parking for the eastern endpoint from I-94, take Exit 301A south toward S. Moorland Road. Go 0.4 mile, and turn left onto WI 59/W. Greenfield Ave., heading east. After 2 miles, turn right onto S. 124th St. Go 0.6 mile, and turn left into Greenfield Park on Park Dr. To reach the New Berlin Recreation Trail, take a small trail north from the parking lot to the West Allis Cross Town Connector, and turn left. The New Berlin Recreation Trail is 0.2 mile ahead.

To reach parking near the western endpoint in Waukesha from I-94, take Exit 294, and head south onto County Road J/Pewaukee Road. Go 2.4 miles—Pewaukee Road becomes E. North St.—and turn left onto NW Barstow St. Go 0.3 mile, crossing the Fox River, and turn left onto W. Main St.; then, in 0.1 mile, turn right onto N. East Ave. Go 1 block, and turn left onto Arcadian Ave. Go 2 miles—Arcadian Ave. joins WI 59—and turn right onto Springdale Road. In 0.3 mile, look for parking on the left. The trail ends 1 mile west of here.

Oak Leaf Trail

The Oak Leaf Trail is the jewel in the crown of Milwaukee County's extensive trail system. The trail meanders for more than 120 miles in and around the city of Milwaukee on a changing terrain of flat rural plains and hilly city streets. Nearly a quarter of the trail hugs the beautiful shores of Lake Michigan.

The trail is mostly smooth asphalt, with dozens of easily accessed connections that take you just about anywhere in the Milwaukee metro area. Three miles of the trail follow the route of an old Chicago and North Western line that was part of the railroad company's long-distance passenger service to Denver, Colorado, and the California coast. The railroad's penchant for purchasing much of its equipment secondhand earned it the nickname "The Cheap and Nothing Wasted." The balance of the trail is made up of parkways and city streets, as well as another 3 miles open on a former Union Pacific corridor.

The Oak Leaf Trail has access points in and around the Milwaukee metro area. The best starting point is the Milwaukee Art Museum, after which you can head either north or south along Lake Michigan, or just a short distance south and west to an additional set of inland trail segments.

In the more remote areas, particularly at dusk, you may spot a coyote or two. Coyotes are common but are

County
Milwaukee

Endpoints
E. Michigan St. at
N. Art Museum Dr.
(Milwaukee) to
W. Brown Deer Road
between N. Arbon Dr.
and N. Deerbrook Trail
(Brown Deer) or
W. Oakwood Road
between W. Oakwood
Pkwy. and S. Howell Ave.
(Oak Creek)

Mileage
120.0

Type
Rail-Trail

Roughness Index
1

Surface
Asphalt

A beautiful starting point for the Oak Leaf Trail is the Milwaukee Art Museum.

wild animals, so maintain your distance and keep your pets close and on a leash. Talking loudly will easily scare coyotes away.

Many species of birds can be found along the trail as well, and Milwaukee County Parks has developed bird trail maps directing you to prime spotting locations.

Near mile 10, hilly city streets wind through an eclectic mix of Milwaukee's middle- and upper-middle-class neighborhoods. You will pass three golf courses in short succession. Just south of downtown there is an old warehouse district that has been converted into lofts and condos, after which the trail carries you down to magnificent Lake Michigan and its beaches. Several kiosks advertise refreshments, and you will find ample parking and restrooms.

In 2015, the Oak Leaf Trail was extended near the northern end of Estabrook Park, home of a popular beer garden, in Whitefish Bay. Heading north from here, you'll traverse elevated grade over I-43 into Glendale and Brown Deer, passing alongside Brown Deer Park to W. Brown Deer Road. Here, you'll connect seamlessly with another section of the Oak Leaf, which then connects with the Ozaukee Interurban Trail, a 30-mile pathway to Cedar Grove.

Additional or nearby connections made by the Oak Leaf Trail include the City of Franklin Hike and Bike Trail, MRK Trail, Forked Aster Hiking Trail System, Wehr Nature Center trail system, Milwaukee Urban Water Trail, Hank Aaron State Trail, Lake Michigan State Water Trail, City of Milwaukee Beerline Trail and Kinnickinnic River Trail, West Allis Cross Town Connector Trail, and numerous mountain biking trails, including Alpha, Bubba's Woods, Hoyt, and Oak Hill.

CONTACT: county.milwaukee.gov/oakleaftrail8289.htm

DIRECTIONS

To reach parking at the Milwaukee Art Museum from I-43, take Exit 72B east toward Lakefront. After 0.8 mile, merge onto I-794 E., and go 0.3 mile. Keep right to stay on I-794 E. another 0.2 mile, and take the exit on the left toward N. Lincoln Memorial Dr. Go 0.3 mile, and turn left onto N. Lincoln Memorial Dr. Go 0.2 mile, and turn right onto E. Michigan St. After 0.1 mile, turn left into the trailhead parking lot.

To reach the trailhead at Dretzka Park Golf Course (and the northwesternmost segment) from I-41 in Menomonee Falls, take Exit 50A for WI 100 E./Main St. Merge onto Main St. heading east, and go 0.8 mile. Turn right (south) onto Old Orchard Road, and go 0.8 mile. Turn right onto N. 124th St., and go 0.1 mile. Turn left, pass Dretzka Park Disc Golf to your left, and turn left into the golf-course parking lot.

To reach the southwestern trailhead at the Milwaukee County Sports Complex Fieldhouse from the intersection of WI 100/W. Ryan Road and S. 60th St. in Franklin, head north on S. 60th St. for 0.5 mile. Parking is available to your right in the complex parking lot.

The Old Abe State Trail rolls for 28 miles along a paved surface from Eau Claire to Cornell. A 3-mile gap (which will one day be closed) between Eau Claire and Chippewa Falls splits the trail into 8.4-mile and 19.7-mile sections. When complete, the Old Abe will be part of a 70-plus-mile-long trail system that also includes the Chippewa River State Trail (Trail 35, page 133), Duncan Creek Parkway Trail, and Red Cedar State Trail (Trail 57, page 215).

The trail begins in Eau Claire's Phoenix Park, where it meets the Chippewa River State Trail on the east landing of a former Chicago, Milwaukee, St. Paul and Pacific Railroad trestle. The trail passes riverfront homes and businesses on its way to Eau Claire's northeast suburbs. After 8 miles, the trail ends at 40th Avenue. *Venturing farther on busy highways with no shoulders or sidewalks is not recommended.*

The trail resumes in Chippewa Falls at the intersection of Seymour Cray Sr. and Wissota Green Boulevards. As you head north, the trail passes farmland and industrial areas on a flat, easy route as it crosses or travels near the Chippewa River, also known as the Old Abe Flowage. About 6 miles north of the trailhead, you'll encounter Jim Falls; here you'll find food options near the post office on County Road S and parking at the Jim Falls–Anson Town Hall.

Counties
Chippewa, Eau Claire

Endpoints
Riverfront Terrace south of Wisconsin St./ Chippewa River State Trail in Phoenix Park (Eau Claire) to 40th Ave. between 126th St. and WI 124 (Chippewa Falls) or Seymour Cray Sr. Blvd./ WI 178 and Wissota Green Blvd. (Chippewa Falls) to Park Road north of Adrian Road at Brunet Island State Park (Cornell)

Mileage
28.1

Type
Rail-Trail

Roughness Index
1

Surface
Asphalt

A forested route leads to Brunet Island State Park.

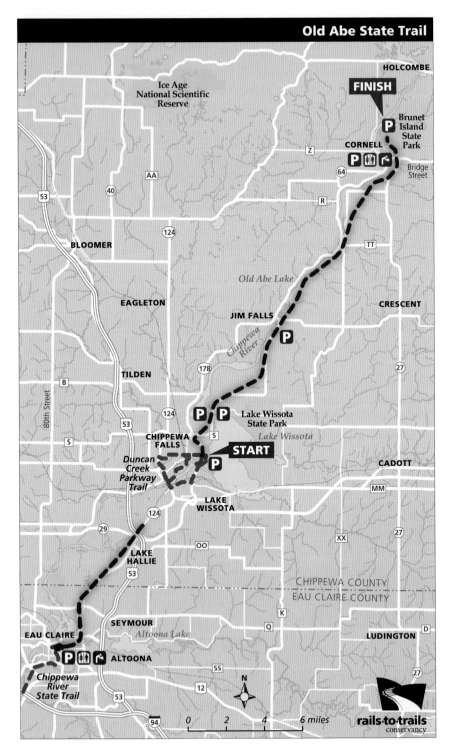

Old Abe State Trail

Farmland and woods greet you for much of the rest of your journey to the city of Cornell. Upon reaching Bridge Street, head west off the trail to the Cornell Visitors' Center, where you can catch a nice sunset over the water and learn about the city's paper milling past. You can also view the world's only stationary pulpwood stacker—now listed in the National Register of Historic Places—as it would have looked in the early 1900s when the Cornell Wood Products Company set up shop (it ceased operations in 1972). Signs in Cornell invitingly point you to the quaint downtown area along Main Street, where you'll find several restaurants, ice-cream shops, and pubs. Parking, restrooms, and water are available next door to the visitor center at Mill Yard Park.

Upon leaving Cornell, the trail continues north a short ways and then bends left to cross Park Road before heading northwest, briefly sharing space with the roadway. Park Road is a lightly traveled street that leads directly to Brunet Island State Park. The trail leaves the road after approximately 0.5 mile and then weaves its way another 0.5 mile through forestland to the Brunet Island State Park entrance. You can continue into the park and enjoy a circular trail system around the island to extend the trip.

NOTE: A State Trail Pass ($25 annually/$5 daily) is required for bicyclists, horseback riders, and in-line skaters ages 16 and older. Snowmobilers must display either Wisconsin registration or a snowmobile State Trail Pass. For information, go to dnr.wi.gov/topic/parks/trailpass.html.

CONTACT: dnr.wi.gov/topic/parks/name/oldabe or **co.chippewa.wi.us /government/land-conservation-forest-management/forest-trails**

DIRECTIONS

In Eau Claire, metered parking is available in a municipal lot just east of the trailhead off N. Farwell St. From I-94, take Exit 70 onto northbound US 53. In 3.8 miles, take Exit 89 toward River Prairie Dr. Head west on River Prairie Dr. for 0.6 mile, and turn left onto Galloway St. just after crossing the Eau Claire River. In 1.8 miles, turn left onto N. Farwell St. The Railroad Street parking area is located midblock to your right.

To reach parking in Chippewa Falls near the southern endpoint from the intersection of Wissota Green Blvd. and WI 178/Seymour Cray Sr. Blvd. heading north, turn right onto Wissota Green Blvd., and take another right immediately onto Beach Dr. In 0.1 mile, turn right into the parking lot. Head west for 0.2 mile on the short spur trail in the back of the parking lot to the starting point for the Old Abe State Trail.

To access the northern trailhead at Brunet Island State Park from the four-way "bird foot" intersection of WI 64 E. and WI 27 in Cornell, southwest of Cornell Municipal Airport, head west on WI 27 S./WI 64 W., and go 2 miles. Turn right (north) onto Park Road, and follow for 1.2 miles. Turn right into the trailhead.

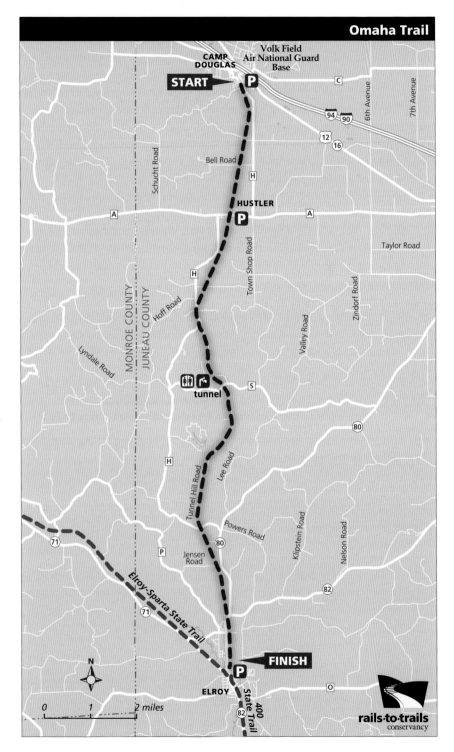

Omaha Trail

The 12.5-mile Omaha Trail passes through a wonderland of towering buttes, mesas, and pinnacles that seem more at home in an arid desert than in fertile farmland. The steep sandstone formations, some 100–200 feet high, served as landmarks for early pioneers traveling through Wisconsin. They have names like Lookout Tower, Castle Rock, and Twin Bluffs. You'll skirt them as you leave Camp Douglas bound for the Elroy trailhead, passing through a tunnel midway.

The Omaha Trail is maintained by Juneau County, which sealed the loose screened-limestone surface usually found on state rail-trails. Although it is built to be smoother than gravel, watch for cracks and potholes that have developed over the years.

The trail follows a spur route that the Chicago and North Western Railway acquired when it bought the

This tunnel along the Omaha Trail is a rare feature for rail-trails in the state.

County
Juneau

Endpoints
Murray St. at Eddy Ave.
(Camp Douglas) to
N. Limits Road at Second
Main St. (Elroy)

Mileage
12.5

Type
Rail-Trail

Roughness Index
2

Surface
Asphalt, Gravel

The route follows a former spur of the Chicago and North Western Railway.

Chicago, St. Paul, Minneapolis and Omaha Railway (known as the Omaha Road) in 1882. The railroad stopped using the rail bed in 1987, and the county adopted the original railway's name when the trail opened in 1992.

Beginning in Camp Douglas, an old logging town that's now home to Volk Field Air National Guard base, you'll head south to the first and only town on the trail at 2.8 miles. Hustler has a pleasant public park right near the trail.

You'll probably notice that the grade increases after you leave Hustler and climb past the weathered bluffs that are unlike anything east of the Mississippi River. You'll gain 200 feet over the next 4 miles, arriving at an 875-foot-long tunnel at the summit. The only other trails in Wisconsin with tunnels are the Elroy-Sparta and Badger State Trails. A small park just before the tunnel's domed entrance provides restrooms and water and a sign encouraging bicyclists to dismount.

Leaving the tunnel, it's all downhill for the next 5.4 miles to the town of Elroy. You'll cross more than a dozen bridges and pass through a dense forest where you might spot white-tailed deer. Closer to Elroy the valley widens, and you'll return to farm country.

The trail ends at the north end of Elroy, where you'll turn left onto Second Main Street and go 0.9 mile to Cedar Street. You'll find the 400 State Trail (Trail 38, page 145) a half block to the left and the Elroy-Sparta State Trail (Trail 37, page 141) one block to the right at the Main Street intersection. The 400 State Trail passes Elroy Commons Trail Shop, which serves as a trailhead for all three trails; here you'll find parking, an information center, and bike rentals.

NOTE: A Juneau County Trail Pass ($10 annually/$2 daily) is required for bicyclists ages 18 and older on the Omaha Trail. The passes are available at Home Front Travel Mart (608-427-6555) in Camp Douglas, Hustle Inn (608-427-3424) and Hustle Stop (608-427-3521) in Hustler, and Elroy Commons Trail Shop (608-462-2410) and Hansen's IGA (608-462-8200) in Elroy.

CONTACT: www.co.juneau.wi.gov/trails.html

DIRECTIONS

To reach the northern trailhead in Camp Douglas from I-90/94, take Exit 55 toward Camp Douglas onto County Road C. Go 0.1 mile south, and turn right onto US 12; immediately turn left onto Castle St. and then left again onto Douglas St. Go 0.1 mile, and turn right onto N. Washington St. Take the first right onto Eddy Ave., and look for on-street parking. The trail begins directly across the street from Eddy Ave., heading south.

To reach the southern trailhead in Elroy from I-90/94, take Exit 69 toward Mauston on WI 82/Gateway Ave., heading west. In 0.6 mile, bear left on WI 82/N. Union St. to head south across the Lemonweir River. In 0.2 mile, turn right on E. State St., go 0.3 mile (4 blocks), and turn left to head south on WI 82/Division St. In 0.6 mile, bear right around the traffic circle, and take the first right to continue east on WI 82/Grayside Ave. In 10.5 miles, turn left to continue south on WI 82. In 1.6 miles, turn left onto Franklin St. in Elroy. Take the first left into the parking lot, located behind the Elroy Commons Trail Shop on Railroad St. After parking, take the 400 State Trail north to Cedar St., turn left, and then, in half a block, turn right onto Second Main St. Go 0.9 mile and look for the Omaha Trail on the right.

Ozaukee Interurban Trail

If you're going to visit the historical communities that lie just west of Lake Michigan, why not use the former route of the venerable interurban railroad? The Ozaukee Interurban Trail stretches the length of Ozaukee County and links communities known for a lighthouse, Civil War–era downtowns, surviving railroad depots and gristmills, as well as a popular 1920s recording studio for Mississippi Delta blues singers.

The 30-mile paved trail passes through Belgium, Port Washington, Grafton, Cedarburg, Thiensville, and Mequon. It mostly follows the route of a Milwaukee–Sheboygan interurban railway launched in 1908 and taken over in 1922 by the Milwaukee Electric Railway & Light Company as a rapid-transit line. Falling victim to the declining rail business after World War II, the owner terminated the line in 1948. The corridor still carries the

County
Ozaukee

Endpoints
County Road K/ Sheboygan Interurban Trail between County Road KW and Temaat Road (Cedar Grove) to W. County Line Road/ Brown Deer Recreational Trail between Garden Dr. and N. Arrowwood Road (Mequon)

Mileage
30.1

Type
Rail-Trail, Rail-with-Trail

Roughness Index
1

Surface
Asphalt

The Ozaukee Interurban Trail spans the length of Ozaukee County.

A highlight of the rail-trail is passing over this 1907 bridge.

power lines, operated today by We Energies, and by 1975 a few towns used the rights-of-way as trails. The Ozaukee Interurban Trail combined these in 2002.

The trail connects with the Brown Deer Recreational Trail in the south and the Sheboygan Interurban Trail in the north. It runs alongside railroad tracks most of the distance. Unlike most rail-trails, this one has steeper than normal grades as it enters and leaves Port Washington.

Beginning in the north at County Road K, you'll immediately realize why the trail is known for its birding hot spots; it starts at the Cedar Grove Waterfowl Production Area, a wetland habitat for sandhill cranes, green heron, and more. You'll pass through the small town of Belgium in 3 miles (where the closest public parking to the northern endpoint is available at the Community Park on Beech Street) and then through another 6 miles of farm country to the outskirts of Port Washington.

The trail heads downhill after you cross I-43 and arrive at the harbor on East Jackson Street. A bustling port since Civil War times and now a tourist destination, its centerpiece is the 1930s Art Deco lighthouse out on the breakwater. Follow the BIKE ROUTE signs on city streets for 1.5 miles uphill to regain the Ozaukee Interurban Trail on West Oakland Avenue between South Park and South Spring Streets.

You'll pass through open country for 5 miles until you cross the Milwaukee River and enter Grafton. You'll have to pass through this old mill town on a mile of city streets, too, but this won't be a problem if you're a music lover. In the 1920s, Grafton was home to Paramount Records, a leading recorder of early Delta blues artists such as Charley Patton and Blind Lemon Jefferson. Their music is celebrated in a statue and piano keyboard–style Walk of Fame in Paramount Plaza, located a block from the bike route on Wisconsin Avenue between Beech and Bridge Streets.

Returning to the trail on Seventh Avenue between Maple Street and Wisconsin Avenue, you'll pass through residential areas for the next 2 miles to a restored trestle over Cedar Creek in Cedarburg. The downtown has developed a vibrant tourism economy; many buildings, such as the woolen mill, date to the Civil War era. On Center Street, watch for the cream-colored brick 1907 railroad depot; it's the last building related to the railway on the trail.

It's about 5 miles to Thiensville, and about halfway there you'll cross over the Union Pacific Railroad tracks. Another 3 miles reaches the Brown Deer Recreational Trail, which joins the Oak Leaf Trail (Trail 51, page 195) and goes all the way to Milwaukee's downtown waterfront.

CONTACT: **interurbantrail.us**

DIRECTIONS

Public parking is available in Belgium, about 3 miles south of the northern endpoint in Cedar Grove. To reach the parking lot from I-43, take Exit 107 onto westbound County Road D. Go 1.1 miles, and turn right onto Beech St. Turn left into the parking area by the tennis courts. To reach the trail endpoint, head south on Main St., and turn right. Go about 2 blocks, and turn right onto the Ozaukee Interurban Trail, located just less than 1 block past Elm St. Head 3.2 miles north on the trail to reach the endpoint at County Road K, which is also the southern endpoint for the Sheboygan Interurban Trail.

To reach the southern endpoint from I-43, take Exit 85 onto WI 57/WI 167/Mequon Road toward Thiensville. After 3.2 miles, turn right a half block past N. Cedarburg Road at a sign for CITY HALL PARKING, and look for parking on the left. Go south on the trail for 2.2 miles to locate its southern endpoint, at W. County Line Road.

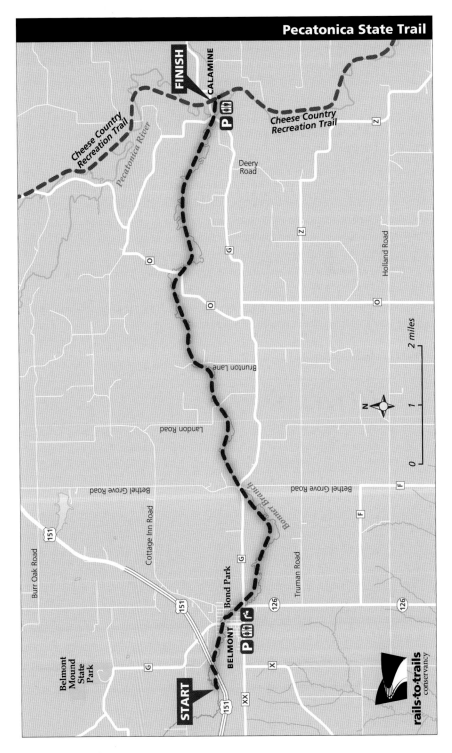

Pecatonica State Trail

The Pecatonica State Trail is never far from water as it takes the easygoing Bonner Branch Valley through the rolling hills and rocky bluffs of southwest Wisconsin's Driftless Area, a region that the glaciers didn't scrape flat in the last Ice Age.

The 10-mile trail from Belmont to Calamine follows a branch line of the Mineral Point Railroad that the Chicago, Milwaukee, St. Paul and Pacific Railroad (Milwaukee Road) later acquired to haul lead from area mines. The railroad builders avoided the rugged terrain by keeping to the valley of this Pecatonica River tributary.

Like its cousin the Cheese Country Recreation Trail (Trail 34, page 131), the Pecatonica State Trail is shared by ATVers (April 1–November 15), mountain bikers, horseback riders, and hikers in warmer months. When the snow flies, snowmobilers and cross-country skiers use the trail. Motorized use can make the trail passage rough in places, so it's best to use the widest possible tires if you're mountain biking.

County
Lafayette

Endpoints
US 151 underpass south of W. Liberty St. (Belmont) to Cheese Country Recreation Trail junction south of County Road G and west of Prospect St. (Calamine)

Mileage
10.0

Type
Rail-Trail

Roughness Index
2

Surface
Asphalt, Crushed Stone

The Pecatonica State Trail is never far from water as it travels through the Bonner Branch Valley.

You're starting in Belmont, the home of the First Capitol, where the Wisconsin Territory was established. The two-story white clapboard capitol and adjacent Supreme Court buildings still stand, but nearly 3 miles north of town in the midst of cornfields. After Belmont had its year of glory in 1836, many residents followed the government to its new home in Madison or just drifted away. The final blow came in 1867 when the railroad laid its tracks to the south. Anyone who was left relocated to be near the railroad.

The trail starts on the west side of town where the railroad continued its route to Platteville, but the best parking and facilities are in shady Bond Park on the east side. Be sure to stock up on water and snacks, as there's nothing east of Belmont unless you're passing through Calamine on the Cheese Country Recreation Trail to Darlington (5.6 miles south) or Mineral Point (9 miles north).

Beginning at Bond Park, you'll notice the asphalt trail turns to crushed stone on the way out of town. The trail twists and turns along the sluggish waters and crooked banks of the Bonner Branch as you cross 24 bridges.

Oak and hickory trees shade parts of the trail. Elsewhere you'll pass rolling farmland and tall grasses. Together this creates a good habitat for such birdlife as flycatchers, vireos, quail, and turkey. The valley deepens as you head east, and you'll notice Bonner Branch spreading out into a marshy area as it joins the Pecatonica River right before you hit the Cheese Country Recreation Trail junction. A left turn takes you to Calamine and the trailhead there.

NOTE: ATVers must carry Wisconsin DNR registration to use the Pecatonica and Cheese Country Trails. A State Trail Pass ($25 annually/$5 daily) is required for bicyclists and horseback riders ages 16 and older. Snowmobilers must display either Wisconsin registration or a snowmobile State Trail Pass. For information, go to dnr.wi.gov/topic/parks/trailpass.html. Use of the Cheese Country Recreation Trail requires a separate Cheese Country Trail sticker.

CONTACT: dnr.wi.gov/topic/parks/name/pecatonica

DIRECTIONS

To reach the western trailhead at Bond Park in Belmont from US 151, take Exit 26 toward Belmont onto southbound County Road G/First Capitol Ave., which becomes N. Mound Ave. Go 0.8 mile, and turn left (east) onto E. Platteville Ave. Go 0.3 mile, turn left onto S. Park St., and go 0.1 mile to parking for Bond Park on the left. The endpoint is located 1.1 miles west along the trail.

To reach the eastern trailhead near the town of Calamine from US 151, follow the directions above through the second sentence, but instead of turning left onto S. Park St., continue straight (east) on County Road G/E. Platteville Ave. In 5.3 miles, bear right at the Y to continue east on County Road G. In another 3.8 miles, look for the trailhead on your left, after you cross the Pecatonica River and just before you reach Calamine.

The 26-mile Pine Line Trail calls to mind a time when trains loaded with timber chugged out of northern Wisconsin's great white pine forests. The local economy still depends on lumber, as sawmills are at work in Medford and Prentice, located at either end of the trail.

The trail follows a section of the Wisconsin Central Railway, which launched rail service in 1876 between Lake Superior and Chicago. The Soo Line took over until 1985, when the Wisconsin Central Ltd. got the rail bed, but it ceased to use the line in 1988. Price and Taylor Counties then acquired it for use as a trail.

In the mid-1800s, lumberjacks had been somewhat selective in harvesting timber because of difficulties in getting the lumber to market. The arrival of the railroad changed that and ushered in the so-called Cutover period of the late 1800s and early 1900s, when whole forests were reduced to stumps. Immigrants later cleared that land for

Counties
Price, Taylor

Endpoints
W. Allman St. and River Dr. (Medford) to Morner Road between WI 13 and Prentice Road (Prentice)

Mileage
26.2

Type
Rail-Trail

Roughness Index
2

Surface
Crushed Stone

Naturally, forest growth is a backdrop of the Pine Line Trail.

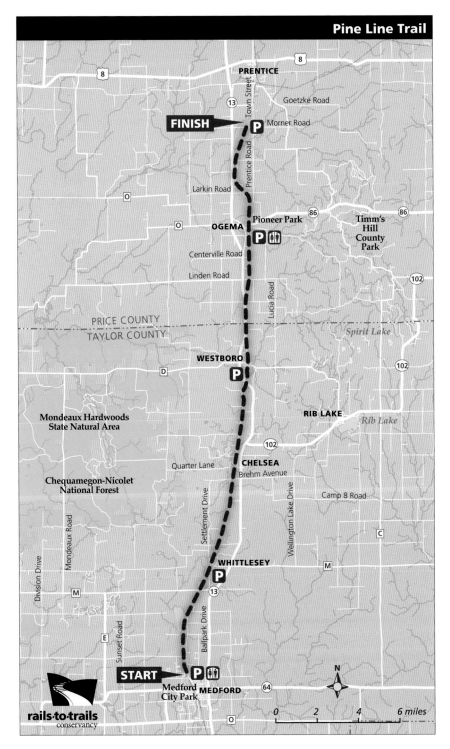

Pine Line Trail

farms, while conservation methods, begun in the 1930s, created new forests. You'll see farms and second-growth forests from the trail.

The city of Medford at the trail's southern end dates from the 1870s. Much of the downtown streetscape, including the 1913 vintage Soo Line railroad depot located between East Broadway Avenue and West State Street, appears much as it did in the early 20th century.

Beginning in Medford, you'll travel on screened limestone for the first 3 miles; after that it's crushed gravel. Dairyland farming dominates the landscape as you leave Medford. At 5 miles, you'll pass through the crossroads community of Whittlesey as the land around the trail alternates between farms, forests, and the Black River wetlands where you may see beavers at work.

Five miles up the trail, you'll arrive at the Chelsea community, a former railroad stop where the second-growth forest becomes the dominant feature. Another 4 miles and you're in Westboro, another former whistlestop with cafés. If you take County Road D about 8 miles west, you'll find camping and hiking in the Mondeaux Hardwoods State Natural Area of the Chequamegon-Nicolet National Forest, where the Civilian Conservation Corps planted trees in the 1930s.

In the 6 miles between Westboro and Ogema, you might notice a slight grade as you head over a glacial moraine. A restored railroad depot provides a welcome rest area in Ogema. If you're hungry, hit a nearby restaurant for some true Wisconsin fare: fried cheese curds.

The last 5 miles from Ogema is slightly downhill as the trail ends at a parking lot on Morner Road.

The trail in Price and Taylor Counties is open to snowmobiles and ATVs from December through March when the temperature is below 28 degrees. UTVs are allowed on the trails during those conditions only in Price County.

CONTACT: www.co.taylor.wi.us/pdf/rail_trail.pdf or co.price.wi.us/427 /pine-line-price-taylor-rail-trail

DIRECTIONS

To reach the southern trailhead in Medford from US 51, take Exit 208 onto westbound WI 64 in Merrill. In 9.3 miles, bear left (south) onto WI 64/WI 107. In 1.9 miles, bear right to continue west on WI 67/WI 107. In 25.2 miles, turn right onto Luepke Way. Go 0.9 mile—Luepke Way becomes Centennial Parkway, and you'll pass restrooms in Medford City Park—and turn right onto W. Allman St. Go 0.2 mile and look for trailhead parking on the left. Parking also is available on River Drive, just past the trail on your left.

To reach the northern trailhead in Prentice from US 8, exit just west of Prentice on WI 13, heading south. Go 2.7 miles, and turn left onto Morner Road. Go 0.7 mile, and look for parking on your left and the trail across the road on your right.

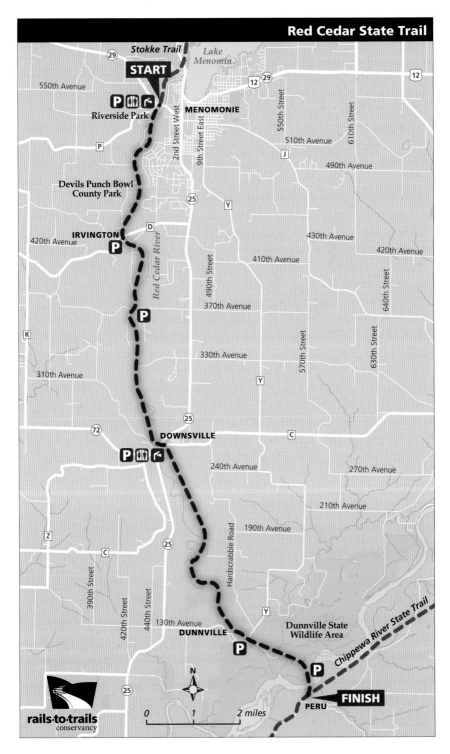

One of Wisconsin's earliest rail-trail conversions, the 14.5-mile Red Cedar State Trail is built on the former corridor of the Red Cedar Junction railway, which served Knapp, Stout & Co. in the 1880s—then the world's largest timber producer. Since the late 1970s, the trail has offered a serene experience for trail users from Menomonie to Peru, where it meets with the southern end of the Chippewa River State Trail (Trail 35, page 133), just south of the Dunnville State Wildlife Area.

Start your journey at the old train depot turned visitor center at Riverside Park in Menomonie. Here, you can

A bridge at Dunnville State Wildlife Area provides gorgeous views of the Chippewa River.

Counties
Dunn

Endpoints
WI 29 Trunk east of Hofland Road/County Road P at Riverside Park (Menomonie) to the Chippewa River State Trail north of 50th Ave. and Weber Road, just south of Dunnville State Wildlife Area (Peru)

Mileage
14.5

Type
Rail-Trail

Roughness Index
2

Surface
Crushed Stone, Asphalt (last 1,000 feet)

Bridge over the Red Cedar River in Downsville

access ample parking and purchase a State Trail Pass, required for all bikers, snow-mobilers, and cross-country skiers. (Note that hybrid bikes are recommended for an optimal experience on the crushed-limestone route.) You can also connect with the Stokke Trail, just across WI 29 Trunk/Hudson Road, which leads north to Lake Menomin.

Snowmobiles are permitted on the 2 miles of the trail between the Chippewa River State Trail and County Road Y. Hunting is also permitted along a 4-mile section through the Dunnville State Wildlife Area.

Heading south, the Red Cedar State Trail pulls you into a peaceful riverside corridor with scenic views of the water to your left and sandstone cliffs to your right. You'll soon cross the first of several bridges built over the tributaries that feed the Red Cedar River. The crushed-sandstone trail remains level for the duration of your trip, and there are several benches along the way for rest and respite. Take some time to sit and watch the river flow by as you listen to the sounds of songbirds and small animals scurrying about in the surrounding woods.

The first 3 miles of trail to Irvington wind along the river in deciduous forest, which provides shade in the warmer months and a beautiful palette of birch, maple, elm, and aspen leaves in the fall. On the trail, you might spy some unexpected "trail users" enjoying the tranquility, including white-tailed deer, foxes, and raccoons.

As you travel 5 miles farther south to Downsville, the forest opens up to a view of surrounding farmland. Just before the Downsville trailhead, you'll cross the 200-foot Red Cedar Trestle, which has well-maintained plank decking and an iconic rusty-but-solid steel frame.

Just north of Dunnville, you'll pass a small waterfall, a reward for your journey from one of the state's most beautiful trails. Nearing the southern endpoint, you're sure to marvel at the sweeping views as you pass through the Dunnville State Wildlife Area and cross over a spectacular trestle on the Chippewa River.

NOTE: A State Trail Pass ($25 annually/$5 daily) is required for bicyclists, snowmobilers, and cross-country skiers ages 16 and older on the Red Cedar State Trail. Snowmobilers must display either Wisconsin registration or a snowmobile State Trail Pass, and hunters must have a license. For information, go to dnr.wi.gov /topic/parks/trailpass.html.

CONTACT: dnr.wi.gov/topic/parks/name/redcedar or wisconsintrailguide.com /bicycle/red-cedar-state-trail.html

DIRECTIONS

To access the northern trailhead in Menomonie from I-94, take Exit 41 for WI 25 toward Menomonie and Barron. Head south on WI 25/N. Broadway St. for 2.3 miles, crossing Lake Menomin; then turn right onto 11th Ave. W. and continue west across the Red Cedar River—11th Ave. W. turns into Hudson Road. In 0.5 mile, turn left into Riverside Park. The trailhead is just west of the parking area.

Parking is unavailable at the southern endpoint, and there is no direct access to the trail from nearby 50th Ave. The closest trailhead is located in the Dunnville State Wildlife Area along the Chippewa River. From the intersection of WI 25/S. Broadway St. and 11th Ave. W. in Menomonie, take WI 25 south for 11.6 miles. Turn left onto County Road Y; go east 2 miles, crossing the Red Cedar River; and turn right onto Dunnville Road. Dunnville Road loosely parallels the trail for 1.8 miles (crossing the trail after about 1 mile) and then dead-ends just after the parking area and before a trestle bridge over the Chippewa River.

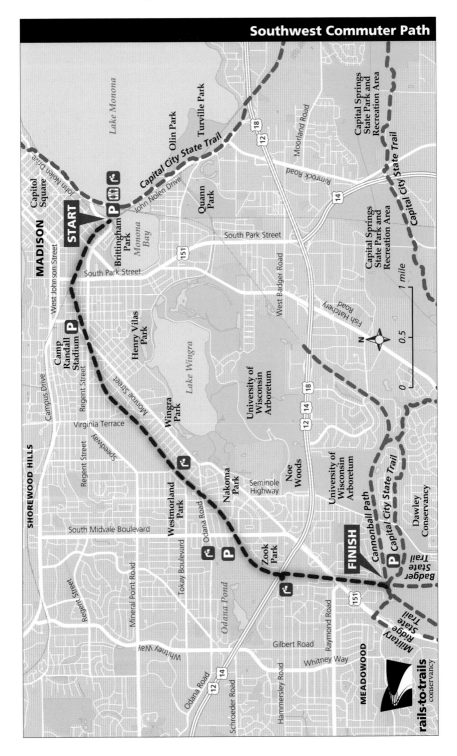

Southwest Commuter Path

All it takes is a short ride on Madison's 5.6-mile Southwest Commuter Path to understand the critical role it plays in getting people around town. Not only does it pass within a mile of the State Capitol complex and through the southern part of the University of Wisconsin–Madison campus, but it also connects with a handful of trails that loop the city or head across the countryside.

The paved path follows the route of the Illinois Central Railroad branch built in 1887 between Freeport, Illinois, and Madison. The crushed-stone Badger State Trail (Trail 30, page 115) uses that route as it heads 40 miles south to the Illinois border, where it meets the Jane Addams Trail. Financial difficulties in 1980 forced the railroad (by now the Illinois Central Gulf) to stop using the line. A succession of railroads—the Chicago, Madison and Northern, the Central Wisconsin, and the Wisconsin and Calumet—all

County
Dane

Endpoints
Brittingham Park on Lake Monona west of N. Shore Dr. and S. Bedford St. (Madison) to Capital City State Trail at Arrowhead Park near near Chalet Gardens Court south of Chalet Gardens Road (Fitchburg)

Mileage
5.6

Type
Rail-with-Trail

Roughness Index
1

Surface
Asphalt

The commuter path is a pleasant source of transportation and recreation for residents of and visitors to Madison.

Wooded residential lots line the Southwest Commuter Path as you head out of Madison.

failed to return the line to profitability. The tracks were pulled in 1999, and the trail opened two years later.

Beginning where the Southwest Commuter Path meets a scenic trail through Brittingham Park on Monona Bay, you'll head through a warehouse district alongside a still-active rail yard where some old buildings have been upgraded to loft apartments. In 0.3 mile, you'll cross West Washington Avenue with its view of the Capitol dome, about a mile away.

Across the tracks you'll see a vintage depot for the Chicago, Milwaukee, St. Paul and Pacific Railroad. Designed by noted Chicago architect Charles Sumner Frost, the imposing 1903 structure is listed in the National Register of Historic Places. Closed in the 1960s, it's now home to several shops, including one that rents, sells, and repairs bicycles. A diesel engine and railroad cars flank the depot.

After the depot, the path passes the university's Kohl Center for basketball and hockey and Camp Randall Stadium, home of the Badgers football team and named for a Civil War–era Army training camp at the site. Other university-related buildings are scattered about, and students regularly use the trail.

In a couple of blocks, you enter established residential neighborhoods with wooded lots and homes that back up to the trail. Residents have planted wild-flowers along several stretches of trail. The Dudgeon-Monroe neighborhood, for instance, plants and maintains a prairie-themed border.

Although there could be frequent street crossings, you'll find that the rail-trail rolls below the major roads as you're heading out of town. The spans

are labeled so you can track your location. Ramps and stairways lead up to the neighboring streets.

At 5.5 miles from the start, you'll come to a mixing zone for three trails that collect bike commuters on their way into town. First, the Badger State Trail merges from the left. In another 500 feet you hit the path's end at the Capital City State Trail (Trail 33, page 127), where you can connect with the Cannonball Path or the Military Ridge State Trail (Trail 48, page 183). Now you can see why this is one of the busiest trails in Madison.

Unlike other trails in the region, the Southwest Commuter Path requires no State Trail Pass.

CONTACT: **cityofmadison.com/bikemadison**

DIRECTIONS

To reach the eastern trailhead from US 12/US 18, take Exit 263 toward downtown Madison on John Nolen Dr. Go 1.9 miles and turn left onto N. Shore Dr. Go 0.4 mile, and turn left onto W. Brittingham Place. Take an immediate left into Brittingham Park (3-hour parking at all times). The trail is 0.1 mile east.

Parking near the western endpoint is available near the Capital City State Trail at Dawley Conservancy in Fitchburg. To reach the western trailhead from the intersection of US 18/US 151/ Verona Road and County Road PD/McKee Road, take McKee Road east. Go 0.9 mile to S. Seminole Hwy., turn left, and then go 0.4 mile and turn left into the parking lot for Dawley Conservancy. To find the trail, take the short path in back of the parking lot north for 0.1 mile, turn left onto the Capital City State Trail, and then go 0.5 mile to the junction with the Southwest Commuter Path. Turn right (north) toward Madison.

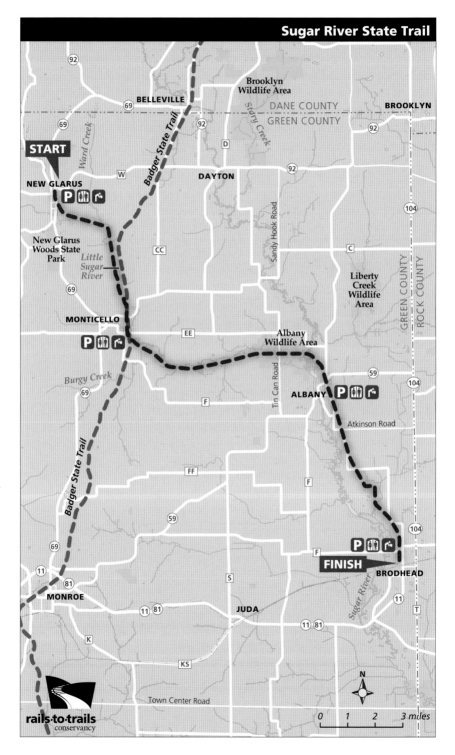

Sugar River State Trail

I f you can't make it to Switzerland, then you can do the next best thing: take the Sugar River State Trail to "America's Little Switzerland," New Glarus, Wisconsin. Settled in 1845 by a small group of Swiss pioneers, New Glarus today is a living monument to all things Swiss, with chalet-style buildings, restaurants dishing up savory Swiss fare, and annual celebrations including Polka Fest, the Heidi Festival, and Volksfest, which marks the Swiss independence day.

The Sugar River State Trail follows the route of the New Glarus Branch of the Chicago, Milwaukee, St. Paul and Pacific Railroad. Known locally as the "Limburger Special," the railroad laid tracks from Brodhead to Albany in 1880 and extended the line a few years later to New Glarus.

The scenic Sugar River State Trail crosses the Little Sugar and Sugar Rivers as it rolls southeast nearly 23 miles

The Sugar River State Trail takes trail users on a scenic 23-mile journey through Green County.

County
Green

Endpoints
Railroad St. just north of Fifth Ave. (New Glarus) to W. Exchange St. and W. Third Ave. (Brodhead)

Mileage
22.7

Type
Rail-Trail

Roughness Index
2

Surface
Asphalt, Crushed Stone

The Sugar River State Trail begins in "America's Little Switzerland."

past gently rolling hills and meadows and through the farming communities of Monticello and Albany to Brodhead.

Beginning at the restored railroad depot in New Glarus, you'll ride a paved trail for 0.3 mile until it crosses WI 69 and becomes screened limestone. (Remaining on the paved path alongside WI 69 takes you on a side trip to the New Glarus Brewing Company in 1 mile.) From here, the trail follows the course of the Little Sugar River. Near mile 6, approaching Monticello, you arrive at a brightly painted railroad depot (not open to the public). You'll also be running alongside the Badger State Trail (Trail 30, page 115), which you'll cross south of Monticello nearly 7 miles after leaving New Glarus.

About 12 miles from New Glarus you'll enter a 3-mile stretch of the Albany Wildlife Area, where hunting is allowed. Bright bicycling wear is recommended. Between Monticello and Albany there are five stream crossings with views of scenic farmland. At mile 14, the trail crosses the Sugar River on a long, curving bridge that provides spectacular views of lowlands of cattails and reeds, and woods of oak, hickory, walnut, cherry, and willow.

At mile 21, the trail crosses Norwegian Creek on a replica of a covered bridge built in 1984 from wood supplied by the DNR from demolished old barns and other buildings in the state.

You'll arrive in Brodhead at the crossing of Decatur Road. Cross the street and take West Third Avenue south for about a mile to the trailhead parking lot at the corner of West Exchange Street.

The town was named for Edward Brodhead, chief engineer of the Milwaukee Road's predecessor, the Milwaukee and Mississippi Railroad. Hopping off your bike to take in the sights, be sure to visit the Depot Museum at 1108 First Center Ave., open in the summer, which chronicles the trail's Milwaukee Road railroad days. Also worth a visit is the Half-Way Tree, located on Halfway Tree Road between WI 81 and County Road T south of the town, designated by American Indians as the halfway point between the Great Lakes and the Mississippi River.

NOTE: A State Trail Pass ($25 annually/$5 daily) is required for bicyclists ages 16 and older on the Sugar River State Trail. In-line skaters ages 16 and older must also have a pass, although there is only 1 mile of paved trail. Snowmobilers must display either Wisconsin registration or a snowmobile State Trail Pass. For information, go to dnr.wi.gov/topic/parks/trailpass.html.

CONTACT: dnr.wi.gov/topic/parks/name/sugarriver

DIRECTIONS

To reach the trailhead in New Glarus from US 18/US 151, take Exit 79, and head south toward Paoli on Old County Road PB. Go 3.3 miles, turn right across the Sugar River onto Paoli Road, and then, in 0.2 mile, turn left to follow County Road PB south through Paoli. Go 5.3 miles, turn right onto WI 69/WI 92, and then, in 2.2 miles, bear left to stay on WI 69. Go 4.3 miles, and turn right onto Sixth Ave. in New Glarus. Go about 250 feet, and turn right onto Railroad St. Look for parking on your right.

To reach the southern endpoint parking in Brodhead from I-90/I-39, take Exit 171A in Janesville to southbound WI 26/Milton Ave. Go 0.3 mile, and turn right (west) onto US 14. Go 6.9 miles, crossing the Rock River along the way, and turn left onto County Road H; after 3 miles, turn right to continue west on H. In 0.9 mile, bear left at the Y to continue south on H. In 1 mile, turn right onto WI 11. Go 13.3 miles west all the way into Brodhead, bearing left (south) at 12.7 miles to continue on WI 11, and, in 0.6 mile, turn right onto W. Exchange St. Go 0.1 mile (2 blocks), and look for Sugar River State Trail Southern Terminus parking on the right, just before W. Third Ave. The off-road trail heads north on W. Third Ave. for 0.9 mile and reaches the on-road portion of trail at Decatur Road.

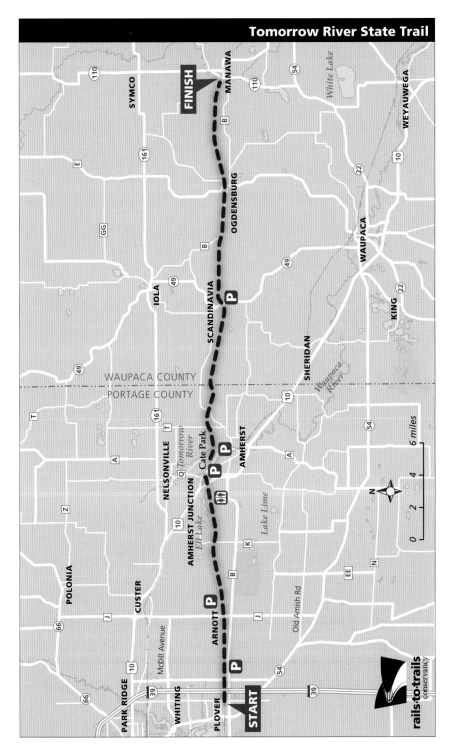

Tomorrow River State Trail

Despite its futuristic name, the Tomorrow River State Trail takes users on a tour of a historic rail-trail through beautiful Portage and Waupaca Counties. Trail users will find a good start at the trailhead along Twin Towers Drive in Plover, just south of Water Way, about 1.5 miles from the trail's start at Hoover Avenue South. However, those starting on Hoover Avenue South will be rewarded with the sweet smells coming from a nearby food-processing plant.

This rural trail alternates between open fields and shaded woodlands. There is a separate adjacent path for horseback riders—who, along with cyclists, need a State Trail Pass to use the trail.

Rural fields and shaded woodlands make up the landscape of the Tomorrow River State Trail.

Counties
Portage, Waupaca

Endpoints
Hoover Ave. S. just north of Plover Road (Plover) to Wolf Road just north of Westwood Dr. (Manawa)

Mileage
29.2 miles

Type
Rail-Trail

Roughness Index
2

Surface
Crushed Stone

After about 10 miles, you'll reach Amherst Junction, where the trail crosses over an active rail line adjacent to a trailhead with parking. Here, the trail takes a brief on-road detour to bypass an incomplete section between Second Street and Alm Road. From the parking area, turn left onto Second Street, right onto County Road KK, left onto School Road, and left onto Alm Road to complete the 1.5-mile detour and return to the off-road trail.

The trail's namesake, the Tomorrow River, flows under the trail at a bridge 1.5 miles east of Amherst Junction. Just to the south, you'll find Cate Park, with parking and restrooms, along Tomorrow River Road.

The town of Scandinavia lies another 8.5 miles down the trail from the Tomorrow River crossing. A trailhead with parking is available at the WI 49 overpass, and users can take a brief detour into town to the general store and Viking statue (a great photo op). Other Scandinavia-themed businesses give the town some color and embrace the town name.

The last 10 miles of trail cut through fields and forests and provide solitude and quiet, even with County Road B nearby. The trail ends just outside the town of Manawa, east of Wolf Road. There is no trail parking here, and the direct connection to Manawa is incomplete due to a closed bridge crossing at the Little Wolf River. However, rail enthusiasts are encouraged to take a look at the bridge, which provides a great slice of railroad history and a view of what could be in the future.

NOTE: A State Trail Pass ($25 annually/$5 daily) is required for bicyclists and horseback riders ages 16 and older on the Tomorrow River State Trail. Snowmobilers must display either a Wisconsin registration or a snowmobile State Trail Pass. For information, go to dnr.wi.gov/topic/parks/trailpass.html.

CONTACT: dnr.wi.gov/topic/parks/name/tomorrowriv

DIRECTIONS

To access the western trailhead at Twin Towers Drive from I-39, take Exit 153 for County Road B toward Plover/Amherst. Head east on County Road B/Plover Road for 1 mile, and turn left onto Twin Towers Dr. The trailhead parking area is 0.2 mile north, on the right side of the road just past the trail. The endpoint is 1.5 miles west along the trail.

To access the Scandinavia trailhead from I-39, follow the directions above through the second sentence, but follow County Road B/Plover Road east for 10.4 miles. Turn right to merge onto US 10 E. toward Waupaca/County Road B, and go 1.8 miles. Take the County Road A exit toward Amherst/County Road B, and head east 8.3 miles on County Road B. Continue right (south) onto N. Main St. After 0.4 mile, look for a small parking lot on your left, just past where the trail intersects N. Main St. The eastern endpoint is just under 11 miles along the trail, just past Wolf Road.

The White River State Trail is composed of two separate segments: a 12-mile stretch that runs between Elkhorn and just west of Burlington in Walworth County, and a 7-mile section that connects the unincorporated community of Kansasville near Eagle Lake to downtown Burlington in Racine County.

In Racine County, the eastern endpoint begins at Vandenboom Road in Kansasville, where a stretch of unused rail corridor is clearly visible from the parking lot on the east side of the road. Heading west toward Burlington, riders will be treated to classic Wisconsin farmland along a gentle grade, crossing bridges and passing by scenic vistas and wetlands along the way. Football fans will recognize

You'll pass quaint bridges with scenic vistas on the White River State Trail.

Counties
Racine, Walworth

Endpoints
Vandenboom Road south of Durand Ave./WI 11 (Kansasville) to Congress St. between Delaware Ave. and Maryland Ave./ Seven Waters Trail (Burlington); Spring Valley Road and Burlington Bypass (Burlington) to County Road H south of Pinecrest Lane (Elkhorn)

Mileage
19 miles

Type
Rail-Trail

Roughness Index
2

Surface
Concrete, Crushed Stone, Gravel

White River State Trail

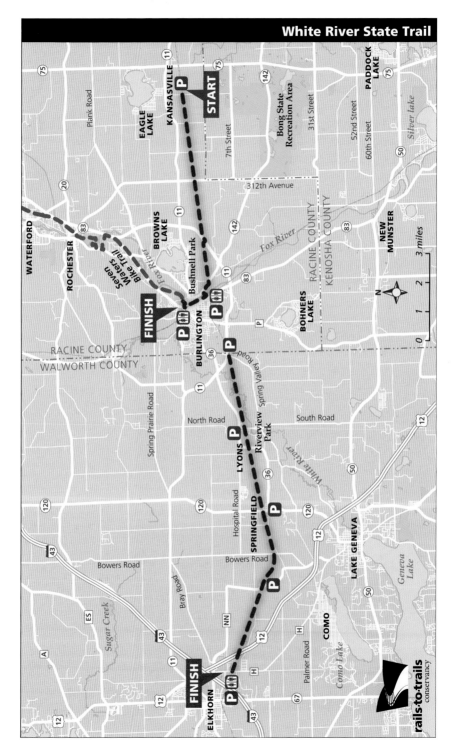

The well-maintained trail offers a pleasant, friendly journey between Kansasville and Elkhorn.

Burlington as the hometown of NFL quarterback Tony Romo. Chocolate fans will be welcomed by the strong scent of chocolate chip cookies as they approach Burlington from the east, due to the ongoing production of a Nestlé plant in town (Burlington hosts its annual ChocolateFest every Memorial Day weekend).

The trail is open to snowmobilers, cross-country skiers, and snowshoers; however, note that the trail is not groomed. A separate trail for horseback riding runs between the towns of Springfield and Lyons (Walworth County).

After passing through Bushnell Park—which offers sports fields, walking trails, picnic facilities, a playground, and restrooms—you'll cross the Fox River and remain on an off-street section that parallels Calumet Street. Just south of Adams Street, the trail continues on city sidewalks. You'll continue for several blocks and then head right onto Fox Street and enter Wehmhoff Jucker Park, where the trail connects with the Seven Waters Bike Trail and proceeds north toward the Village of Waterford.

The 12-mile western segment in Walworth County begins on the western outskirts of Burlington where Spring Valley Road meets the Burlington Bypass in Walworth County. Lake Geneva is located approximately 5 miles south of the trail after passing the historic villages of Lyons and Springfield. The scenic trail then rolls through the glaciated landscape of southern Wisconsin, featuring woodlands, farm fields, creeks, and its namesake White River.

NOTE: A State Trail Pass ($25 annually/$5 daily) is required for bicyclists and horseback riders ages 16 and older. Snowmobilers must display either a Wisconsin registration or a snowmobile State Trail Pass. For information, go to dnr.wi.gov /topic/parks/trailpass.html.

CONTACT: dnr.wi.gov/topic/parks/name/whiteriver

DIRECTIONS

To reach the eastern endpoint in Kansasville from I-94, take Exit 340 toward WI 142/Burlington. Head west onto WI 142, and go 8.4 miles. (Parts of this road may be closed at certain times or days.) Make a right onto WI 75 N., heading north. After 2.1 miles, turn left onto First St./County Line Road, and go 1 mile. Turn right onto Vandenboom Road, and go 0.8 mile. Turn right into the parking lot just across the street from where the trail begins.

To reach the Burlington trailhead from the intersection of Milwaukee Ave. and WI 36/ WI 83 heading south (about 0.3 mile after crossing the Fox River), take a slight right onto Milwaukee Ave., and go 3.2 miles. Turn left onto Maryland Ave., and go 0.3 mile. Turn right onto Congress St., and make an immediate left into the trailhead parking lot.

To reach the Spring Valley Road trailhead from I-43, take Exit 29 toward WI 11/Elkhorn/ Burlington. Head east on WI 11/Wisconsin Trunk Hwy. 11 E. for 10.5 miles, and take the exit on the left to get on WI 36. Turn right onto WI 36, and go 0.4 mile; then turn right onto Mormon Road/Spring Valley Road and go 0.6 mile. Turn right into the small trailhead parking lot.

To reach the western trailhead in Elkhorn from I-43, take Exit 27A for US 12 E. toward Lake Geneva. Follow signs for County Road NN/Elkhorn for 0.2 mile, and turn left onto County Road NN/E. Geneva St.—note the signs for Gateway Tech. After 0.2 mile, turn left (south) onto County Road H, and go 0.7 mile. Turn left into the trailhead parking lot.

E xpect to see the Wild Goose State Trail's namesake waterfowl flying overhead in V formations as you travel 34 miles across the rural landscape between Clyman Junction and Fond du Lac. Canada geese are just one of nearly 300 bird varieties that migrate through the Horicon National Wildlife Refuge, which you pass midway. The trail follows part of a historic Chicago and North Western Railway line that linked Oshkosh and Chicago as early as 1859. The section from Fond du Lac to just north of Clyman Junction fell into disuse by the early 1980s.

Nearly the entire trail is screened limestone, with short paved sections in some towns. Partial to dense tree canopies shade the trail in the summer and give way to colorful displays in autumn. A wood-chip horse path parallels the trail for 14 miles from WI 60 north to Pautsch Road in Burnett—the only section where horses are allowed. Snowmobiles and winter ATVs are permitted in Dodge County when conditions permit; in Fond du Lac County, snowmobiles are allowed but ATVs are prohibited.

Starting at the southern endpoint on WI 60, you'll head north through farmland for 4.2 miles to the town of Juneau,

Tree canopies along the route give way to colorful autumn displays.

Counties
Dodge, Fond du Lac

Endpoints
WI 60 and Junction Road
(Juneau) to W. Pioneer
Road and S. Hickory St.
(Fond du Lac)

Mileage
34.4

Type
Rail-Trail

Roughness Index
2

Surface
Asphalt, Crushed Stone,
Wood Chips

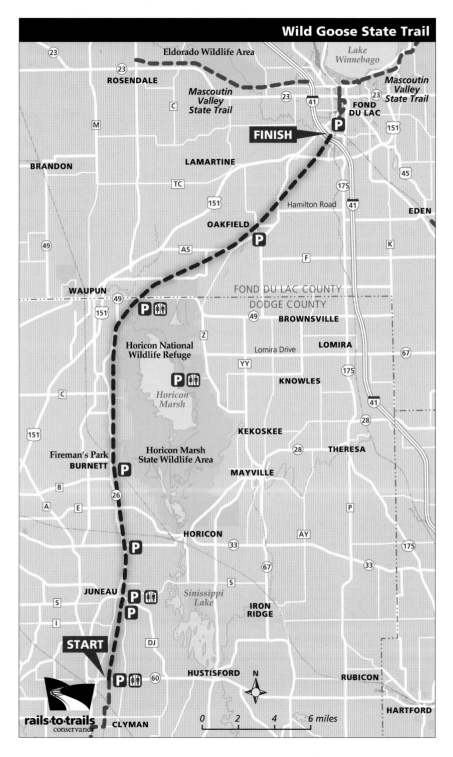

Wild Goose State Trail

which has a few cafés and grocery stores, as well as a shady park. Where the trail ends at East Oak Grove Street, turn left for a half block, turn right onto South Depot Street and go two blocks, and then turn right onto County Road S; look for the trail on the left in a half block.

About 4 miles after leaving Juneau, you'll begin skirting the edge of the Horicon National Wildlife Refuge and Horicon Marsh State Wildlife Area (not visible from the trail) for 14 miles. Ranked as the largest cattail marsh in the nation, it attracts hundreds of thousands of birds that stop here on their annual migratory flights. Turtles, frogs, and toads make their homes here, as do mink, muskrat, and river otters.

Look for a marked path to the right near WI 49 if you want to tour the northern part of the wetlands. You can also visit the Marsh Haven Nature Center, located 0.4 mile east of the trail crossing at WI 49. The Wildlife Refuge Headquarters and Visitor Center is located on County Road Z on the east side of the refuge (watch for busy traffic). Canoe and kayak tours also are offered.

WI 49 also is the border between Fond du Lac and Dodge Counties. Although the state owns the trail, each county takes care of its own trail maintenance.

The last 15 miles of the journey in Fond du Lac County is similar to the first, with farmland and frequent woodlots for shade. At 4.1 miles past WI 49, you'll come to Oak Center, which doesn't have services, followed in 3 miles by Oakfield, which does. The agricultural countryside remains a constant until you arrive at the office parks and warehouses on the edge of the city of Fond du Lac.

A newer trail extension takes trail users via a bridge over I-41 to West Pioneer Road. A short distance north, a network of bike paths and bike lanes leads to Lakeside Park on Lake Winnebago and the Fond du Lac Lighthouse.

NOTE: Snowmobilers and ATV/UTV users must display either a Wisconsin registration or an ATV/UTV or snowmobile State Trail Pass. For information, go to dnr .wi.gov/topic/parks/trailpass.html.

CONTACT: dnr.wi.gov/topic/parks/name/wildgoose

DIRECTIONS

To reach the southern trailhead and parking in Juneau from I-94, take Exit 267 to WI 26 toward Watertown, heading north. Go 18.9 miles, and take Exit 52 to WI 60, heading east. Go 1.7 miles, and turn left into the parking lot just past where the trail begins, with Junction Road on your right.

To reach the northern trailhead parking in Fond du Lac from I-41, take Exit 97 to southbound S. Hickory St. Go 0.1 mile, and turn right onto W. Rolling Meadows Dr. Go 0.4 mile, and turn left into the parking lot. Turn left on the trail to go 0.5 mile to the northern endpoint on W. Pioneer Road in Fond du Lac, or turn right to the southern endpoint in Clyman Junction.

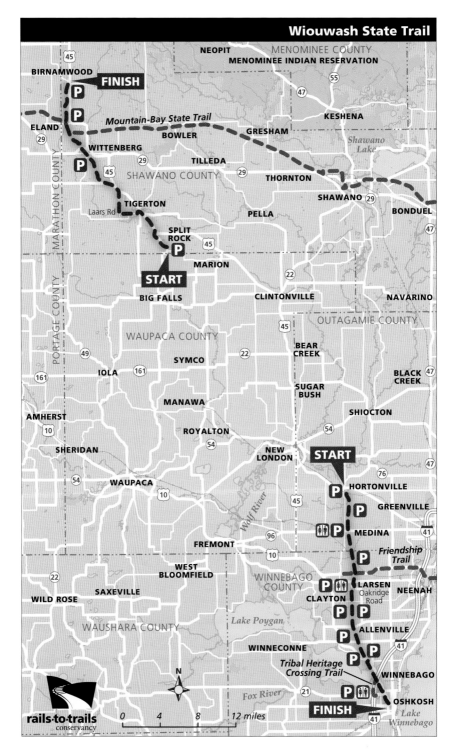

Wiouwash State Trail

NEOPIT
MENOMINEE COUNTY
MENOMINEE INDIAN RESERVATION

BIRNAMWOOD
FINISH

P
P

ELAND
Mountain-Bay State Trail
BOWLER
GRESHAM
KESHENA

WITTENBERG

P

29
TILLEDA
SHAWANO COUNTY
29
THORNTON

TIGERTON
Laars Rd
PELLA

SHAWANO
BONDUEL

SPLIT ROCK
P
MARION

START
MARATHON COUNTY
PORTAGE COUNTY

BIG FALLS
CLINTONVILLE
NAVARINO

OUTAGAMIE COUNTY
WAUPACA COUNTY
45

49
SYMCO
22
BEAR CREEK

IOLA
161
SUGAR BUSH
BLACK CREEK

AMHERST
MANAWA
SHIOCTON

ROYALTON
54

SHERIDAN
NEW LONDON
START

54
WAUPACA
10
HORTONVILLE
76

P

GREENVILLE
P

MEDINA
P

FREMONT
Friendship Trail
P

WEST BLOOMFIELD
WINNEBAGO COUNTY
LARSEN
Oakridge Road
NEENAH

SAXEVILLE
P
CLAYTON

WILD ROSE
P

WAUSHARA COUNTY
Lake Poygan
ALLENVILLE
P

WINNECONNE
P
P

Tribal Heritage Crossing Trail
WINNEBAGO

N

Fox River
21
P
OSHKOSH

FINISH
Lake Winnebago

rails-to-trails
conservancy

0   4   8   12 miles

The Wiouwash State Trail is appropriately named for the four counties through which it passes: Winnebago, Outagamie, Waupaca, and Shawano. Currently, 41 miles of the rail-trail are open in two disconnected sections separated by a gap of approximately 40 miles.

Split Rock to Birnamwood: 19 miles

The northern segment of the Wiouwash State Trail follows along WI 45 in the western part of Shawano County. Most of the trail is crushed stone but is not heavily used, so grass grows freely on the trail.

Parking is available near the southern endpoint in the unincorporated town of Split Rock, the best place to start your journey. A few miles north, the trail reaches the town of Tigerton, where it is only open in the winter for snowmobiling. Cyclists must take County Road M west

Counties
Outagamie, Shawano, Waupaca, Winnebago

Endpoints
County Road SS between Kersten Lake Road and County Road EE (Split Rock) to County Road N/ State Road and N. Railroad Ave. (Birnamwood); Lakeview Ave. east of S. Nash St. (Hortonville) to the University of Wisconsin–Oshkosh at Osceola St. just west of Pearl Ave. (Oshkosh)

Mileage
41.0

Type
Rail-Trail

Roughness Index
2

Surface
Asphalt, Crushed Stone

A farm view along the northern segment of the Wiouwash near WI 45

of Tigerton, remain straight on Laars Road where M turns to the south, and turn right onto Malueg Road. The trail is open again where Malueg Road meets US 45. Heading north to the town of Wittenberg, follow the city streets, East Reed Street and then Howard Street, to continue on the trail.

Just north of Wittenberg, the trail again follows rural roads, heading north on Hummingbird Road and then turning west on Hemlock Road; follow the directions carefully, as the trail is poorly marked. The off-road trail picks up again from Hemlock Road and heads north to Eland, where it connects and shares a pathway with the more popular 83-mile Mountain-Bay State Trail (Trail 49, page 187), which heads west to Weston and east to Howard. Follow the Mountain-Bay State Trail until the two trails split at the site of a historic railroad just past Cedar Street. A few miles north of Eland, the existing portion of the trail terminates in Birnamwood, where there is parking available 0.1 mile north of the trail, along with several bars and restaurants.

NOTE: Snowmobilers must display either a Wisconsin registration or a snow-mobile State Trail Pass. For information, go to dnr.wi.gov/topic/parks/trailpass.html.

CONTACT: dnr.wi.gov/topic/parks/name/wiouwash

DIRECTIONS

To reach the southern trailhead near Split Rock from the intersection of US 45 and County Road SS, head south and then west on County Road SS for 0.4 mile. Turn left to stay on County Road SS, and go 1.7 miles—the road briefly merges with Kersten Lake Road after about 1 mile and then merges left (southeast) into County Road SS again. Just after the bend, turn right into the grassy parking lot, which is easy to miss.

To reach parking near the northern endpoint in Birnamwood from the intersection of US 45 and County Road N/State Road, head west on County Road N/State Road for 0.1 mile. Turn right onto Railroad St., and go 0.1 mile. Turn right into the paved parking lot just after passing Birch St. to your left. The trail endpoint is 0.1 mile south, at the corner of Railroad St. and County Road N/State St.

Hortonville to Oshkosh: 22 miles

The southern segment of the Wiouwash State Trail is located approximately 40 miles southeast of Split Rock, beginning in Hortonville. Heading south from the trailhead, you'll embark on a journey through a mostly shaded corridor of Outagamie County. A highlight for movie buffs: about halfway along the trail near Oakridge Road in Clayton is a commemorative area where footage was shot for the movie *Public Enemies* in 2008.

Just past I-41 and before Marine Drive in Oshkosh, you can head right onto the Tribal Heritage Crossing Trail, which travels on the eastern side of Lake Butte Des Morts Drive on I-41 and terminates on Omro Road in Oshkosh. Opened in 2013, the Tribal Heritage Crossing Trail provides access to fishing and kiosk overlooks highlighting the natural history of Wisconsin's 11 American Indian tribes.

Continuing south on the Wiouwash State Trail, you'll reach River Mill Road in Oshkosh, where signs will lead you to an on-street section along Summit Avenue and to another short off-road section of trail, which terminates at Rockwell Avenue near the University of Wisconsin–Oshkosh. A short trail spur continues south to the university campus and terminates at Osceola St.

NOTE: Snowmobilers must display either a Wisconsin registration or a snowmobile State Trail Pass. For information, go to dnr.wi.gov/topic/parks/trailpass.html.

CONTACT: **dnr.wi.gov/topic/parks/name/wiouwash**

DIRECTIONS

To reach the northern trailhead from the intersection of WI 15/Main St. and S. Nash St./County Road M in Hortonville, head south on S. Nash St. for 0.2 mile. Turn left onto Lake Shore Dr., and go 0.3 mile. Turn left onto Lakeview Ave. and, after 0.2 mile, turn right into the trailhead.

Parking is also available at the southern endpoint at the Westwind Road trailhead, near the Tribal Heritage Crossing Trail. To reach the trailhead from I-41 heading north, take Exit 120 for US 45/Algoma Blvd. toward US 10 W./New London. Keep right and follow signs for US 45/ New London. Turn right (south) onto US 45 S./Algoma Blvd., and go 0.2 mile. At the traffic circle, take the first exit onto Lake Butte Des Morts Dr., and go 0.2 mile. Turn left onto Westwind Road, and take an immediate right into the trailhead. The trail's endpoint, at Osceola St., is about 2.8 miles south.

To reach the same trailhead from I-41 heading south, take Exit 120 for US 45/Algoma Blvd., and keep left to continue south toward Algoma Blvd. At the traffic circle, take the third exit south onto Algoma Blvd., and go 0.4 mile. At the second traffic circle, take the first exit onto Lake Butte Des Morts Dr., and follow the directions above to the trailhead.

Index

Sites in Michigan are indicated by (MI); sites in Wisconsin are indicated by (WI); page numbers followed by *m* indicate maps.

A

Aaron, Hank ("The Hammer"), 169
active railroad icon, 3
Adventure Mine (old copper mine) (MI), 19
Ahnapee State Trail (WI)
description of the, 113–114
directions to the, 114
map of the, 112*m*
Albany Wildlife Area (WI), 222*m*, 224
Aloha State Park, 74*m*, 76
Alpena Wildlife Sanctuary (MI), 74*m*, 76
"America's Cereal City" (Battle Creek, MI), 8–11
Amherst Junction (WI), 226*m*, 228
Amsterdam Sloughs State Wildlife Area (WI), 152*m*, 155
Amtrak's *Empire Builder,* 171
Ann Arbor Railroad (MI), 17
apple and peach production (MI), 65
Apple Fest (MI), 66
Apple Island (MI), 104*m*, 105
arboretums. *See* gardens/arboretums (MI); gardens/arboretums (WI)
Art & Apples Festival (MI), 79
ATVs
Badger State Trail (WI), 117
Cheese Country Recreation Trail (WI), 130*m*–132
Gandy Dancer Trail: Southern Section (WI), 152*m*–155
map icon indicating use of, 5
Pecatonica State Trail (WI), 132, 208*m*–210
Pine Line Trail (WI), 211–213
Wild Goose State Trail (WI), 163, 233–235
Wisconsin passes information, 114

B

Badger State Trail (WI)
description of the, 115, 117–118
directions to the, 118
map of the, 116*m*
Bailey Park, 8*m*, 11
Bald Mountain State Recreation Area (MI), 78*m*, 79
Barton Pond (WI), 136*m*, 139
Battle Creek ("America's Cereal City") (MI), 8–11
Battle Creek Linear Park trail (MI)

description of the, 9–11
directions to the, 11
map of the, 8*m*
Battle Creek River (MI), 9
Bay County Riverwalk/Railtrail System trail (MI)
description of the, 13–15
directions to the, 15
map of the, 12*m*
Bearskin State Trail (WI)
description of the, 119, 121
directions to the, 121
map of the, 120*m*
Belmont (WI), 208*m*, 210
"Ben Bikin' " statue (Sparta, WI), 142, 174
Berlin Fen State Natural Area (WI), 180*m*, 181
Betsie River State Game Area (MI), 16*m*, 18
Betsie Valley Trail (MI)
description of the, 17–18
directions to the, 18
map of the, 16*m*
bike rentals
Elroy Commons Trail Shop (WI), 142
Kendall (WI) restored depot museum and, 143
biking. *See* mountain biking/cycling (MI); mountain biking/cycling (WI)
Bill Nicholls Trail (MI)
description of the, 19, 21
directions to the, 21
map of the, 20*m*
Black Hawk War (1832), 185–186
Black Hawk (Sauk war chief), 186
Bloomingdale Depot museum (MI), 44
Blue Mound State Park (WI), 184*m*, 186
blueberry industry (MI), 44
The Blues Brothers (film), 169
Bogue Flats Recreation Area (MI), 86*m*, 87
Bradley House (MI), 83
Brodhead, Edward, 225
Brodhead (WI), 222*m*, 225
Brown County Historical Society (WI), 150
Brown Deer Recreational Trail (WI), 204*m*, 206
Bruemmer Park (WI), 112*m*, 114
Brunet Island State Park (WI), 198*m*, 199
Bugline Trail (WI)
description of the, 123–125
directions to the, 125
map of the, 122*m*

Photo Credits

Page x: Ken Bryan; *page 7:* Brian Housh; page 9: C. Phillip Houck; *page 10:* Rails-to-Trails Conservancy; *pages 13 and 14:* Jim Rugenstein; *page 17:* D. V. Goodwin; *page 19:* Martin Beek; *page 23:* Roger Klyn; *pages 24 and 27:* Rails-to-Trails Conservancy; *page 28:* Vicki E. Schooley; *page 31:* Kevin Mills; *pages 35 and 36:* Brian Housh; *page 39:* Patrick Wojahn; *page 43:* Russell Cooper; *page 45:* Patrick Wojahn; *page 49:* DNemo Photography; *page 51:* Rails-to-Trails Conservancy; *page 53:* Naohiro Inohara; *page 55:* Rails-to-Trails Conservancy; *page 57:* TART Trails Inc.; *page 61:* Chuck Gulker; *page 62;* Rails-to-Trails Conservancy; *page 65:* Dan Pieniak; *page 67:* Joel VanAntwerpen; *page 69:* Rachel Kramer; *page 71:* Michigan Trails & Greenways Alliance; *page 75:* Brian Housh; *page 77:* Tom Hughes; *pages 81 and 83:* Isabella County Parks; *page 85:* Wayne A. Kuntzman; *page 89:* Sharlene Smeage; *page 90:* Ed Beaumont; *page 93:* Ken Laughlin; *page 94:* Pam Darling; *page 97:* Bruce Bodjack; *page 98:* Bonnie Withrow; *page 101:* Dennis C. Delor; *page 103:* Kathleen Nalon; *pages 107 and 108:* White Lake Area Chamber of Commerce; *page 111:* Eric Reischl Photography; *page 113:* Ken Bryan; *pages 115 and 117:* Patrick Wojahn; *page 119:* Laura and Nick Kazynski; *page 123:* Dave Jonasen; *page 124:* Joseph James; *page 127:* Ashley Robertson; *page 128:* Barbara Richey; *page 131:* Rails-to-Trails Conservancy; *page 133:* Derek Strout; *page 137:* Kathy Cornell; *page 138:* Rails-to-Trails Conservancy; *page 141:* Eric Reischl Photography; *page 142:* Amy Henschen; *page 145:* Sandor Weisz; *page 146:* Wisconsin Department of Natural Resources; *page 149:* Heather Deutsch; *page 150:* Jane Brookstein; *pages 153 and 154:* Chris Hanser; *pages 157 and 158:* Barbara Richey; *pages 161 and 162:* Jane Brookstein; *page 165:* Tracy L. Coyle; *page 166:* Dave Jonasen; *page 169:* John Siegert; *pages 171 and 173:* Rails-to-Trails Conservancy; *page 175:* Charles Morlock; *page 177:* Cindy Dickerson; *page 179:* John Siegert; *page 183:* Barbara Richey; *page 185:* Dave Jonasen; *pages 187 and 189:* Derek Strout; *page 191:* Eric Tank; *page 195:* Rails-to-Trails Conservancy; *page 197:* Ken Bryan; *pages 201 and 202:* Rails-to-Trails Conservancy; *page 205:* Cindy Dickerson; *page 206:* Michael Murray; *page 209:* Barbara Richey; *page 211:* J. Leas; *pages 215 and 216:* Derek Strout; *page 219:* Heather Deutsch; *pages 220 and 223:* Barbara Richey; *page 224:* Dave Jonasen; *page 227:* Ken Bryan; *pages 229 and 231:* John Siegert; *page 233:* Dave Jonasen; *page 237:* Patrick Wojahn.

Support Rails-to-Trails Conservancy

T he nation's leader in helping communities transform unused rail lines and connecting corridors into multiuse trails, Rails-to-Trails Conservancy (RTC) depends on the support of its members and donors to create access to healthy outdoor experiences.

Your donation will help support programs and services that have helped put more than 22,000 rail-trail miles on the ground. Every day, RTC provides vital assistance to communities to develop and maintain trails throughout the country. In addition, RTC advocates for trail-friendly policies, promotes the benefits of rail-trails, and defends rail-trail laws in the courts.

Join online at **railstotrails.org,** or mail your donation to Rails-to-Trails Conservancy, 2121 Ward Court NW, Fifth Floor, Washington, DC 20037.

Rails-to-Trails Conservancy is a 501(c)(3) nonprofit organization, and contributions are tax deductible.

Find your next trail adventure on TrailLink

Visit TrailLink.com today.